# THE CITIZENSHIP DEBATES

# THE CITIZENSHIP DEBATES

*A Reader*

GERSHON SHAFIR, EDITOR

UNIVERSITY OF MINNESOTA PRESS

*Minneapolis • London*

Published by the University of Minnesota Press
111 Third Avenue South, Suite 290
Minneapolis, MN 55401-2520

http://www.upress.umn.edu/

Library of Congress Cataloging-in-Publication Data

The citizenship debates : a reader / Gershon Shafir, editor.
    p.    cm.
    Includes index.
    ISBN 978-0-8166-2880-3 (hc : alk. paper)–ISBN 978-0-8166-2881-0 (pbk. : alk. paper)
    1. Citizenship.  I. Shafir, Gershon.
    JF801.C5733   1998
    323.6 — dc21                    97-35656

Printed in the United States of America on acid-free paper

The University of Minnesota is an equal-opportunity educator and employer.

14 13 12                    10 9 8 7 6

# CONTENTS

# 1

## *Introduction: The Evolving Tradition of Citizenship*
### GERSHON SHAFIR

Imagine that you have been invited to draw up, through intensive consultation with a group of strangers, the blueprints for a new society. Your task is to delineate the legal framework, institutions, and social relations around which the members of the new society would coalesce. That would probably require you and your cofounders to debate how virtuous ordinary people are and can be made. You and your cofounders would then need to ask how the members of the new society would learn to cooperate and settle their conflicts. Subsequently, you are likely to puzzle over the best way of emending these arrangements once the circumstances of the society change. Raising and answering such questions is part of the long tradition that addresses society as a partnership of free citizens.[1]

The theme of citizenship and the kinds of questions raised herewith have reemerged into the center of public debate in the past few years (together with the concept of civil society) as the focus of policies and studies regarding a number of major contemporary processes: democratization and its consolidation in Eastern Europe and parts of Africa and Latin America; the rise of sometimes vicious ethnic and national conflicts concomitantly with the unprecedented integration of Western Europe's nation-states in the European Union; the debate over welfare entitlements; and global migration to developed industrial states. Effective democracy, nationalism, the reform of the welfare state, and immigration all pose challenges to our understanding of individual rights, political and social conflicts, and the nation-state; they can be, and have been, addressed through the prism of citizenship discourses.

The appeal of the theme of citizenship is not surprising. Citizenship, as the legal and social framework for individual autonomy and political democracy, has been a central axis of Western political philosophy. This long tradition of citizenship is a bridge between antiquity and the modern era, linking the civic and political self-conception of the Greek *polis* and the Roman Empire with the French Revolution and Enlightenment emphasis on the equal moral worth of all individuals. Citizenship, then, is an intellectual and political tradition that has been repeatedly revisited and updated and, therefore, today consists of a string of citizenship discourses. The resilience of the study of citizenship is further demonstrated by the fact that it is becoming the new abode of some of the Marxian preoccupations with conflict, oppression, and resistance.

But it was a theoretical renewal — John Rawls's systematic revision of the theory of liberal individualism — that helped give the issues we associate with citizenship pride of place in current intellectual and political debates. Rawls's philosophical writings facilitated and catalyzed the resurgence of interest in citizenship as a central theme for comprehending social change at the end of the twentieth century and supplied some of the theoretical language for analyzing contemporary social processes. Rawls's invigorated liberal theory continues to serve as a major impetus for a considerable portion of the new citizenship debates.

The cross between an age-old theme and current public concerns rendered the citizenship nexus into the node of five modern debates (which are presented in Parts III to VII). The first goal of this reader is to present the perspectives of those who are engaged in these polemics. As part of each debate, the demand to expand liberal individual citizenship rights, in order to provide new or sturdier rights to individuals or to fully incorporate the individual members of another group into society, is criticized from the perspective of yet another collectivist version of citizenship rights. Complex communitarian, social democratic, nationalist, feminist, and multiculturalist critiques of liberal citizenship extend into debates over the proper nature of citizenship.

The theme of citizenship is frequently treated in relative isolation within separate academic disciplines, and most theorists participate in debates that take place within a single citizenship discourse. Case studies, however, frequently demonstrate that in most societies alternative discourses of citizenship coexist with and constrain one another. I believe, therefore, that bringing together alternative citizenship frameworks and pitting them against each other would increase theoretical cross-fertilization among disciplines. The second goal of this reader is to juxtapose these debates in order to inquire how competing citizenship discourses affect one another and the society in question. And, given the conflicting views of these discourses, we need to conclude by asking what is left today of the universalist claims made on behalf of citizenship as full membership in society. In Part VIII, therefore, theoretical and empirical articles seek to examine the interaction of multiple citizenship frameworks within one society.

As we proceed from historical origins to contemporary debates, we will observe a growing emphasis on social pluralism and cultural diversity that typifies our modern society and correspondingly the analysis of citizenship. While some of the theorists argue that for the citizenship tradition to survive it needs to ignore or at least to bypass this potentially fragmenting diversity, others hold that diversity has to be, and can be, integrated into the framework of citizenship itself. It is here, on the cutting edge of the debates on contemporary citizenship, its limits and potential for extension, that the fiercest debates are joined and the character of our society in the future is contested.

## HISTORICAL ORIGINS AND ANTECEDENTS

Already in the earliest formulation, as J. G. A. Pocock's and Max Weber's essays in Part I suggest, we can locate the most enduring themes associated with citizenship. The tradition of citizenship commences as a framework of political life. But it also doubles as a sociological perspective and becomes one with humanism itself. Organizing social life around the political goal of securing freedom for the citizen generates a general vision of humanity.

In the context of the Greek city-state, the *polis,* citizenship appeared as a double process of emancipation. First, it was the liberation of a portion of humanity from tribal loyalties and its fusion into a voluntary civic community. Citizenship is the legal foundation and social glue of the new communality. It is founded on the definition of the human being as "a creature formed by nature to live a political life" and, in Pocock's words, this is "one of the great Western definitions of what it is to be human." Second, it was the transcendence of the instrumental sphere of necessity, in which we toil to satisfy our material wants, into the sphere of freedom where the practice of freedom, in collective rational and moral deliberation over a common destiny, is its own reward. This contrast has been conceptualized in multiple forms—for example, as emancipation from the private sphere of the household (*oikos*) into the public sphere of political life (*polis*) or, as

Pocock chooses to designate it, from the world of things into the world of persons and actions. This definition of freedom as an aim sought after for its own sake shows, in his words, that "citizenship is not just a means to being free; it is the way of being free itself" and has remained an enduring view of freedom as a value in itself regardless of other conditions in which we find ourselves.

The Greek concept of citizenship enshrined freedom, but only for a portion of mankind. The elevation of the public domain of political life over the private sphere of the family and economic life signaled the emancipation of free male citizens at the expense of women and slaves, who remained excluded from citizenship. The purview of Greek citizenship was limited and never amounted to more than a participatory aristocracy. The legacy of Greek citizenship, consequently, remained contradictory. The civic notion of membership established a framework for the incorporation of new members or categories of members into the "realm of freedom." At the same time, the early identity of citizenship and privilege left us with the question of just how possible it is to accommodate the practice of citizenship with broader notions of inclusion, such as the reduction of the barrier between the private and public, without having to abandon the citizenship tradition altogether.

The historical record indicates that when social conditions change, some aspects of the theme of citizenship change with them. Consequently, multiple historical conceptions of citizenship are available. Two of these transformations, the Roman imperial and the medieval, and their citizenship discourses are examined by Pocock and by Weber respectively.

In the *polis* all citizens possessed the same privileges, but the heterogeneity of empires is reflected in multiple and diverse types of memberships. In the Roman Empire various gradations of citizenship were granted to individuals and groups with the aim of incorporating the upper strata into the imperial institutions as loyal supporters of the emperor. The nature of citizenship itself had also been drastically revised as the conception of freedom was altered in the transition from the small Greek self-governing city-state to the massive Roman Empire. Instead of enabling one to freely participate in political decision making, citizenship became a legal *status* that provided protection from the emperor and his representatives' arbitrary rule. In addition, Roman citizenship was defined, for example by the jurist Gaius, not by the freedom to deliberate with other people but by the right to be a proprietor. Roman law became the regulation over freedom to take and dispose of possessions, including slaves.

The comparison of the Roman and Greek experiences already suggests many of the issues we will encounter in contemporary citizenship debates. In many ways the Greek approach resembles the communitarian discourse of citizenship while the Roman approach is like the liberal version of our times; in fact, as we shall see in Parts II and III, the liberal-communitarian debate might be fruitfully seen as a modern reenactment of the imperial-*polis* division. The contrast between political freedom and legal freedom raises intriguing questions. Could it be that where legal protection of rights is available, civic-mindedness suffers? Does security, and security in our possessions in particular, override people's aspiration to be free? Is the aspiration for political freedom less compelling than Greek political theory makes it out to be?

Pocock and Weber concur that the political freedom associated with citizenship emerged at first in the Western world. The rest of their analyses diverge. In Weber's comparison of citizenship in the city-states of antiquity and the Middle Ages, in contrast to Pocock's analysis of the cultural significance of citizenship, we benefit from a sociological explanation of the unique conditions under which citizenship came into existence. While Pocock places great emphasis on the importance of transcending tribal loyalties, Weber draws a broader picture in which the elimination of all magically (or religiously) sanctioned social divisions is seen as crucial for allowing the free association and solidarity on which communities of citizens are founded.

Unlike Pocock, Weber locates the impetus toward the development of citizenship in the military dimension of the Greek *polis.* The city-state is based on the association of those who can afford to purchase their own weapons and military equipment first for the protection of the city and later for conquest and the acquisition of land and booty (a venture Weber terms political or military capitalism). Equal access to arms led to the demand for the granting of effective citizenship rights to the armed plebeians. The democratic character of the *polis* reflects the further desire to ensure that growing economic inequality will not undermine the ability of free men to participate in the military, that is, to ensure the survival of the partnership of soldiers (termed by Weber a soldiers' guild). The identity of soldier and citizen was firmly established in the *polis,* and participation in the military became the foundation for ancient freedoms.

Medieval cities, like the *polis,* also legislated their own law, and their citizens, mostly guild members and therefore still only a fraction of the inhabitants, elected their own officials. But in important respects the two institutions and their citizenship frameworks differed. The divergence of the *polis* and the medieval cities reflected the changing relationship of military and civilian occupations. Medieval military technologies privileged feudal knights and reduced the armies of medieval cities to defensive tasks, and, conversely, the weight of the artisans' guilds and the role played by them in the city was enhanced. The medieval city was founded on the peaceful arts of the citizens, scorned in antiquity, and produced economic resources and mobile capital that were the key to urban ascendance and modern progress. Allied with the political power of the rising modern states, the bourgeoisie or the first national citizenry emerged out of the cities. The possibility of its expansion into a truly all-encompassing national citizenry and the consequent transformations of citizenship will be the focus of all subsequent chapters.

## The Revisited Liberal Position

John Rawls's *A Theory of Justice,* which was published in 1971, its 1993 sequel, *Political Liberalism,* and his many articles commenced a reassessment of our thinking about public life in modern democratic liberal society and inspired many subsequent studies — some sympathetic, others critical — that focused on the theme of citizenship. Rawls has revisited liberalism with the intention of replacing its self-interested justification by *utilitarian* philosophy with a public morality that focuses on the attainment of justice in liberal society. At the same time, Rawls's philosophical approach, like other forms of liberalism, continues to accent personal liberty — that is, individuals as the bearers of rights — and the toleration of religious, cultural, and political diversity. The centrality of his work and its relative complexity warrant a detailed exposition of its central arguments.[2]

In contrast with most liberals who are content with deliberating over ways of ensuring rights for individuals, Rawls seeks to discuss the rights of free and equal individuals as part and parcel of a theory of social cooperation. He proposes to do so by identifying justice with the simple idea of *fairness.* When cooperation between individuals is fair — that is, based not only on individuals' freedom to contract with one another but also on mutually benefiting from their cooperation (for example, by acquiring some of the *primary goods* they need to shape their lives in a way that is meaningful) — justice is ensured while justice itself becomes fairness. Rawls's approach of *justice as fairness* permits a shift in the liberal perspective from private to public life while still retaining the traditional concern with individual rights that animates liberalism.

One of the main reasons for Rawls's rejection of the foundation of liberalism on a utilitarian psychology and its goal of maximizing the psychological well-being of "happiness" for all is his disagreement with the notion that all rational and well-informed individuals have an identical view of what is good. Presuming principled diversity, the question Rawls faces is how the cooperation of a multitude of individuals can be secured when, frequently, the efforts necessary for the attainment of their different goals lead to conflict among them. May diverse goods be attained through cooperation and still benefit all?

In seeking to lay out the *basic structure* of an ideal or *well-ordered society* — a modern constitutional democracy — Rawls recreates the classical thought experiment (in Rawls's own terms, it is a "device of representation") of Hobbes, Locke, and Rousseau. Like his illustrious predecessors, Rawls seeks a social contract type of agreement as the foundation of the social order. Rawls suggests that, in order to be fair, individuals in the *original position* of contracting have to be behind a *"veil of ignorance"* as to their social situation in the new society: they must not know whether they will be rich or poor, a member of the majority or a minority, and so on. Under such conditions of imaginary equality, he argues, individuals will evolve from their basic intuitive ideas of cooperation in a democratic society a framework of political justice. As reasonable moral individuals — with capacities for justice (to act from the public conception of justice) and a capacity for a conception of the good (to rationally pursue a view of what is valuable in human life) — they will construct a society of free and equal citizens.

The ensuing conception of justice (or social contract, in the traditional language of political theory), he argues, would include the two principles according to which political and economic institutions of a fair modern liberal democracy may be set up: the possession, by individuals, of (1) "a fully adequate scheme of equal basic rights and liberties," and (2) equal opportunity combined with the most clearly distinguishing feature of Rawls's approach of justice as fairness, *"the difference principle,"* namely, that "social and economic inequalities" would be acceptable only insofar as they operate "to the greatest benefit of the least advantaged members of society." These two principles are listed in order of priority. In practical terms this means that of the alternative social orders that safeguard the individual's basic liberties, we should select the one that provides the most equal access to those positions that provide unequal rewards and in which social and economic inequalities work to the advantage of society's least advantaged members.[3] Once basic liberties, or what in this volume will repeatedly be called civil citizenship rights, are safeguarded, the rights of the least advantaged, or their social citizenship rights, should be our main consideration in contracting for a just society.

For Rawls's theory of justice as fairness to work, he repeatedly admonishes us, it has to be viewed as a political theory for a democratic citizenry. The reason is that the political life of citizens in a liberal democracy is not dominated by a single comprehensive moral — whether religious, nationalist, or other — vision, in contrast to other areas, such as our private or communal lives, where monolithic views are permissible. According to Rawls, justice as fairness is not intended as a comprehensive moral doctrine but as a practical modus vivendi that allows the emergence of an *overlapping consensus* of moral principles between opposing comprehensive doctrines.

It is not possible to attain agreement in a pluralistic modern society on disputed moral and religious questions without resorting to the repression that exists in nondemocratic societies. The strength of liberal society is precisely its ability to tolerate diversity by creating a self-limited political realm of individual rights and by setting an institutional framework within which disputes are avoided by permitting the political expression of only those conceptions of the good that are not monopolistic. Whereas in *A Theory of Justice* Rawls went as far as arguing that his theory gave priority to right over good, in his more recent *Political Liberalism* he holds that rights are not opposed to the good, but only very limited notions of the good, such as the practical attainment of an overlapping consensus, are compatible with rights.[4]

The embodiment of the moral person in the liberal democratic society is the citizen who is free, self-originating, and responsible in exercising rights and discharging duties. Rawls argues that the citizen was formed in this limited political arena and operates to uphold it. Since rights are attached to an individual's public identity as a free and equal citizen and not to one of the features that determine her identity, such as religion or nationality, she is free to change her view of the good life (e.g., convert from one religion to another) without being deprived of these rights. Indeed, only in a democratic society do citizens have the right to make claims that are valid; in nondemocratic societies only the views of those in positions of leadership carry authority. Finally, citizens take into account the need for cooperation (political justice is based on notions of social cooperation) and are responsible for making demands that are not excessive. This last point allows Rawls to argue that though the focal point of his theory is individual rights, the very same individuals possess what we would call cooperative virtues, which allow the citizens to create not just a loose partnership of ad hoc associations between individuals but a type of society with fairly stable and strong bonds between the members. Social unity and the allegiance of the citizens to their common institutions evolves only when they all share the same political conception of justice. The acceptance of the moral principle of fairness through an overlapping consensus, and not just adherence to the formal aspects of the political and institutional framework, is the foundation of social unity.

Some of the new liberal theorists, like Stephen Macedo, argue that democratic liberal society is in fact less divided and more robust than Rawls's surface-level approach, seeking no more than an overlapping consensus, makes it out to be. Rawls's theory focuses on the original position, the stage in which a reasonable political consensus is constructed. There is, however, a second stage in which the established liberal social order comes up against competing comprehensive religious and political moral orders. It is then that liberalism as a regime—namely, its principles that shape our goals and lives and its institutions that embody those principles and help us reach them—leads its citizens to oppose comprehensive conceptions of the good because they are incompatible with liberalism itself. In Macedo's view, then, Rawls has not avoided but only deferred conflict, since liberalism cannot remain only a means but will also install its practice of justifying and accepting conceptions of the good only when they are reasonable. Liberal citizenship, therefore, possesses its own virtues, and those who publicly advocate its standards in effect construct their own moral community around those reasoned political positions.[5]

Rawls's approach is obviously normative—he constructs a well-ordered, or ideal, society, in part through a thought experiment. This question arises: how can one compare the kinds of empirical studies that are found in this volume with his and with other normative approaches, such as Walzer's? Though it is normative, Rawls's theory is also historically situated: he clearly and repeatedly states that he strove to work out a basic structure for a modern liberal citizenry from the intuitive ideas of a political culture that continues the Greek tradition of citizenship and was reconstituted in the early modern era out of the confluence of religious toleration following the Wars of Religion, the market economy, and the constitutional principles of government. There is, in short, enough communality between his theory and the other works to make comparison possible. At the same time, the empirical studies in this volume are also not devoid of normative dimensions and concerns: they frequently study and often critique existing legal frameworks and principles on which the allocation of rights depends. The gap, then, between the normative and the empirical studies in the area of citizenship is limited and many bridges lead across it.

## THE COMMUNITARIAN CRITIQUE

Modern civic republicanism is driven by longing for the communal life that seems to have been lost in the transition to the modern world. The source of many of the ailments of liberal society, in the view of many of its critics, is found in the decline of solidarity between citizens and their limited involvement in governing themselves, which leads to the loss of the sense of a common destiny. True communal life is possible, according to the civic republican discourse, only if citizens are *virtuous* and society is organized in a fashion that will ensure that they are and remain so.

If the utilitarian version of liberalism, and in important respects even Rawls's revisited liberalism, resemble in their individualistic accent and legalistic framework the Roman imperial conception of citizenship, many of their opponents derive their inspiration from, and seek to make relevant to modern life, the Greek *polis*'s citizenship ideal. Greek civic republicanism, which was given expression most coherently by Aristotle, has sustained a vibrant political tradition in the writings of Machiavelli, Rousseau, Tocqueville, and others all the way to American republican thought in the eighteenth century. Adrian Oldfield's essay expresses the views of civic republicanism, or the communitarian approach.

The debate between the liberal and the communitarian schools is a debate between two normative conceptions of the citizen. The individual, in either the utilitarian or the contractual liberal view, is the sovereign author of her life who pursues her private rational advantage or conception of the good. The role of politics in this approach remains negative: only to aid and protect individuals from interference by governments in exercising the rights they inalienably possess and in return for which they have to undertake certain minimal political duties (pay taxes, vote periodically, obey the law, serve in the military). Consequently, citizenship, in the liberal view, is an accessory, not a value in itself.

Oldfield uncovers one major limitation of this perspective. Oldfield emphasizes that individuals are members of social units larger than themselves, and one of these larger units — and it is here that the character of the communitarian approach emerges most clearly — is the *political community*. Communitarians retain the Greek view of politics as the hub of human existence and as life's supreme fulfillment. Politics is a communal affair, and it is enduring political attachment that provides the citizen with her *identity* — and hereby another important term that will recur in many of the essays in this volume is introduced. Citizens are who they are by virtue of participating in the life of their political community, and by identifying with its characteristics. Pursuing the common good is the core of the communal citizens' civic virtue. If we amplify political life by demanding more from the citizen, as Oldfield's emphasis on duties indicates, her existence will be richer and she will lead a more fulfilling and morally inspired life.

One of the highlights of the communitarian perspective is the considerable attention devoted to identifying the kinds of social bonds, commitment, and education, maybe even molding, necessary to create and maintain such a community. Oldfield concludes that the citizen's *autonomy* has to be balanced with "*concord*" or friendship, and the citizenry's shared life and common aims have to be secured through the ongoing exercise of collective political *judgment*. Citizenship, in sum, communitarians contend, should be an activity or a *practice* and not, as liberals hold, simply a *status* of membership. Precedence is to be given not to individual rights but to the pursuit of the common good.

Liberals and communitarians are famous for their polemics over the priority of right versus good. Rawls's and Oldfield's essays in this volume seek to find common ground between their respective versions of liberalism and communitarianism and are willing to accept goals that are more modest than those sought by other liberals or communitarians. Oldfield is at pains to point out that modern communities must allow for the pursuit of alternative forms of individual good life, that is, to stay consistent with the autonomy of individuals and their diversity, which is also a starting point of Rawls's justice as fairness approach. Rawls, for his part, constructs a theory of social cooperation and believes that in a society based on political justice rights complement the good. Individuals' attitude toward one another in such a society is not instrumental but is based on moral principles that also serve to provide social unity. But even Rawls's approach, satisfied as it is with the search for an overlapping moral consensus, has been criticized for not paying sufficient attention to the communal aspects of social life.

The contention between the liberal and the communitarian views of citizenship is many-sided and raises many questions. Would the pursuit of a single conception of the good, which communitarians hunger after and of which Rawls remains fearful, inevitably bring on an authoritarian state or, as Oldfield believes, could it be obtained voluntarily? Can the balance between individual autonomy and social cohesion, as is drawn by Oldfield, be maintained over time? How fallible is collective political judgment, and how susceptible is the public to demagogy? In general, what is the appropriate balance of freedom and control within both liberal societies and communities?

There are also many questions communitarians debate among themselves. One of the central ones is what kind of community of citizens communitarians should wish for and under what circumstances it would rise and prevail. Oldfield mentions two such communities. First, historically, political communities of engaged citizens, as Oldfield notes, have frequently emerged in the context of revolutions or wars of liberation that perforce educated the citizenry to cooperate against their enemies and, in the process, endowed them with a new political identity. The French Revolution was the first of such experiences, and the Jacobin radical political clubs provided the model for generating sweeping commitment in the modern era. But such revolutionary origin is hardly a recipe for begetting continuously active and free citizens. How long would it be possible to avert the danger of the community's members being forced to endorse a collective interest that they don't necessarily view as their own? When would such community come to exist outside, and therefore above, the individuals who constitute it and come to resemble a closed, hierarchical, preindustrial society?

Oldfield recognizes that in the modern world it is well nigh impossible to construct a true community on the national level and, consequently, it is necessary to seek communal forms of life in smaller units. Relying on Platt's view that in the modern world functional units should replace territorial communities, Oldfield offers a second model of modern communities, professional associations. It seems mildly naive, however, to suggest that professions have a "common identity, stable membership, shared values, a common language, and acknowledged authority." Even if the members of a profession successfully maintain a common front toward outsiders, they may engage in bitter struggles over the legitimate authority and the criterion of authority that should govern them.

The same question can be raised, in more general form, in regard to the capability of small, decentralized communities to accommodate diversity. Will not small communities' desire to preserve their distinct identity lead their members to reject minorities that hold different conceptions of the good? What would be the status of immigrants? Will a communitarian approach lead to the enforcement of popular morality at the exclusion of alternative ways of life; will it lead to the tyranny of the majority? Will prejudice and ignorance replace moral argumentation over reasonableness? Conversely, will the admission of diversity into the community allow its members to reach consensus through collective political judgment? Since communal citizenship also takes precedence over larger, especially universal, identities, will there be an impetus toward the evolution of new, broad rights; or will small communities stagnate and remain inward-looking?

Beyond criticizing what they see as the willingness of liberalism to sacrifice social solidarity and the virtuous behavior of citizens to the protection of individual rights, even the best-known communitarians such as Sandel and McIntyre are hard-pressed to put forth "some substantial vision of a common political good."[6] In fact, they seem apt to reject many of the existing comprehensive conceptions of the good as detrimental to liberal citizenship rights. This lacuna of civic republicanism is filled by others.[7] In Parts IV, V, VI, and VII, alternative versions of communities of modern citizens are put forth by social democrats, nationalists, feminists, and multiculturalists.

## THE SOCIAL DEMOCRATIC CRITIQUE

In 1949, in a series of lectures entitled "Citizenship and Social Class," the British sociologist T. H. Marshall opened a new debate over citizenship by producing a theory that owes little to antiquity and a great deal to modern industrial experience.[8] The historical context of Marshall's work was the post–Second World War era when the British Labour Party and its social-democratic program of a welfare state and universal provision of welfare services predominated.

The strength of Marshall's and the social-democratic approach is that they go beyond the conventional idea that membership in a community is predominantly a political matter. Marshall's theory is at once legal, political, and socioeconomic, and since it is also historical, it introduces into the study of citizenship the element of social change that was missing from the more one-dimensional and static normative approaches. Marshall surveys and analyzes the *expansion* of the rights of citizens as a process of incorporating new groups — in the case of England, the working classes — into society and the body politic. New rights make the possession and wielding of previous rights more effective, and the accession to such rights removes fences between groups previously separated by legal barriers or social custom. Each time citizenship is expanded it becomes stronger and richer.

The expansion of citizenship is connected with the incorporation of new groups into the *state,* a concept that had been only touched upon so far but now has to be introduced into the center of the citizenship debates. In our historical survey this will be the third time the political and territorial unit in which citizenship is embedded has changed: in antiquity from the Greek *polis* to the Roman Empire, during the Middle Ages from the Roman Empire to towns, and, finally, in the modern era from towns to states. The modern state emerges around the time of the Renaissance, usually through a political process of centralization that replaces fragmented and overlapping feudal authority with uniform practices within its boundaries. With the growth of citizenship from a local into a statewide institution, the freedoms conferred on citizens in the medieval towns were radically expanded, and freedom itself was converted from a privilege into a right. Simultaneously, argues Marshall, the expansion of rights is part and parcel of the process of democratization, of the attainment by the lower classes, specifically the working class, of the modern rights originally fashioned by the upper classes for themselves.

Marshall distinguishes between three sets, or what we might term three generations, of citizenship rights: civil, political, and social. *Civil rights* are the bundle of rights necessary for individual freedom that emerged in the eighteenth century. *Political rights* originated in the nineteenth century and guaranteed participation in the exercise of political power as voter or representative. Finally, in the twentieth century, *social rights* of citizenship — Marshall's original conceptual contribution to the theory of citizenship — make possible the attainment of a modicum of economic welfare and security or, as gracefully expressed by Marshall: "the right to share to the full in the social heritage and to live the life of a civilized being according to the standards prevailing in society." Marshall's emphasis on the common standard of civilization allows us to avoid the common mistake of conflating welfare rights with social citizenship: the former are means-based and single out vulnerable individuals as needing protection; the latter is universal and attained as a right by virtue of membership in the community.

Marshall's work explores the relations that emerge from the expansion of rights that are at once cumulative and contradictory. He is especially concerned with the contradiction between civil rights, which are in harmony with class inequalities, and social rights, which established "a universal right to real income which is not proportionate to the market value of the claimant" and, therefore, modify "the whole pattern of social inequality." Their operation is also antithetical: civil rights provide protection from the state; social rights establish claims for benefits guaranteed by the state. The question that drove Marshall's theoretical quest was, To what extent can the reduction of class equality, through the expansion of citizenship rights, reconcile people to the remaining inequality? He concluded that social citizenship and capitalism are at war, and the exercise of citizenship rights will continue to generate social conflict. At the same time, Marshall argues that citizenship and social class are compatible in our society "so much so that citizenship has itself become ... the architect of legitimate social inequality." Marshall's own ambiguity echoes the debate over citizenship between the radical followers of Marx and the more moderate social democrats.

Nancy Fraser and Linda Gordon examine the evolution of citizenship rights in the United States and note contrasts with Marshall's evolutionary framework. Fraser and Gordon show that a strongly rooted civil rights tradition, instead of leading to the attainment of social rights, as was the case in Britain, may in fact hinder the growth of social rights of citizenship. The emphasis on contract — the predominant social relationship — and on property rights — the model for other kinds of legitimate rights — relegates other relations to a less esteemed status and restricts the emergence of alternative public languages that could legitimate social citizenship rights. Fraser and Gordon's study suggests that the relationship of social citizenship rights to civil and political rights has been complex and cannot be reduced to a single pattern.

There is now a rich body of empirical studies that criticize Marshall's work for presenting the British case as a universal model and the expansion of citizenship as a linear and irreversible process, thus opening a debate over the relationship between the different types of rights and, correspondingly, over different types of modern societies. Michael Mann has shown that modernizing absolutist elites, for example, granted civil rights; provided, and sometimes even pioneered, limited social rights; but bestowed only sham political citizenship. In other cases social citizenship rights have served to constrain, or even were conceived of outright as substitutes for, civil citizenship. For example, fascism and communism provided no civil or political rights but went furthest toward social citizenship, fascist regimes hesitantly and communist ones aggressively.[9] Even in Britain, it has been argued, highlighting internal regional variation and giving greater emphasis to the impact of political culture and the public sphere would alter the pattern of the evolution of citizenship rights that was painted by Marshall.[10] And not only social democratic regimes such as those in Great Britain and Scandinavia but, *pace* Fraser and Gordon, also the New Deal in the United States "revolutionized" social rights and thus acquired the loyalty of masses of voters.[11] We need to inquire how both in Britain and in the United States social citizenship rights and welfare rights that seemed secure for decades have been recently abrogated. The study of each country then has to examine the history of the struggle for rights, the conditions under which they were given, the type of regime or state that granted or conceded them, and the local configuration of citizenship rights. But scholars and policy makers will continue to test and inquire: How intense is the conflict between civil, political, and social rights? How deeply are social rights ingrained and how far have they expanded or contracted? And have additional types of citizenship rights been demanded or granted as part of the full social heritage and the life of a civilized being under contemporary circumstances? Finally, the history of modern citizenship is more extensive than the history of industrial class conflict since it also contains the struggles of national and ethnic movements, women, and minorities, which will be studied in their own right. We will proceed now to examine the similarities and differences between the rights demanded by the British working class and those sought by these groups.

## THE NATIONALIST CRITIQUE

Another crucial dimension of modern citizenship, as Weber had already indicated and Marshall clearly noted, is the coincident emergence of civil rights and the birth of "modern national consciousness," which awoke people for the first time to a "sense of community membership and common heritage."[12] The extension of other citizenship rights also paralleled the growth of the institutions of the state for national justice and a common law to all, national markets and economy, national education, and finally national planning. The framework for modern citizenship rights is the state that is gradually transformed into a state for a nation, a nation-state.

The French revolutionaries were the first to introduce the term *nation* with its modern meanings into the political lexicon. The Declaration of the Rights of Man and Citizen spelled out within the Enlightenment's rational philosophical framework simultaneously the democratic sovereignty of the nation and the civil rights of its citizens. As Rogers Brubaker's essay in this volume notes, this overlap between the "national" of a country and its "citizen" was the result of the long existence of the old French regime and the active role it played in the homogenization of its population, a process that was continued with greater vigor by the state administration, schools, and army in the nineteenth century. The Enlightenment's civic framework of citizenship is another embodiment of the values of liberal individualism, in the form of of liberal nationalism.

In contrast, in the fragmented German kingdoms and principalities, the void between political citizenship and the nation gave rise to the alternative tradition of the Romantic, or *völkisch*, nationalism. In place of the Enlightenment's view of the nation as a partnership of individual citizens who possess identical, universal civil rights, the ethnic *Volk* was posited as an organic body with a life of its own. Nations, in Romantic nationalism, are all radically different from one another because their members possess distinct cultural markers, such as language, religion, and history. Since in this view nations are inscribed into the *identity* of their members, individuals were regarded as beholden to their nation and were required to demonstrate an ever-growing loyalty to the nation-state at the price of an ever-growing denial of their individual rights. The most extreme denial of individualism was advocated by fascist nationalism, an exaggerated and distorted version of Romantic nationalism.

Clearly, civic or liberal and Romantic or ethnocultural nationalism have given rise to conflicting theories of nationhood and citizenship. The rights demanded for the individual members of the nation by the former were bestowed on the national collective by the latter; whereas in the former individuals are known through their rights, in the latter individuals are characterized more by their identities.

In Brubaker's study we are shown how these conflicting versions of nationalism, mediated by alternative legal definitions of citizenship, lead to different approaches to the naturalization of immigrants in France and Germany. Whereas French civic nationalism is based on the French experience that political incorporation and assimilation into the national language and culture go hand in hand, German ethnic nationalism denies the possibility of cultural assimilation. Consequently, in France the nation was seen as a territorial community and the criterion of *jus soli* was used to grant citizenship to those born on its territory. Germany is an extreme case in that its citizenship is based exclusively on *jus sanguinis* — on descent or blood line. German law, consequently, makes no provisions for granting citizenship to second-generation immigrants because that would contradict its dominant nationalist conception. It has to be emphasized that though the French and German nationalists disagree as to how best to achieve their goal — politically or culturally — that goal is the same and it is shared by nationalists elsewhere: the creation and maintenance of a homogeneous nation.

In the past few years, however, a process of revision began in both countries. In France, the automatic right of second-generation immigrants to become French citizens upon maturity has been abolished, and those who wish to become citizens will be required to ask expressly. In Germany, a yet inconclusive debate is carried on over the tradition of restricting citizenship to "foreigners" who were born in the country or lived there most of their adult lives. These changes and debates seem to be instances of contrary tendencies for responding to the kind of diversity that nationalists oppose. The changes in French and debates over German naturalization practices raise the question of how fixed national traditions and conceptions of citizenship are. Are they likely to change and, if so, under what conditions? And if change is possible, can liberal individual citizenship replace the Romantic, *völkisch* citizenship, or vice versa, completely? Finally, placing these questions in broad terms, just how fixed are individuals' social and national identities? Does and should citizenship represent the deepest layers of cultural identity or proclaim the surface layers of political life?

## The Immigrant and Multiculturalist Critiques

The examination of national citizenship has demonstrated that traditions of national identity, though divided into opposing camps, are animated by the desire to homogenize the state's population by producing a fundamental overlap between citizens and nationals. In the post–Second World War era, however, global factors frustrate this goal. Contemporary waves of migration pose a clear challenge to the European conception of the nation-state as the political framework of a culturally homogenous citizenry. The growing number of migrants and their descendants, having forsaken one nation-state but not yet merged into another, are legal and cultural anomalies according to any national conception. On top of the still ongoing debates within many countries between adherents of the Enlightenment's liberal and Romanticism's *völkisch* versions of nationhood and citizenship, the diversification of industrial nation-states' populations produces new demands for the extension of the rights of citizens in yet new directions. Will Kymlicka's and Yasemin Soysal's essays outline two such directions that, nonetheless, are potentially opposed to each other. But there is also continuity between the nationalist and the postnationalist debates: the multiculturalist aspirations examined by Kymlicka share some, though not all, features of ethnic citizenship, whereas the global citizenship rights studied by Soysal seem to further expand the liberal framework of citizenship.

Kymlicka's multiculturalist perspective on polyethnicity, simply stated, calls for reforming social institutions in a way that will allow the accommodation of the cultural distinctiveness of multiple ethnic groups in a single state. Such an approach requires that rights be bestowed not only on individuals, as is done in the liberal mold, but on groups as well, thus leading to *differentiated citizenship*. Kymlicka's illustrations demonstrate that most democracies already confer rights on distinct groups when their members live in close proximity and, in fact, the claims of homogeneity made by nation-states had never been fully met and are in the process of rapid erosion. Multiculturalists would like to go further by instituting rights for groups that are not concentrated territorially; theirs is a new goal for a new era of diversity. Though multiculturalism in many ways signals a further extension of the religious tolerance that Rawls also cited as a basis of liberalism, it is also a step beyond, and in some views away from, the liberal tolerance of "pluralism."

Kymlicka's main purpose is to show that the apprehension that liberal society will be fragmented if group-based rights are granted is largely unfounded. The goal of ethnic groups, frequently composed of new immigrants, is not withdrawal from the mainstream, argues Kymlicka, but, on the contrary, the kind of inclusion that does not require the denial of their culture. Rawls already suggested that the creation of an overlapping consensus was the way to create cooperation in the face of pluralism. Kymlicka seeks a new, broader cultural consensus by extending Marshall's scheme. This would be attained by awarding what we might characterize as a *fourth citizenship right* (or, in the corresponding legal lingo, a fourth-generation right): adding cultural citizenship rights to the congeries of civil, political, and social citizenship rights.

Though multiculturalism in Kymlicka's view implies a willingness on the part of both immigrants and hosts to traverse part of the cultural gap between them, frequently multiculturalism is defined in a more sweeping and radical fashion. In such view, Western societies committed to multiculturalism must allow and facilitate each ethnic group's right to develop its own culture and, in the process, accede to the reduction of its Western-centrism. This multiculturalist perspective seeks not simply diversification of the majority's culture, so that it can include the contributions made by immigrants, but abandonment of the very notion of a majority culture. Radical multiculturalists hold that citizenship as identity takes precedence over citizenship as a legal status of membership.

The divergence of opinions among multiculturalists raises critical questions: Can citizenship itself be overextended to the point where it loses its integrative role, or is further democratization always the best solution to crises of democracy and alienation from the mainstream? Will increased participation by new groups compensate for the loss of the single status of citizenship for all? When religious and legal practices in the immigrants' cultures — such as those that violate gender equality — are incompatible with the civil rights of the host societies, which should prevail? And, turning to Marshall's scheme, will differentiated rights undermine the universal definition of citizenship rights on which the welfare system is based?

Kymlicka's approach to group-based citizenship rights of national minorities leads him to embrace at least some aspects of the radical definition of multiculturalism. In the debate between the adherents of the malleability of national identities and those arguing their "givenness," Kymlicka comes down on the side of the latter, seeing collective identities as generally very stable. Equally telling is his argument that a shared conception of justice and the rights based on it, as developed by Rawls, might not suffice for attaining social unity, whereas shared identity will unify the members of a society. Rights based on membership status in the political community seem to steadily recede, in his mind, before rights allocated on the basis of identity.

This preference becomes even clearer in Kymlicka's discussion of national minorities. Multiculturalism for immigrants can be, and usually is, combined with a commitment to common political institutions that provide social unity; thus polyethnicity does not threaten the state's political unity. In contrast, states with national minorities that, viewing themselves as a separate people, also seek some measure of self-government are under such threat. The coexistence of multiple political communities in one state may definitely lead to demands of ever-increasing autonomy, sovereignty, and, eventually, secession. Thus, paradoxically, the progression from *common citizenship,* typical to liberal societies, to *differentiated citizenship,* awarded to immigrant groups, to *dual citizenship,* granted to national minorities, as part of growing respect for cultural diversity, might lead from multicultural to unicultural states. Such development would defeat Kymlicka's stated goal.

Soysal's study of guest workers, many of whom became permanent residents of their host Western European societies, also shows that the character of the nation-state is challenged. Immigrants in Europe, even when they are not formally citizens, possess a modicum of civil and social rights (though not yet political ones) and, consequently, enjoy a measure of incorporation into their societies. They are a new category between citizens and immigrants, called by Hammar *denizens.* Soysal identifies the contemporary phenomenon of the decoupling of citizenship rights and identity as the key to their emergence.

Immigrants are the beneficiaries of the evolution of a new model of membership, seen in the transition from individual rights to *universal personhood.* Universal human rights replace national rights when universal personhood replaces nationhood as the defining site of citizenship. The incorporation of guest workers into their host societies, in contrast to Kymlicka's approach, is not sought through the expansion of rights within the nation-state but as the latter's transcendence in important respects. Nation-states decline in importance as states become increasingly interdependent, as illustrated by the rise of transnational political structures (like the United Nations and the European Union) and the spread of inter- and transnational market and security arrangements.

Soysal's study leads her to point to yet another, the fourth, transition in the site of citizenship: so far it was embedded in the *polis,* empire, town, and nation-state; now its purview is transnational or global. Not only immigrants but also citizens of the member states of the European Union, as agreed to in the 1991 Maastricht treaty, will be able to carry with them their rights as they move from state to state within the union. This ongoing transition, Soysal warns us, is partial: nation-states are declining but not disappearing. No new structure has emerged to replace the nation-state. The sovereign nation-state still remains the sole institution that administers and enforces rights, even those conceived to be universally held. Soysal, therefore, cautiously calls hers a *postnational* model, one in which state sovereignty is contested but not yet replaced. The postnational and the national frameworks remain concurrent.

Soysal's work raises new questions: Is the importance placed by multiculturalists on identity as the basis of citizenship exaggerated, and is there a return to the liberal emphasis on citizenship granted according to membership status? How far is the eclipse of nation-states likely to proceed? Will we ever possess a single world society, and what would the meaning of citizenship in such a world be? In general, which of the respective directions in which immigrants' rights are expanding, as documented by Kymlicka and Soysal, is likely to prevail?

## THE FEMINIST CRITIQUE

The last direction from which the liberal conception and practice of citizenship comes under intense and rigorous criticism is feminism. Feminists concur that women remained second-class citizens even in Western democracies, and only a few of them see the continued extension of liberal citizenship rights as sufficient to foster women's full integration into society in the future.

This skepticism is based on an identified male bias in the tradition of citizenship—found in the dichotomy between the private household (*oikos*) and the public sphere (*polis*)—that was central to the citizenship tradition from its inception in ancient Greece.[13] The consequent portrayal of the *public sphere* as transcendent, rational, and ultimately masculine and of the *private sphere* as the feminine realm of emotions and the weak body has not disappeared. The association of citizenship with military service, as in the Greek *polis,* or with labor market participation, as in Marshall's model, or the customarily narrow definition of politics and political participation as interaction with the state and its institutions prevents the full incorporation of women into the body politic. Fraser and Gordon point out that the independence gained by married men as male heads of nuclear families in the nineteenth century went hand in hand with and was predicated on making their spouses into their dependents. And even when women gain citizenship rights, their ability to act in the public realm is curtailed and their rights remain ineffective or only partially effective. Though citizenship was finally proclaimed to be universal, its erstwhile character as privilege keeps resurfacing. But beyond this agreement, as Jones's article asserts, alternative feminist schools emerge — communitarian, social democratic, multicultural, and neoliberal — and, consequently, the contending schools in the debate over the character of citizenship have been reproduced within the feminist discourse. All these schools probe the margins of liberalism.

Jones seeks to gather, as well as critique, the various perspectives and direct attention to the relevance of those empirical studies that highlight women's citizenship status and rights. Essays by Fraser and Gordon and by Young also address issues found in the feminist literature.

Feminists working within the framework of Marshall's approach probe the extent to which women's social citizenship rights can alter gender stratification. Some argue that allegedly gender-neutral welfare policies in fact create a two-tiered system in which women lose the autonomy that typifies citizens and become dependent on the welfare state and, consequently, gender stratification is increased. Conversely, others point to the disbursement of non-income-tested services as empowering their recipients and, furthermore, leading to solidarity among them. Finally, some take Marshall's argument further by suggesting that as social rights shield workers from the adverse effects of the labor market by decommodifying them, so women need to be shielded from the failure of marriage — for example, by establishing secure income for women engaged in full-time domestic work or child rearing.[14]

The strongest opposition to the liberal perspective comes from "difference feminism," whose adherents emphasize the unique aspects of women's social world and of female culture and call for the transformation of the citizenship tradition itself in order to make these features into the tradition's constituent parts. The liberal demand for equal rights, as Young notes, leads to the denial of differences and creates the paradoxical situation in which equal treatment is based on the repudiation of women essential's needs — for example, for maternity leave from the workplace.

Alternatively, in the communitarian approach, the formation of a women's community is proposed. This notion of community is based on voluntary, strong primary ties between women themselves. This approach expects to attenuate or replace the conflictual paradigm of politics with a model derived from the more intimate and particularistic bonds typical to kinship. Obligation to other women, in the latter view, may sometimes override the rights of the individual citizen. When the feminist community is international, the framework of the nation-state and its war-making focus are also challenged.

Since citizenship in antiquity, the Middle Ages, and the early modern era was identified with the masculine principle, many feminist works suggest that liberal and even revisited liberal attempts to extend citizenship as an abstract and disembodied practice, in disregard of concrete identities, are bound to fail. Feminist critiques of citizenship suggest that citizenship theories recognize the embodied self — its concrete identity, and the body itself — by reconstructing the public sphere to include the private or personal issues of concern to women. But the incorporation of private or embodied concerns, such as control over the body, alters the Greek, Roman, medieval, and early modern notions of citizenship, which essentially meant the replacement of particularistic identities with a public and universal identity. Would such extension of citizenship rights to cover biological matters and concerns, in the past considered private but now politicized by feminists and other social movements, make the citizenship tradition even broader and richer, or would it negate it altogether? Can the sphere of politics remain true to general concerns by seeking to focus on issues of concern to only part of the citizenry? Can the citizenship tradition be extended by being made true to its purportedly universalist promise, or does the very conception of citizenship need radical overhauling in order to accommodate gender equality, and thus be changed beyond recognition?

## MULTIPLE CITIZENSHIPS

The modern preoccupation with citizenship is an expression of a desire to create, and the capability to imagine, comprehensive membership frameworks that are capable of replacing the weakened communities of traditional society. But the aspiration to recover small and close-knit communities continues to coexist with the new citizenship frameworks, the most authoritative of which is the nation-state, while others are revised and new ones are imagined. Global citizenship discourses are also typical of the modern era, and they live at times in accommodation and at other times in conflict with the nation-state. In most societies these multiple citizenship frameworks coexist uneasily and sometimes in outright conflict with each other. By "citizenship," therefore, we need to understand not only a bundle of formal rights, but the entire mode of incorporation of a particular individual or group into society. By focusing on the multivalence of citizenship we will gain access to a major feature of modern society: a simultaneous and interconnected struggle for membership or identity or both with the intention of ensuring access to rights that are disbursed by state (and, occasionally, local and transnational) institutions. As a result of the coexistence of multiple citizenship discourses, we will see the citizenship tradition not as necessarily leveling, universalizing, and dignifying for all but as a complex system of status gradations.

The final part of this volume will examine the relationship between alternative citizenship discourses that most often have been analyzed in isolation from one another. We have already observed how Kymlicka's and Soysal's approaches share the conviction that in multicultural or postnational states citizenship is no longer a single status but rather a multiplicity of memberships (even among immigrants some are more privileged than others). Kymlicka characterizes modern polyethnic and multinational societies as alternating between differentiated and dual citizenship; Soysal portrays the push and pull of global and national institutions that leads to a multilevel citizenship structure. Both versions depict modern societies as full of unresolved tensions. We will turn now to an examination of the coexistence and tensions inherent in the multiplicity of citizenship traditions based, alternately, on status, participation, and identity.

We will contrast two approaches: Iris Young's, which calls for the institutionalization of multiple citizenships in order to enhance justice and fairness, with Michael Walzer's insistence that in light of such diversity one type of citizenship — political — should be preserved as a common foundation without, however, using it to supplant other versions. Where Young is concerned with group rights, Walzer's own survey of social pluralism concludes with a focus on the profound importance of public life: the common sphere of otherwise competing groups. Theirs are alternative notions of emancipation!

Young provides the most comprehensive and far-reaching criticism of the liberal promise of universal inclusion yet and of the very possibility of citizenship as equal rights for all. Citizenship even in its universal phase, she asserts, cannot but retain its character as privilege. Exclusion from citizenship does not result from an unwillingness to live up to the original pledge but, both in the liberal and in the republican tradition, was made in the name of universalism itself. The formation of a universal "public" presumes an ability and a willingness on the part of individuals to transcend their particular identities. In spite of "the near achievement of equal rights for all groups" nowadays, exclusion, Young asserts, will not disappear as long as there are, and unavoidably there always will remain, groups that have not assimilated to the requisite level of universality. Consequently, their members are faced with "the dilemma of difference": they have to deny that they are different from others since citizenship rights are based on the equal moral worth of citizens, but they have to affirm their difference from other groups since formal equal treatment puts them at a disadvantage. Formal equality, ironically, creates substantive inequality.

In Young's perspective, differences matter, and we cannot disregard them or successfully minimize their full impact as Rawls suggested. Instead, we should accept the unavoidability of social heterogeneity and the ensuing multiplicity of perspectives. Any concept of justice as fairness has to acknowledge that diversity by institutionalizing group-based representation enables groups to learn from each other and communicate to each other their multiple viewpoints and interests. True inclusion necessitates *group representation,* whereas equal treatment requires special *group rights,* leading Young to argue in favor of the *differentiation of citizenship.* Whereas Kymlicka bases the same demand for group representation on the grounds of cultural differences, Young seeks such rights for all oppressed groups in the United States, among which she lists women, blacks, Native Americans, Chicanos, Puerto Ricans and other Spanish-speaking Americans, Asian Americans, gay men, lesbians, working-class people, poor people, old people, and mentally and physically disabled people.

An empirical study by Peled and Shafir examines the reality of several citizenships in the context of Israel and the Israeli-Palestinian conflict and demonstrates both the dangers and the promises of multiplicity. The coexistence of citizenship discourses in Israel — republican, nationalist, and liberal — as well as lack of citizenship rights in the Israel-controlled Occupied Territories allows both for the incorporation of various hierarchically stratified groups and for the complete exclusion of other groups. Differentiated citizenship is just as likely to be hierarchical as it is to be vertical or sectional. Such hierarchy of citizenships leads to struggle over the types of citizenship rights distinguished by Marshall, not all of which can be taken for granted by all and a few of which cannot be taken for granted by some of the groups. This analysis provides a possible model for studying citizenship dynamics as a framework for social research. It also raises the question of whether the multiplication of group rights or their collapse into a single liberal framework is most likely to ensure effective incorporation.

Young is aware of the danger that dividing political rights on the basis of group rights might lead to multiple criteria of inclusion and, consequently, to citizens with varying rights. She seeks to eliminate such a danger by transferring the site of the disadvantage from the group itself to society: instead of viewing oppressed groups as deviant cases in need of special treatment, she wishes to assert the heterogeneity of society and the "plural circumstances" of its members as a natural condition of society itself. To remove the homogenizing tendency of universal citizenship, majority culture itself has to be replaced with a truly heterogenous culture.

Walzer compares and critiques four ideals of the "good life" — citizen, producer, consumer, and member of the nation — and examines their relationship to each other. The first is the realm of active engagement in the public life of society, whereas the other three have more detached and ambiguous relations to politics. Though Walzer associates citizenship, as in the Greek tradition, with politics as moral behavior and, therefore, as the highest form of humanity, in fact each of the four versions of the good life possesses its own citizenship discourse. The contention between these versions of the good life is, in fact, the citizenship debate.

And yet, political citizenship plays a crucial role in Walzer's multidimensional framework. It is in this sphere of citizenship where individuals "think about a common good, beyond their own conceptions of the good life" and employ the state as a political tool for shaping their common life. "Hence" concludes Walzer, "citizenship has a certain practical preeminence among all our actual and possible memberships." After all the alterations, transformations, and additions to citizenship theory, the Greek tradition lost its unique position but, as Walzer shows, it continues to provide the common core of social membership. Walzer returns us to the starting point of the tradition to confirm the enduring power of the Greek conception of citizenship as the principle of incorporation and social unity. But he rounds out the tradition of citizenship with the modern concept of civil society — "a setting of settings" — to provide another, less formalistic, version of the quest for toleration pursued by Rawls. Whereas citizenship is the basis of social unity, civil society, Walzer asserts, by allowing competing exclusive claims to accent one another's inherent limits, fulfills its classical task of generating civility. Citizenship, therefore, retains a privileged position among our multiple membership commitments.

In Walzer's and Young's respective essays, the contours of the contemporary debate are most sharply illuminated. Though Walzer and Young share the premise that citizenship discourses need to acknowledge the social pluralism and diversity that typify our modern society, they disagree about the proper way of doing so. Walzer views the political framework of citizenship as the arena in which a modicum of social unity is established since all individuals in society are its members and sometimes are active participants. Citizenship, however, cannot serve as the vehicle for the communitarian desire for the pursuit of a common good, not so much because of cultural or ethnic diversity but, as Rawls suggested, because there exist significantly different ideals of the good life and the common good. Within the voluntary civil society their plurality will be respected. The moderate goal of mutual respect is within reach within a modern civil society that is animated by the unifying authority of the citizenship tradition.

In contrast, citizenship for Young, even when its reach is well neigh universal, will always retain part of its character as privilege for those who fall within its implicit criterion of adhering to the elusive common good. Consequently, she argues, the allegedly universal character of citizenship, which as Kymlicka has shown is in many ways more illusion than reality even in modern industrial societies, should be replaced by differentiated citizenship. She suggests a changed focus: instead of being concerned with commonality and, consequently, ignoring or at least bypassing diversity, priority should be given to making the public sphere truly representative not only of individuals but of groups as well. Though Young opposes fundamental features of citizenship as we know it, she is, in fact, asserting that the citizenship tradition has not yet exhausted its potential to liberate oppressed groups. This can be accomplished by integrating diversity into the framework of citizenship itself. Walzer's and Young's perspectives represent the cutting edge of the debates on contemporary citizenship, its hopes and fears, its limits and potential for extension. Their essays are a fitting summary to the debates in which the character of our future society is contested.

## NOTES

1. For a similar mental exercise, see David Johnstone, *The Idea of Liberal Theory: A Critique and Reconstruction* (Princeton, N.J.: Princeton University Press, 1994), pp. 11–12.

2. For two helpful overviews of Rawls's approach, see Johnstone, *The Idea of Liberal Theory,* chapter 4, and Michael Pakaluk, "The Liberalism of John Rawls: A Brief Exposition," in Christopher Wolfe and John Hittinger, eds., *Liberalism at the Crossroads* (Lanham, Md.: Rowman & Littlefield), pp. 1–21.

3. See Johnstone, *The Idea of Liberal Theory,* p. 109.

4. John Rawls, *A Theory of Justice* (Cambridge, Mass.: Belknap, 1971), Pars. 1, 68; *Political Liberalism* (New York: Columbia University Press, 1993), Lecture V.

5. Stephen Macedo, *Liberal Virtues: Citizenship, Virtue, and Community in Liberal Constitutionalism* (Oxford: Clarendon, 1990), pp. 29–35, 50–64.

6. Macedo, *Liberal Virtues,* p. 17.

7. An exception is Robert D. Putnam's *Making Democracy Work: Civic Traditions in Modern Italy* (Princeton, N.J.: Princeton University Press, 1993), which seeks to alleviate one of the major problems of the communitarian

approach: its vagueness about the choice of the community that will fulfill the civic republican vision. Putnam's study of effective democracy in Italy leads him to locate the effective community at the regional level. Local civic tradition of participatory citizenship enhances regional democracy and conceivably can do so on a state level as well. But while his work is empirical and the studies of most communitarians remain abstract, Putnam shares one of their shortcomings: he did not include in his study an examination of the conception of the good pursued by the associations he surveyed, nor is he willing to endorse either a single conception of what is good in life or any and all that arise. Putnam is aware of, and warns against, the coalescence of solidarity and involvement generated by civic traditions around nondemocratic goals (such as the Ku Klux Klan or the Fascist Party), but this warning remains incidental to his theory.

8. For a survey and evaluation of Marshall's work, see J. M. Barbalet, *Citizenship: Rights, Struggle and Class Inequality* (Milton Keynes: Open University Press, 1988).

9. Michael Mann, "Ruling Class Strategies and Citizenship," *Sociology* 21, no. 3 (Aug. 1987):339–54.

10. Margaret R. Sommers, "Citizenship and the Place of the Public Sphere: Law, Community, and Political Culture in the Transition to Democracy," *American Sociological Review* 58 (Oct. 1993):587–620.

11. Gosta Esping-Andersen, *Politics against Markets: The Social Democratic Road to Power* (Princeton, N.J.: Princeton University Press, 1985), pp. 145–78.

12. T. H. Marshall, "Citizenship and Social Class," in *Class, Citizenship, and Social Development: Essays by T. H. Marshall*, ed. Seymour Martin Lipset (Chicago: University of Chicago Press, 1964), pp. 92–93.

13. See Susan Moller Okin, "Women, Equality and Citizenship," *Queens Quarterly* 99, no. 1 (Spring 1992):56–71.

14. For an international comparison of women's welfare rights, see Ann Shola Orloff, "Gender and the Social Rights of Citizenship: The Comparative Analysis of Gender Relations and Welfare States," *American Sociological Review* 58 (June 1993):303–28.

# PART I
## HISTORICAL ORIGINS AND ANTECEDENTS

# 2

## *The Ideal of Citizenship since Classical Times*

### J. G. A. Pocock

When we speak of the "ideal" of "citizenship" since "classical" times, the last term refers to times that are "classical" in a double sense. In the first place, these times are "classical" in the sense that they are supposed to have for us the kind of authority that comes of having expressed an "ideal" in durable and canonical form—though in practice the authority is always conveyed in more ways than by its simple preservation in that form. In the second place, by "classical" times, we always [mean] the ancient civilizations of the Mediterranean, in particular Athens in the fifth and fourth centuries B.C. and Rome from the third century B.C. to the first A.D. It is Athenians and Romans who are supposed to have articulated the "ideal of citizenship" for us, and their having done so is part of what makes them "classical." There is not merely a "classical" ideal of citizenship articulating what citizenship is; "citizenship" is itself a "classical ideal," one of the fundamental values that we claim is inherent in our "civilization" and its "tradition." I am putting these words in quotation marks not because I wish to discredit them, but because I wish to focus attention upon them; when this is done, however, they will turn out to be contestable and problematic.

The "citizen"—the Greek *polites* or Latin *civis*—is defined as a member of the Athenian *polis* or Roman *res publica,* a form of human association allegedly unique to these Mediterranean peoples and by them transmitted to "Europe" and "the West." This claim to uniqueness can be criticized and relegated to the status of myth; even when this happens, however, the myth has a way of remaining unique as a determinant of "western" identity—no other civilization has a myth like this. Unlike the great coordinated societies that arose in the river valleys of Mesopotamia, Egypt, and China, the *polis* was a small society, rather exploitatively than intimately related to its productive environment, and perhaps originally not much more than a stronghold of barbarian raiders. It could therefore focus its attention less on its presumed place in a cosmic order of growth and recurrence, and more on the heroic individualism of the relations obtaining between its human members; the origins of humanism are to that extent in barbarism. Perhaps this is why the foundation myths of the *polis* do not describe its separation from the great cosmic orders of Egypt or Mesopotamia, but its substitution of its own values for those of an archaic tribal society of blood feuds and kinship obligations. Solon and Kleisthenes, the legislators of Athens, substitute for an assembly of clansmen speaking as clan members on clan concerns an assembly of citizens whose members may speak on any matter concerning the *polis* (in Latin, on any *res publica,* a term which is transferred to denote the assembly and the society themselves). In the *Eumenides,* the last play in Aeschylus's *Oresteia,* another fundamental expression of foundation myth, Orestes comes on the scene as blood-guilty tribesman and leaves it as a free citizen capable with his equals of judging and resolving his own guilt. It is, however, uncertain whether the blood-guilt has been altogether wiped out or remains concealed at the foundations of the city—there are Roman myths that express the same ambivalence—and the story is structured in such a way that women easily symbolize the primitive culture of blood, guilt, and kinship which the males, supposedly, are trying to surpass. But the men, as heroes, continue to act out the primitive values (and to blame the women for it).

This is a point that must be made strongly, and made all the time, but it does not remove the fact that, stated as an ideal, the community of citizens is one in which speech takes the place of blood, and acts of decision take the place of acts of vengeance. The "classical" account of citizenship as an Athenian "ideal" is to be found in Aristotle's *Politics,* a text written late enough in *polis* history—after the advent of the Platonic academy and the Macedonian empire—to qualify as one of the meditations of the Owl of Minerva. In this great work we are told that the citizen is one who both rules and is ruled. As intelligent and purposive beings we desire to direct that which can be directed toward some purpose; to do so is not just an operational good, but an expression of that which is best in us, namely, the capacity to pursue operational goods. Therefore it is good to rule. But ruling becomes better in proportion as that which is ruled is itself better, namely, endowed with some capacity of its own for the intelligent pursuit of good. It is better to rule animals than things, slaves than animals, women than slaves, one's fellow citizens than the women, slaves, animals, and things contained in one's household. But what makes the citizen the highest order of being is his capacity to rule, and it follows that rule over one's equal is possible only where one's equal rules over one. Therefore the citizen rules and is ruled; citizens join each other in making decisions where each decider respects the authority of the others, and all join in obeying the decisions (now known as "laws") they have made.

This account of human equality excludes the greater part of the human species from access to it. Equality, it says, is something of which only a very few are capable, and we in our time know, at least, that equality has prerequisites and is not always easy to achieve. For Aristotle the prerequisites are not ours; the citizen must be a male of known genealogy, a patriarch, a warrior, and the master of the labor of others (normally slaves), and these prerequisites in fact outlasted the ideal of citizenship, as he expressed it, and persisted in Western culture for more than two millennia. Today we all attack them, but we haven't quite got rid of them yet, and this raises the uncomfortable question of whether they are accidental or in some way essential to the ideal of citizenship itself. Is it possible to eliminate race, class, and gender as prerequisites to the condition of ruling and being ruled, to participate as equals in the taking of public decisions, and leave the classical description of that condition in other respects unmodified? Feminist theorists have had a great deal to say on this question, and I should like to defer to them — and leave it to them to speak about it. At an early point in the exposition of the problem, one can see that they face a choice between citizenship as a condition to which women should have access, and subverting or deconstructing the ideal itself as a device constructed in order to exclude them. To some extent this is a rhetorical or tactical choice, and therefore philosophically vulgar, but there are real conceptual difficulties behind it.

Aristotle's formulation depends upon a rigorous separation of public from private, of *polis* from *oikos,* of persons and actions from things. To qualify as a citizen, the individual must be the patriarch of a household or *oikos,* in which the labor of slaves and women satisfied his needs and left him free to engage in political relationships with his equals. But to engage in those relationships, the citizen must leave his household altogether behind, maintained by the labor of his slaves and women, but playing no further part in his concerns. The citizens would never dream of discussing their household affairs with one another, and only if things had gone very wrong indeed would it be necessary for them to take decisions in the assembly designed to ensure patriarchal control of the households. In the parafeminist satires of Aristophanes they have to do this, but they haven't the faintest idea how to set about it; there is no available discourse, because the situation is unthinkable. What they discuss and decide in the assembly of affairs of the *polis* and not the *oikos*: affairs of war and commerce between the city and other cities, affairs of preeminence and emulation, authority and virtue, between the citizens themselves. To Aristotle and many others, politics (alias the activity of ruling and being ruled) is a good in itself, not the prerequisite of the public good, but the public good in *res publica* correctly defined. What matters is the freedom to take part in public decisions, not the content of the decisions taken. This nonoperational or noninstrumental definition of politics has remained part of our definition of freedom ever since and explains the role of citizenship in it. Citizenship is not just a means to being free; it is the way of being free itself. Aristotle based his definition of citizenship on a very rigorous distinction between ends and means, which makes it an ideal in the strict sense that it entailed an escape for the *oikos,* the material infrastructure in which one was forever managing the instruments of action, into the *polis,* the ideal superstructure in which one took actions that were not means to ends but ends in themselves. Slaves would never escape from the material because they were destined to remain instruments, things managed by others; women would never escape from the *oikos* because they were destined to remain managers of the slaves and other things. Here is the central dilemma of emancipation: does one concentrate on making the escape or on denying that the escape needs to be made? Either way, one must reckon with those who affirm that it needs to be made by others, but that they have never needed to make it. The citizen and the freedman find it difficult to become equals.

If one wants to make citizenship available to those to whom it has been denied on the grounds that they are too much involved in the world of things — in material, productive, domestic, or reproductive relationships — one has to choose between emancipating them from these relationships and denying that these relationships are negative components in the definition of citizenship. If one chooses the latter course, one is in search of a new definition of citizenship, differing radically from the Greek definition articulated by Aristotle, a definition in which public and private are not rigorously separated and the barriers between them have become permeable or have disappeared altogether. In the latter case, one will have to decide whether the concept of the "public" has survived at all, whether it has merely become contingent and incidental, or has actually been denied any distinctive meaning. And if that is what has happened, the concept of citizenship may have disappeared as well. That is the predicament with which the "classical ideal of citizenship" confronts those who set out to criticize or modify it, and they have not always avoided the traps the predicament puts before them. In the next part of this essay, I shall consider how some alternative definitions of citizenship have become historically available, but before I do so, I want to emphasize that the classical ideal was and is a definition of the human person as a cognitive, active, moral, social, intellectual, and political being. To Aristotle, it did not seem that the human — being cognitive, active, and purposive — could be fully human unless he ruled himself. It appeared that he could not do this unless he ruled things and others in the household, and joined with his equals to rule and be ruled in the city. While making it quite clear that this fully developed humanity was accessible only to a very few adult males, Aristotle made it no less clear that this was the only full development of humanity there was (subject only to the Platonic suggestion that the life of pure thought might be higher still than the life of pure action). He therefore declared that the human was *kata phusin zoon politikon,* a creature formed by nature to live a political life, and this, one of the great Western definitions of what it is to be human, is a formulation we are still strongly disposed to accept. We do instinctively, or by some inherited programming, believe that the individual denied decision in shaping her or his life is being denied treatment as a human, and that citizenship — meaning membership in some public and political frame of action — is necessary if we are to be granted decision and empowered to be human. Aristotle arrived at this point — and took us there with him — by supposing a scheme of values in which political action was a good in itself and not merely instrumental to goods beyond it. In taking part in such action the citizen attained value as a human being; he knew himself to be who and what he was; no other mode of action could permit him to be that and know that he was. Therefore his personality depended on his emancipation from the world of things and his entry into the world of politics, and when this emancipation was denied to others, they must decide whether to seek it for themselves or to deny its status as a prerequisite of humanity. If they took the latter course, they must produce an alternative definition of humanity or face the consequences of having none. *Kata phusin zoon politikon* set the stakes of discourse very high indeed.

I want to turn now to a second great Western definition of the political universe. This one is not aimed at definition of the citizen, and therefore, in Aristotle's sense, it is not political at all. But it so profoundly affects our understanding of the citizen that it has to be considered part of the concept's history. This is the formula, ascribed to the Roman jurist Gaius, according to which the universe as defined by jurisprudence is divisible into "persons, actions, and things [*res*]." (Gaius lived about five centuries after the time of Aristotle, and the formula was probably well known when he made use of it.) Here we move from the ideal to the real, even though many of the *res* defined by the jurist are far more ideal than material, and we move from the citizen as a political being to the citizen as a legal being, existing in a world of persons, actions, and things regulated by law. The intrusive concept here is that of "things." Aristotle's citizens were persons acting on one another, so that their active life was a life immediately and heroically moral. It would not be true to say that they were unconcerned with things, since the *polis* possessed and administered such things as walls, lands, trade, and so forth, and there were practical decisions to be taken about them. But the citizens did not act upon each other through the medium of things, and did not in the first instance define one another as the possessors and administrators of things. We saw that things had been left behind in the *oikos,* and that, though one must possess them in order to leave them behind, the *polis* was a kind of ongoing potlatch in which citizens emancipated themselves from their possessions in order to meet face to face in a political life that was an end in itself. But for the Roman jurist it was altogether different; persons acted upon things, and most of their actions were directed at taking or maintaining possession; it was through these actions, and through the things or possessions which were the subjects of the actions, that they encountered one another and entered into relationships which might require regulation. The world of things, or *res,* claimed the status of "reality"; it was the medium in which human beings lived and through which they formed, regulated, and articulated their relations with each other. The person was defined and represented through his actions upon things; in the course of time, the term *property* came to mean, first, the defining characteristic of a human or other being; second, the relation which a person had with a thing; and third, the thing defined as the possession of some person. From being *kata phusin zoon politikon,* the human individual came to be by nature a proprietor or possessor of things; it is in jurisprudence, long before the rise and supremacy of the market, that we should locate the origins of possessive individualism.

The individual thus became a citizen — and the word *citizen* diverged increasingly from its Aristotelian significance — through the possession of things and the practice of jurisprudence. His actions were in the first instance directed at things and at other persons through the medium of things; in the second instance, they were actions he took, or others took in respect of him, at law — acts of authorization, appropriation, conveyance, acts of litigation, prosecution, justification. His relation to things was regulated by law, and his actions were performed in respect either of things or of the law regulating actions. A "citizen" came to mean someone free to act by law, free to ask and expect the law's protection, a citizen of such and such a legal community, of such and such a legal standing in that community. A famous narrative case is that of Saint Paul announcing himself a Roman citizen. Paul not only asserts that as a citizen he is immune from arbitrary punishment, he goes on to remind the officer threatening the punishment that he is a citizen by birth and the officer only by purchase and therefore of lower prestige and authority. Citizenship has become a legal status, carrying with it rights to certain things — perhaps possessions, perhaps immunities, perhaps expectations — available in many kinds and degrees, available or unavailable to many kinds of person for many kinds of reason. There is still much about it that is ideal, but it has become part of the domain of contingent reality, a category of status in the world of persons, actions, and things. One can say in the world of Saint Paul that citizenship is a right to certain things, and say far more than by saying the same in the world according to Aristotle.

We now ask: in what sense does *citizen* remain a political term after it has become a legal or juristic concept? An Aristotelian citizen, ruling and being ruled, took part in the making or determining of the laws by which he was governed. There had been a time when *civis Romanus* had similarly denoted one who participated in the self-governing assemblies of republican Rome. But Paul — who is not a Roman, has never seen Rome, and will find no assembly of the citizens if he ever gets there — means something quite different. By claiming to be a Roman citizen, he means that of the various patterns of legally defined rights and immunities available to subjects of a complex empire made up of many communities, he enjoys access to the most uniform and highly privileged there is. Had he been only a citizen of Tarsus, the officer might have ordered him to be flogged, especially as they were not in Tarsus at the time. But he is a Roman citizen and can claim rights and immunities outside the officer's jurisdiction. The ideal of citizenship has come to denote a legal status, which is not quite the same thing as a political status and which will, in due course, modify the meaning of the term *political* itself. Over many centuries, the *legalis homo* will come to denote one who can sue and be sued in certain courts, and it will have to be decided whether this is or is not the same as ruling and being ruled in an Aristotelian *polis.*

The status of "citizen" now denoted membership in a community of shared or common law, which may or may not be identical with a territorial community. In Paul's case it is not; the status of "Roman citizen" is one of several extended by Roman imperial authority to privileged groups throughout the empire (who enjoy it, wherever they may be, while living and moving — empires can be highly mobile societies — alongside others who enjoy only local and municipal privileges in communities more localized and territorial in terms of the laws that define them). In much later centuries, these municipal communities become known by the medieval French term *bourg,* and one's right of membership in them, one's right of appeal to the privilege and protection of municipal law, comes to be known as one's *bourgeoisie.* In virtue of one of those rhetorical devices that extend meaning from the part to the whole, the universal community of legal privilege to which Saint Paul laid claim, and his right of membership within it, came to be described as his *bourgeoisie Romaine,* the municipal authority of that city having become imperial. But *bourgeois* and *bourgeoisie* came to denote membership in a municipal — rather than an imperial or political — community. While the bourgeois might sue and be sued, it was not clear that he ruled and was ruled, even when his *bourg* might claim to be free and sovereign. In consequence, although many cities and *civitates* had been reduced to the municipal status of *bourgs* within empires and states, and the words *bourgeois* and *citizen* were used interchangeably as a result, there was always room for doubt whether they conveyed the same meanings — whether the *bourgeois* really enjoyed, should enjoy, or wanted to enjoy the absolute liberty to rule and be ruled asserted by the ideal of citizenship in its classical or Aristotelian sense.

It was the notion of law that profoundly altered the meaning of the political. As Paul and Gaius both knew, law denoted something imperial, universal, and multiform; there were many kinds of law, some of which applied everywhere and some of which did not. As soon, therefore, as one employed the term *citizen* to denote the member of a community defined by law, there might be as many definitions of *citizen* as there were kinds of law. There was a community of Roman citizens like Paul, who might claim the same status wherever they went in the empire; there were numerous communities of those whose citizenship was only municipal and did not apply where municipal authority could not be appealed to; there was half the population according to gender and about half according to the distinction between slave and free who were not citizens at all and could not take the initiative in claiming the protection of the law even if it was offered them. And there was the notion — a new "classical ideal" — of a universal community to which all humans belonged as subject to the law of nature. But whether one was a "citizen" of the community defined by the law of nature was a question that strained the resources even of metaphor. Certainly one did not "rule" in it, if by "rule" was meant determining what the law of the community should be; there was no assembly of all mankind, and the very notion of a universal law meant that one could be a citizen only municipally, determining what the local, particular, and municipal application of the law of nature should be. There had by this time appeared the figure, or ideal type, of the philosopher, who, as the word was used as a classical idea, claimed that the cognition of natural law was an intellectual activity, and that by a separation between contemplation and action, theory and practice, the philosopher had acquired in his ideal world the absolute freedom of determination once sought by the citizen in his *polis*. There are those who think the history of political thought has no meaning outside the history of this claim by the philosopher, but my commission is to peruse the history of the concept of the citizen.

The advent of jurisprudence moved the concept of the "citizen" from the *zoon politikon* toward the *legalis homo,* and from the *civis* or *polites* toward the bourgeois or burger. It further brought about some equation of the "citizen" with the "subject," for in defining him as the member of a community of law, it emphasized that he was, in more senses than one, the subject of those laws that defined his community and of the rulers and magistrates empowered to enforce them. It would do little violence to our use of language to suppose that Saint Paul claimed to be a Roman "subject" since by doing so he could claim protection and privilege as well as offering allegiance and obedience. This is why the last action he performs as *civis Romanus* is to exercise his right of appealing to Caesar, after which the local magistrates are obliged to send him to Rome to be judged by Caesar, and we don't know exactly what Caesar did with him when he got there; Caesar's jurisdiction certainly extended to judgment of life or death. All this would be in the minds of Lord Palmerston and his parliamentary hearers when he proclaimed that any British subject might say with Paul "civis Romanus sum." In terms of protection and allegiance, right and authority, *subject* and *citizen* might be interchangeable terms, and when my passport declares me to be a United Kingdom "citizen" as well as a British "subject," I know that it is offering me rights and protections within the United Kingdom which may be denied to other "British subjects," and I am not altogether reassured, even though I am being privileged, by the implied separation between "subject" and "citizen," which once meant the same thing.

What is the difference between a classical "citizen" and an imperial or modern "subject"? The former ruled and was ruled, which meant among other things that he was a participant in determining the laws by which he was to be bound. The latter could appeal to Caesar; that is, he could go into court and invoke a law that granted him rights, immunities, privileges, and even authority, and that could not ordinarily be denied him once he had established his right to invoke it. But he might have no hand whatever in making that law or in determining what it was to be. It can be replied that this is too formal a way of putting it; the law functions in such a way that it is determined in the process of adjudication, and litigants, witnesses, compurgators, pleaders, and so forth play a variety of parts in the process of determining it. The *legalis homo* is not necessarily a subject in the rigorously passive sense. But the growth of jurisprudence decenters and may marginalize the assembly of citizens by the enormous diversity of answers it brings to the questions of where and by whom law is made, and how far it is made — how far determined and how far discovered. It may be found in the order of nature, the revealed will of God, the pleasure of the prince, the judgment of the magistrate, the decree of the assembly, or the customs and usages formed in the processes of social living themselves; and in this majestic hierarchy of lawgivers, the assembly of citizens, meeting face to face in the utter freedom to determine what and who they shall be, can only be one and may sink into entire insignificance. *Legalis homo* is perpetually in search of the authority that may underlie determinations of the law; the need to close off this search within the human world may induce him to locate sovereignty whenever it seems to have come to rest, in prince or people, and there are circumstances in which sovereignty may be lodged in the assembly of the citizens, so that the individual as citizen comes again to be what he was in the classical ideal, a coauthor of the law to which he is subject. But there are so many other possible locations of sovereignty, and so many ways of determining and discovering law other than by the sovereign's decree, that even when the subject is a member of the sovereign, he is unlikely to forget Charles I's dictum that "a subject and a sovereign are clean different things" and may ask whether he is the same person when ruling that he was when being ruled. This is the question repeatedly asked by Jean-Jacques Rousseau, the last great philosopher of early modern politics, and it reminds us that even from the world of Paul and Gaius — let alone from the world of Jean-Jacques — the road back to the heroic simplicities of the *polis* may be too long to be traversed. Yet the meaning of "the ideal of citizenship since classical times" is that we constantly need to explore this road back, even if we cannot travel it, and it is important to understand why we have this need....

# 3
## Citizenship in Ancient and Medieval Cities
### MAX WEBER

The concept of citizenship (*Bürgertum*), as it is used in social history, carries three distinct meanings: [economic, political, and cultural]. First, citizenship may include certain social categories or classes which have a specific communal or economic interest. As thus defined, class citizenship is stratified; there are greater citizens and lesser citizens; entrepreneurs and manual laborers. Second, in the political sense, citizenship signifies membership in the state, with its connotation as the holder of certain political rights. Finally, by citizens . . . we understand those strata which are drawn together, in contrast with the bureaucracy or the proletariat and others outside their circle, as "persons of property and culture," entrepreneurs, recipients of funded incomes, and in general all persons of academic culture, a certain class standard of living, and a certain social prestige.

The first of these meanings is economic in character and is peculiar to Western civilization. There are and have been everywhere manual laborers and entrepreneurs, but never and nowhere were they included in a unitary social class. The [second meaning], the notion of the citizen of the state, has its forerunners in antiquity and in the medieval city. Here there were citizens as holders of political rights, while outside of the West only traces of this relation are met with. . . . The farther east we go the fewer are these traces; the notion of citizens of the state is unknown to the world of

Islam, and to India and China. Finally, [the third meaning], the social signification of citizen as the man of property and culture, [as a "man with class,"]
or of one or the other, in contrast with the nobility, on the one hand, and
the proletariat, on the other, is likewise a specifically modern and Western
concept, similar to that of the bourgeoisie. At the same time, in antiquity
and in the Middle Ages, citizen was also an [economic] class concept; membership in specific class groups made the person a citizen.

     ... The citizen in the quality of membership in a class is always a
citizen of a particular city, and the city in this sense has existed only in the
Western world, or elsewhere, as in the early period in Mesopotamia, only
in an incipient stage.... Outside the West there have not been cities in the
sense of a unitary community. In the Middle Ages, the city's distinguishing
characteristic was the possession of its own law and court and an autonomous
administration of whatever extent. The citizen of the Middle Ages was a
citizen because and insofar as he came under this law and participated in
the choice of administrative officials. That cities have not existed outside
the West in the sense of a political community is a fact calling for explanation. That the reason was economic in character is very doubtful. . . .

     For the fact that this development took place only in the West there
are two reasons. The first is the peculiar character of the organization for
defense. The Western city is in its beginnings first of all a defense group, an
organization of those economically competent to bear arms, to equip and
train themselves.

     [In general], whether the military organization is based on the prin-
ciple of self-equipment or on that of equipment by a military overlord who
furnishes horses, arms, and provisions is a distinction quite as fundamental
for social history as is the question whether the means of economic production are the property of the worker or of a capitalistic entrepreneur. Everywhere outside the West the development of the city was prevented by the
fact that the army of the prince is older than the city. The earliest Chinese
epics do not, like the Homeric, speak of the hero who fares forth to battle
in his own chariot, but only of the officer as a leader of the men. Likewise
in India an army led by officers marched out against Alexander the Great.
In the West, the army equipped by the warlord, and the separation of soldier
from the paraphernalia of war in a way analogous to the separation of the
worker from the means of production, arises only in the modern era, while
in Asia it stands at the apex of the historical development. There was no
Egyptian or Babylonian-Assyrian army which would have presented a picture similar to that of the Homeric mass army, the feudal army of the West,
the city army of the ancient *polis,* or the medieval guild army.

The difference is based on the fact that the question of irrigation was crucial in the cultural evolution of Egypt, western Asia, India, and China. The water question led to the rise of the bureaucracy, the compulsory service of the dependent classes, and the dependence of the subject classes upon the functioning of the bureaucracy of the king. That the king also expressed his power in the form of a military monopoly is the basis of the distinction between the military organization of Asia and that of the West. In the first case the royal official and army officer is from the beginning the central figure of the process, while in the West both were originally absent. [Consequently,] the forms of religious brotherhood and self-equipment for war made possible the origin and existence of the city. It is true that the beginnings of an analogous development are found in the East. In India we meet with relations which verge upon the establishment of a city in the Western sense, namely, the combination of self-equipment and legal citizenship; one who could furnish an elephant for the army is in the free city of Vaiçali a full citizen. In ancient Mesopotamia, too, the knights carried on war with each other and established cities with autonomous administration. But in the one case as in the other these beginnings later disappear as the great kingdom arises on the basis of water regulation. Hence only in the West did the development come to complete maturity.

The second obstacle which prevented the development of the city in the East was formed by ideas and institutions connected with magic. In India the castes were not in a position to form ritualistic communities and hence a city, because they were ceremonially alien to one another. The same facts explained the peculiar position of the Jews in the Middle Ages. The cathedral and the Eucharist were the symbols of the city's unity, but the Jews were not permitted to pray in the cathedral or take part in the Communion and hence were doomed to form diaspora communities. The condition which enabled cities to develop in the West in antiquity was the extensive freedom of the priesthood, the absence of any monopoly in the hands of the priests over communion with the gods, such as obtained in Asia. In Western antiquity the officials of the city performed the rites, and the resultant proprietorship of the *polis* over the things belonging to the gods and the priestly treasures was carried to the point of filling the priestly offices by auction, since no magical limitations stood in the way as in India. For the later period in the West three great facts were crucial. The first was prophecy among the Jews, which destroyed magic within the confines of Judaism; magical procedure remained real but was devilish instead of divine. The second was the Pentecostal miracle, the ceremonial adoption into the spirit of Christ which was a decisive factor in the extraordinary spread of the early Christian enthusiasm. The final factor was the day in Antioch when Paul, in opposition to Peter, espoused fellowship with the uncircumcised. The magical barriers between clans, tribes, and peoples, which were still known in the ancient *polis* to a considerable degree, were thus set aside and the establishment of the Western city was made possible.

Although the city in the strict sense is specifically a Western institution, there are fundamental distinctions among the cities of antiquity and the Middle Ages. . . . During the early years of the ancient and medieval cities the similarity between them was very great. In both, it is those of knightly birth, the families leading an aristocratic existence, who alone are active members in the group, while all the remaining population is merely bound to obedience. . . .

Medieval development and antiquity part ways with the establishment of democracy, though even here at first there is a great deal of similarity. . . . The basis of democratization is everywhere purely military in character; it lies in the rise of disciplined infantry, the hoplites of antiquity, the guild army in the Middle Ages. The decisive fact was that military discipline proved its superiority over the battle between heroes. Military discipline meant the triumph of democracy because the community wished and was compelled to secure the cooperation of the nonaristocratic masses and hence put arms, and along with arms political power, into their hands. . . .

[On their part], the *popolani* know that they have fought and won the great wars of the city along with the nobility; they are armed, and hence feel themselves discriminated against and are no longer content with the subordinate class position that they have previously accepted. Similarities exist also, finally, in securing the right of intervention in legal processes for plebeians' representatives, as part of their opposition to the aristocrats. . . .

Alongside the points of agreement there are categorical differences. At the outset there is an ultimate distinction as regards the divisions into which the city falls. In the Middle Ages these consist of the guilds, while in antiquity they never possessed the guild character. . . .

Under the domination of the guilds, the medieval city pursued a special type of policy, called town-economy. Its objective was in the first place to maintain the traditional access to occupation and livelihood, and, in the second place, to make the surrounding country subservient to the town interest to the utmost extent through *banalités* and compulsory use of the town market. It sought further to restrict competition and prevent the development toward large-scale industry. In spite of all, an opposition developed between trading capital and craft work organized in guilds, with a growth of domestic industry and of a permanent journeyman class as a forerunner of the modern proletariat. Nothing of all this is to be found in antiquity under the rule of democracy.... Thus in antiquity the guild, as the ruling power in the town, is absent, and with it guild policy, and also the opposition between labor and capital which is present even at the close of the Middle Ages.

In place of this conflict we find in antiquity the opposition between the land owner and the landless. The proletarian is not, as Mommsen avers, a man who can only serve the state by providing children, but rather the disinherited descendant of a land owner and full citizen.... The entire policy of antiquity was directed toward the prevention of such proletarians; to this end servitude for debt was restricted and debtor law alleviated. The ordinary contrast in antiquity was that between urban creditor and peasant debtor. In the city dwelt the money-lending patriciate; in the country, the small people to whom it lent its money; and under the ancient law of debt such a condition led readily to the loss of the land and proletarization.

For all these reasons, the ancient city had no subsistence policy like that of the Middle Ages, but only a policy directed to maintaining the *fundus*, on which a man could live and fully equip himself as a soldier. The aim was to guard against weakening the military power of the community. Hence the great reforms of the Gracchi must absolutely not be understood in the modern sense as measures pertaining to a class struggle; their objective is purely military; they represent the last attempt to maintain the citizen army and avoid the substitution of mercenaries. The opponents of the aristocracy in the Middle Ages were, on the one hand, the entrepreneurs and, on the other, the craft workers, while in antiquity they were always the peasantry....

In addition to these distinctions between the ancient and the medieval development, there is a further distinction in class relations. The typical citizen of the medieval guild city is a merchant or craftsman; he is a full citizen if he is also a householder. In antiquity, on the contrary, the full citizen is the landholder. In the guild city, accordingly, class inequality always obtains....

In his personal relations, however, the citizen of the medieval city is free. The principle "town air makes free" asserted that after a year and a day the feudal lord no longer had a right to recover his runaway serf. Although the principle was not everywhere recognized and was subjected to limitations ... the equalization of classes and removal of unfreedom became a dominant tendency in the development of the medieval city.

Antiquity in the early period emphasized class distinctions similar to those of the Middle Ages; it recognized the distinction between the patrician and the client, who followed the knightly warrior as a squire; it recognized relations of dependency and slavery as well. But with the growth of the power of the ancient city and its development toward democracy, the sharpness of class distinctions increases; slaves are purchased or shipped in in large numbers and form a lower stratum constantly growing in numbers, while to them are added the freedmen. Hence the city of antiquity, in contrast with that of the Middle Ages, shows increasing class inequality....

Taken in its entirety, the foregoing argument leads to the conclusion that the city democracy of antiquity is a political guild. It is true that it had distinctive industrial interests and also that these were monopolized; but they were subordinate to military interests. Tribute, booty, the payments of confederate cities, were distributed among the citizens. Thus like the craft guild of the closing period of the Middle Ages, the democratic citizens' guild of antiquity was also interested in not admitting too many participants. The resulting limitation on the number of citizens was one of the causes of the downfall of the Greek city-states. The monopoly of the political guild included cleruchy, the distributing of conquered land among the citizens, and the distribution of the spoils of war; and, in addition, the city paid out of the proceeds of its political activity theater admissions, allotments of grain, and payments for jury service and for participation in religious rites.

Chronic war was therefore the normal condition of the Greek full citizen, and a demagogue like Cleon was conscious of his reasons for inciting to war; war made the city rich, while a long period of peace meant ruin for the citizenship. Those who engaged in the pursuit of profit by peaceful means were excluded from these opportunities. These included the freedmen and metics; among them we first find something similar to the modern bourgeoisie, excluded from the ownership of land but still well-to-do.

Military reasons explain the fact that the city-state of antiquity, so long as it maintained its characteristic form, developed no craft guilds and nothing similar to them, that instead it erected a political-military monopoly for citizens and evolved into a soldiers' guild. The ancient city represented the highest development of military technique in its time; no equivalent force could be sent against a hoplite army or a Roman legion. This explains the form and direction of industry in antiquity with relation to profit through war, and other advantages to be attained by purely political means. Over against the citizen stands the "low-bred"; anyone is low-bred who follows the peaceable quest of profit in the sense of today.

In contrast with this, the center of gravity of military technique in the early Middle Ages lay outside the cities, in the knighthood. Nothing else was equal to an armed feudal host. The result was that the guild army of burghers . . . never ventured offensive operations but was only defensively employed. The burgher army of the Middle Ages could therefore never fulfill the acquisitive guild function of the ancient hoplite or legion army.

In antiquity the freedom of the cities was swept away by a bureaucratically organized world empire. . . . The provision for the economic needs of the state was taken care of through compulsory contributions and compulsory labor of servile persons. . . . A conscript army takes the place of the mercenaries. . . .

Quite different was the fate of the city in the modern era. Here again its autonomy was progressively taken away. The English city of the seventeenth and eighteenth centuries had ceased to be anything but a clique of guilds which could lay claim only to financial and social class significance. The German cities of the same period, with the exception of the imperial cities, were merely geographical entities in which everything was ordered from above. In the French cities this development appeared even earlier, while the Spanish cities were deprived of their power by Charles V. . . . The Italian cities found themselves in the power of the "signory," and those of Russia never arrived at freedom in the Western sense. Everywhere the military, judicial, and industrial authority was taken away from the cities.

In form the old rights were as a rule unchanged, but in fact the modern city was deprived of its freedom as effectively as had happened in antiquity with the establishment of the Roman Empire. In contrast with antiquity, however, it came under the power of competing nation-states in a condition of perpetual struggle for power in peace or war. This competitive struggle created the largest opportunities for modern Western capitalism. The separate states had to compete for mobile capital, which dictated to them the conditions under which it would assist them to power. Out of this alliance of the state with capital, dictated by necessity, arose the national citizen class, the bourgeoisie in the modern sense of the word. Hence it is the closed nation-state which afforded to capitalism its chance for development — and, as long as the nation-state does not give place to a world empire, capitalism also will endure.

# PART II
## THE REVISITED LIBERAL POSITION

# 4
## *Justice as Fairness in the Liberal Polity*
### JOHN RAWLS

... I shall first discuss what I regard as the task of political philosophy at the present time and then briefly survey how the basic intuitive ideas, drawn upon in [the conception of justice that I have called "justice as fairness" (presented in my book *A Theory of Justice*)][1] are combined into a political conception of justice for a constitutional democracy. ...

### I

Justice as fairness is intended as a political conception of justice. While a political conception of justice is, of course, a moral conception, it is a moral conception worked out for a specific kind of subject, namely, for political, social, and economic institutions. In particular, justice as fairness framed to apply to what I have called the "basic structure" of a modern constitutional democracy.[2] (I shall use "constitutional democracy" and "democratic regime" and similar phrases interchangeably.) By this structure I mean such a society's main political, social, and economic institutions, and how they fit together into one unified system of social cooperation. Whether justice as fairness can be extended to a general political conception for different kinds of societies existing under different historical and social conditions, or whether it can be extended to a general moral conception, or a significant part thereof, are altogether separate questions. I avoid prejudging these larger questions one way or the other.

It should also be stressed that justice as fairness is not intended as the application of a general moral conception to the basic structure of society, as if this structure were simply another case to which that general moral conception is applied.[3] In this respect justice as fairness differs from traditional moral doctrines, for these are widely regarded as such general conceptions. Utilitarianism is a familiar example, since the principle of utility, however it is formulated, is usually said to hold for all kinds of subjects ranging from the actions of individuals to the law of nations. The essential point is this: as a practical political matter no general moral conception can provide a publicly recognized basis for a conception of justice in a modern democratic state. The social and historical conditions of such a state have their origins in the Wars of Religion following the Reformation and the subsequent development of the principle of toleration, and in the growth of constitutional government and the institutions of large industrial market economies. These conditions profoundly affect the requirements of a workable conception of political justice: such a conception must allow for a diversity of doctrines and the plurality of conflicting, and indeed incommensurable, conceptions of the good affirmed by the members of existing democratic societies.

Finally, to conclude these introductory remarks, since justice as fairness is intended as a political conception of justice for a democratic society, it tries to draw solely upon basic intuitive ideas that are embedded in the political institutions of a constitutional democratic regime and the public traditions of their interpretation. Justice as fairness is a political conception in part because it starts from within a certain political tradition. We hope that this political conception of justice may at least be supported by what we may call an "overlapping consensus," that is, by a consensus that includes all the opposing philosophical and religious doctrines likely to persist and to gain adherents in a more or less just constitutional democratic society.[4]

## II

There are, of course, many ways in which political philosophy may be understood, and writers at different times, faced with different political and social circumstances, understand their work differently. Justice as fairness I would now understand as a reasonably systematic and practicable conception of justice for a constitutional democracy, a conception that offers an alternative to the dominant utilitarianism of our tradition of political thought.

Its first task is to provide a more secure and acceptable basis for constitutional principles and basic rights and liberties than utilitarianism seems to allow.[5] The need for such a political conception arises in the following way.

There are periods, sometimes long periods, in the history of any society during which certain fundamental questions give rise to sharp and divisive political controversy, and it seems difficult, if not impossible, to find any shared basis of political agreement. Indeed, certain questions may prove intractable and may never be fully settled. One task of political philosophy in a democratic society is to focus on such questions and to examine whether some underlying basis of agreement can be uncovered and a mutually acceptable way of resolving these questions publicly established. Or if these questions cannot be fully settled, as may well be the case, perhaps the divergence of opinion can be narrowed sufficiently so that political cooperation on a basis of mutual respect can still be maintained.[6]

The course of democratic thought over the past two centuries or so makes plain that there is no agreement on the way basic institutions of a constitutional democracy should be arranged if they are to specify and secure the basic rights and liberties of citizens and answer to the claims of democratic equality when citizens are conceived as free and equal persons (as explained in the last three paragraphs of section III). A deep disagreement exists as to how the values of liberty and equality are best realized in the basic structure of society. To simplify, we may think of this disagreement as a conflict within the tradition of democratic thought itself, between the tradition associated with Locke, which gives greater weight to what Constant called "the liberties of the moderns," freedom of thought and conscience, certain basic rights of the person and of property, and the rule of law, and the tradition associated with Rousseau, which gives greater weight to what Constant called "the liberties of the ancients," the equal political liberties and the values of public life. This is a stylized contrast and historically inaccurate, but it serves to fix ideas.

Justice as fairness tries to adjudicate between these contending traditions, first by proposing two principles of justice to serve as guidelines for how basic institutions are to realize the values of liberty and equality, and second by specifying a point of view from which these principles can be seen as more appropriate than other familiar principles of justice to the nature of democratic citizens, viewed as free and equal persons. What it means to view citizens as free and equal persons is, of course, a fundamental question and is discussed in the following sections. What must be shown is that a certain arrangement of the basic structure, certain institutional forms, are more appropriate for realizing the values of liberty and equality when citizens are conceived as such persons, that is, as having the requisite powers of moral personality that enable them to participate in society viewed as a system of fair cooperation for mutual advantage. So to continue, the two principles of justice read as follows: (1.) Each person has an equal right to a fully adequate scheme of equal basic rights and liberties, which scheme is compatible with a similar scheme for all. (2.) Social and economic inequalities are to satisfy two conditions: first, they must be attached to offices and positions open to all under conditions of fair equality of opportunity; and second, they must be to the greatest benefit of the least advantaged members of society.

Each of these principles applies to a different part of the basic structure, and both are concerned not only with basic rights, liberties, and opportunities, but also with the claims of equality, while the second part of the second principle underwrites the worth of these institutional guarantees. The two principles together, when the first is given priority over the second, regulate the basic institutions which realize these values. But these details, although important, are not our concern here.

We must now ask: how might political philosophy find a shared basis for settling such a fundamental question as that of the most appropriate institutional forms for liberty and equality? Of course, it is likely that the most that can be done is to narrow the range of public disagreement. Yet even firmly held convictions gradually change: religious toleration is now accepted, and arguments for persecution are no longer openly professed; similarly, slavery is rejected as inherently unjust, and however much the aftermath of slavery may persist in social practices and unavowed attitudes, no one is willing to defend it. We collect such settled convictions as the belief in religious toleration and the rejection of slavery and try to organize the basic ideas and principles implicit in these convictions into a coherent conception of justice. We can regard these convictions as provisional fixed points which any conception of justice must account for if it is to be reasonable for us. We look, then, to our public political culture itself, including its main institutions and the historical traditions of their interpretation, as the shared fund of implicitly recognized basic ideas and principles. The hope is that these ideas and principles can be formulated clearly enough to be combined into a conception of political justice congenial to our most firmly held convictions. We express this by saying that a political conception of justice, to be acceptable, must be in accordance with our considered convictions, at all levels of generality, on due reflection. . . .[7]

The public political culture may be of two minds even at a very deep level. Indeed, this must be so with such an enduring controversy as that concerning the most appropriate institutional forms to realize the values of liberty and equality. This suggests that if we are to succeed in finding a basis of public agreement, we must find a new way of organizing familiar ideas and principles into a conception of political justice so that the claims in conflict, as previously understood, are seen in another light. A political conception need not be an original creation but may only articulate familiar intuitive ideas and principles so that they can be recognized as fitting together in a somewhat different way than before. Such a conception may, however, go further than this: it may organize these familiar ideas and principles by means of a more fundamental intuitive idea within the complex structure of which the other familiar intuitive ideas are then systematically connected and related. In justice as fairness, as we shall see in the next section, this more fundamental idea is that of society as a system of fair social cooperation between free and equal persons. The concern of this section is how we might find a public basis of political agreement....

The aim of justice as fairness as a political conception is practical, and not metaphysical or epistemological. That is, it presents itself not as a conception of justice that is true, but one that can serve as a basis of informed and willing political agreement between citizens viewed as free and equal persons. This agreement when securely founded in public political and social attitudes sustains the goods of all persons and associations within a just democratic regime. To secure this agreement we try, so far as we can, to avoid disputed philosophical, as well as disputed moral and religious, questions. We do this not because these questions are unimportant or regarded with indifference,[8] but because we think them too important and recognize that there is no way to resolve them politically. The only alternative to a principle of toleration is the autocratic use of state power. Thus, justice as fairness deliberately stays on the surface, philosophically speaking. Given the profound differences in belief and conceptions of the good at least since the Reformation, we must recognize that, just as on questions of religious and moral doctrine, public agreement on the basic questions of philosophy cannot be obtained without the state's infringement of basic liberties. Philosophy as the search for truth about an independent metaphysical and moral order cannot, I believe, provide a workable and shared basis for a political conception of justice in a democratic society....

The hope is that, by this method of avoidance, as we might call it, existing differences between contending political views can at least be moderated, even if not entirely removed, so that social cooperation on the basis of mutual respect can be maintained. Or if this is expecting too much, this method may enable us to conceive how, given a desire for free and uncoerced agreement, a public understanding could arise consistent with the historical conditions and constraints of our social world. Until we bring ourselves to conceive how this could happen, it can't happen.

## III

Let's now survey briefly some of the basic ideas that make up justice as fairness in order to show that these ideas belong to a political conception of justice. As I have indicated, the overarching fundamental intuitive idea, within which other basic intuitive ideas are systematically connected, is that of society as a fair system of cooperation between free and equal persons. Justice as fairness starts from this idea as one of the basic intuitive ideas which we take to be implicit in the public culture of a democratic society.[9] In their political thought, and in the context of public discussion of political questions, citizens do not view the social order as a fixed natural order, or as an institutional hierarchy justified by religious or aristocratic values. Here it is important to stress that from other points of view, for example, from the point of view of personal morality, or from the point of view of members of an association, or of one's religious or philosophical doctrine, various aspects of the world and one's relation to it may be regarded in a different way. But these other points of view are not to be introduced into political discussion.

We can make the idea of social cooperation more specific by noting three of its elements:

1. Cooperation is distinct from merely socially coordinated activity, for example, from activity coordinated by orders issued by some central authority. Cooperation is guided by publicly recognized rules and procedures which those who are cooperating accept and regard as properly regulating their conduct.
2. Cooperation involves the idea of fair terms of cooperation: these are terms that each participant may reasonably accept, provided that everyone else likewise accepts them. Fair terms of cooperation specify an idea of reciprocity or mutuality: all who are engaged in cooperation and who do their part as the rules and procedures require are to benefit in some appropriate way as assessed by a suitable benchmark of comparison. A conception of political justice characterizes the fair terms of social cooperation. Since the primary subject of justice is the basic structure of society, this is

accomplished in justice as fairness by formulating principles that specify basic rights and duties within the main institutions of society, and by regulating the institutions of background justice over time so that the benefits produced by everyone's efforts are fairly acquired and divided from one generation to the next.

3. The idea of social cooperation requires an idea of each participant's rational advantage, or good. This idea of good specifies what those who are engaged in cooperation, whether individuals, families, or associations, or even nation-states, are trying to achieve, when the scheme is viewed from their own standpoint.

Now consider the idea of the person.[10] There are, of course, many aspects of human nature that can be singled out as especially significant depending on our point of view. This is witnessed by such expressions as *homo politicus, homo economicus, homo faber,* and the like. Justice as fairness starts from the idea that society is to be conceived as a fair system of cooperation and so it adopts a conception of the person to go with this idea. Since Greek times, in both philosophy and law, the concept of the person has been understood as the concept of someone who can take part in, or who can play a role in, social life, and hence exercise and respect its various rights and duties. Thus, we say that a person is someone who can be a citizen, that is, a fully cooperating member of society over a complete life. We add the phrase "over a complete life" because a society is viewed as a more or less complete and self-sufficient scheme of cooperation, making room within itself for all the necessities and activities of life, from birth until death. A society is not an association for more limited purposes; citizens do not join society voluntarily but are born into it, where, for our aims here, we assume they are to lead their lives.

Since we start within the tradition of democratic thought, we also think of citizens as free and equal persons. The basic intuitive idea is that in virtue of what we may call their moral powers, and the powers of reason, thought, and judgment connected with those powers, we say that persons are free. And in virtue of their having these powers to the requisite degree to be fully cooperating members of society, we say that persons are equal.[11] We can elaborate this conception of the person as follows. Since persons can be full participants in a fair system of social cooperation, we ascribe to them the two moral powers connected with the elements in the idea of social cooperation noted above: namely, a capacity for a sense of justice and a capacity for a conception of the good. A sense of justice is the capacity to understand, to apply, and to act from the public conception of justice which characterizes the fair terms of social cooperation. The capacity for a conception of the good is the capacity to form, to revise, and rationally to pursue a conception of one's rational advantage, or good. In the case of social cooperation, this good must not be understood narrowly but rather as a conception of what is valuable in human life. Thus, a conception of the good normally consists of a more or less determinate scheme of final ends, that is, ends we want to realize for their own sake, as well as of attachments to other persons and loyalties to various groups and associations. These attachments and loyalties give rise to affections and devotions, and therefore the flourishing of the persons and associations who are the objects of these sentiments is also part of our conception of the good. Moreover, we must also include in such a conception a view of our relation to the world — religious, philosophical, or moral — by reference to which the value and significance of our ends and attachments are understood.

In addition to having the two moral powers, the capacities for a sense of justice and a conception of the good, persons also have at any given time a particular conception of the good that they try to achieve. Since we wish to start from the idea of society as a fair system of cooperation, we assume that persons as citizens have all the capacities that enable them to be normal and fully cooperating members of society. This does not imply that no one ever suffers from illness or accident; such misfortunes are to be expected in the ordinary course of human life, and provision for these contingencies must be made. But for our purposes here I leave aside permanent physical disabilities or mental disorders so severe as to prevent persons from being normal and fully cooperating members of society in the usual sense.

Now the conception of persons as having the two moral powers, and therefore as free and equal, is also a basic intuitive idea assumed to be implicit in the public culture of a democratic society. Note, however, that it is formed by idealizing and simplifying in various ways. This is done to achieve a clear and uncluttered view of what for us is the fundamental question of political justice, namely, what is the most appropriate conception of justice for specifying the terms of social cooperation between citizens regarded as free and equal persons, and as normal and fully cooperating members of society over a complete life. It is this question that has been the focus of the liberal critique of aristocracy, of the socialist critique of liberal constitutional democracy, and of the conflict between liberals and conservatives at the present time over the claims of private property and the legitimacy (in contrast to the effectiveness) of social policies associated with the so-called welfare state.

## IV

I now take up the idea of the original position.[12] This idea is introduced in order to work out which traditional conception of justice, or which variant of one of those conceptions, specifies the most appropriate principles for realizing liberty and equality once society is viewed as a system of cooperation between free and equal persons. Assuming we had this purpose in mind, let's see why we would introduce the idea of the original position and how it serves its purpose.

Consider again the idea of social cooperation. Let's ask: How are the fair terms of cooperation to be determined? Are they simply laid down by some outside agency distinct from the persons cooperating? Are they, for example, laid down by God's law? Or are these terms to be recognized by these persons as fair by reference to their knowledge of a prior and independent moral order? For example, are they regarded as required by natural law, or by a realm of values known by rational intuition? Or are these terms to be established by an undertaking among these persons themselves in the light of what they regard as their mutual advantage? Depending on which answer we give, we get a different conception of cooperation.

Since justice as fairness recasts the doctrine of the social contract, it adopts a form of the last answer: the fair terms of social cooperation are conceived as agreed to by those engaged in it, that is, by free and equal persons as citizens who are born into the society in which they lead their lives. But their agreement, like any other valid agreement, must be entered into under appropriate conditions. In particular, these conditions must situate free and equal persons fairly and must not allow some persons greater bargaining advantages than others. Further, threats of force and coercion, deception and fraud, and so on, must be excluded.

So far so good. The foregoing considerations are familiar from everyday life. But agreements in everyday life are made in some more or less clearly specified situation embedded within the background institutions of the basic structure. Our task, however, is to extend the idea of agreement to this background framework itself. Here we face a difficulty for any political conception of justice that uses the idea of a contract, whether social or otherwise. The difficulty is this: we must find some point of view, removed from and not distorted by the particular features and circumstances of the all-encompassing background framework, from which a fair agreement between free and equal persons can be reached. The original position, with the feature I have called "the veil of ignorance," is this point of view.[13] And the reason why the original position must abstract from and not be affected by the contingencies of the social world is that the conditions for a fair agreement on the principles of political justice between free and equal persons must eliminate the bargaining advantages which inevitably arise within background institutions of any society as the result of cumulative social, historical, and natural tendencies. These contingent advantages and accidental influences from the past should not influence an agreement on the principles which are to regulate the institutions of the basic structure itself from the present into the future.

Here we seem to face a second difficulty, which is, however, only apparent. To explain: from what we have just said it is clear that the original position is to be seen as a device of representation and hence any agreement reached by the parties must be regarded as both hypothetical and nonhistorical. But if so, since hypothetical agreements cannot bind, what is the significance of the original position? The answer is implicit in what has already been said: it is given by the role of the various features of the original position as a device of representation. Thus, that the parties are symmetrically situated is required if they are to be seen as representatives of free and equal citizens who are to reach an agreement under conditions that are fair. Moreover, one of our considered convictions, I assume, is this: the fact that we occupy a particular social position is not a good reason for us to accept, or to expect others to accept, a conception of justice that favors those in this position. To model this conviction in the original position the parties are not allowed to know their social position; and the same idea is extended to other cases. This is expressed figuratively by saying that the parties are behind a veil of ignorance. In sum, the original position is simply a device of representation: it describes the parties, each of whom is responsible for the essential interests of a free and equal person, as fairly situated and as reaching an agreement subject to appropriate restrictions on what are to count as good reasons.

Both of the above mentioned difficulties, then, are overcome by viewing the original position as a device of representation: that is, this position models what we regard as fair conditions under which the representatives of free and equal persons are to specify the terms of social cooperation in the case of the basic structure of society; and since it also models what, for this case, we regard as acceptable restrictions on reasons available to the parties for favoring one agreement rather than another, the conception of justice the parties would adopt identifies the conception we regard — here *and now* — as fair and supported by the best reasons. We try to model restrictions on reasons in such a way that it is perfectly evident which agreement would be made by the parties in the original position as citizens' representatives....

## V

I can ... sketch a positive account of the political conception of the person, that is, the conception of the person as citizen (discussed in section III), involved in the original position as a device of representation. To explain what is meant by describing a conception of the person as political, let's consider how citizens are represented in the original position as free persons.... I have said elsewhere that citizens view themselves as free in three respects, so let's survey each of these briefly and indicate the way in which the conception of the person used is political.

First, citizens are free in that they conceive of themselves and of one another as having the moral power to have a conception of the good. This is not to say that, as part of their political conception of themselves, they view themselves as inevitably tied to the pursuit of the particular conception of the good which they affirm at any given time. Instead, as citizens, they are regarded as capable of revising and changing this conception on reasonable and rational grounds, and they may do this if they so desire. Thus, as free persons, citizens claim the right to view their persons as independent from and as not identified with any particular conception of the good, or scheme of final ends. Given their moral power to form, to revise, and rationally to pursue a conception of the good, their public identity as free persons is not affected by changes over time in their conception of the good. For example, when citizens convert from one religion to another, or no longer affirm an established religious faith, they do not cease to be, for questions of political justice, the same persons they were before. There is no loss of what we may call their public identity, their identity as a matter of basic law. In general, they still have the same basic rights and duties; they own the same property and can make the same claims as before, except insofar as these claims were connected with their previous religious affiliation. We can imagine a society (indeed, history offers numerous examples) in which basic rights and recognized claims depend on religious affiliation, social class, and so on. Such a society has a different political conception of the person. It may not have a conception of citizenship at all; for this conception, as we are using it, goes with the conception of society as a fair system of cooperation for mutual advantage between free and equal persons.

It is essential to stress that citizens in their personal affairs, or in the internal life of associations to which they belong, may regard their final ends and attachments in a way very different from the way the political conception involves. Citizens may have, and normally do have at any given time, affections, devotions, and loyalties that they believe they would not, and indeed could and should not, stand apart from and objectively evaluate from the point of view of their purely rational good. They may regard it as simply unthinkable to view themselves apart from certain religious, philosophical, and moral convictions, or from certain enduring attachments and loyalties. These convictions and attachments are part of what we may call their "nonpublic identity." These convictions and attachments help to organize and give shape to a person's way of life, what one sees oneself as doing and trying to accomplish in one's social world. We think that if we were suddenly without these particular convictions and attachments we would be disoriented and unable to carry on. In fact, there would be, we might think, no point in carrying on. But our conceptions of the good may and often do change over time, usually slowly but sometimes rather suddenly. When these changes are sudden, we are particularly likely to say that we are no longer the same person. We know what this means: we refer to a profound and pervasive shift, or reversal, in our final ends and character; we refer to our different nonpublic, and possibly moral or religious, identity. On the road to Damascus Saul of Tarsus becomes Paul the Apostle. There is no change in our public or political identity, nor in our personal identity as this concept is understood by some writers in the philosophy of mind.

The second respect in which citizens view themselves as free is that they regard themselves as self-originating sources of valid claims. They think their claims have weight apart from being derived from duties or obligations specified by the political conception of justice, for example, from duties and obligations owed to society. Claims that citizens regard as founded on duties and obligations based on their conception of the good and the moral doctrine they affirm in their own life are also, for our purposes here, to be counted as self-originating. Doing this is reasonable in a political conception of justice for a constitutional democracy; for provided the conceptions of the good and the moral doctrines citizens affirm are compatible with the public conception of justice, these duties and obligations are self-originating from the political point of view.

When we describe a way in which citizens regard themselves as free, we are describing how citizens actually think of themselves in a democratic society should questions of justice arise. In our conception of a constitutional regime, this is an aspect of how citizens regard themselves. That this aspect of their freedom belongs to a particular political conception is clear from the contrast with a different political conception in which the members of society are not viewed as self-originating sources of valid claims. Rather, their claims have no weight except insofar as they can be derived from their duties and obligations owed to society, or from their ascribed roles in the social hierarchy justified by religious or aristocratic values. Or to take an extreme case, slaves are human beings who are not counted as sources of claims, not even claims based on social duties or obligations, for slaves are not counted as capable of having duties or obligations. Laws that prohibit the abuse and maltreatment of slaves are not founded on claims made by slaves on their own behalf, but on claims originating either from slaveholders, or from the general interests of society (which does not include the interests of slaves). Slaves are, so to speak, socially dead: they are not publicly recognized as persons at all. Thus, the contrast with a political conception which allows slavery makes clear why conceiving of citizens as free persons in virtue of their moral powers and their having a conception of the good goes with a particular political conception of the person. This conception of persons fits into a political conception of justice founded on the idea of society as a system of cooperation between its members conceived as free and equal.

The third respect in which citizens are regarded as free is that they are regarded as capable of taking responsibility for their ends, and this affects how their various claims are assessed.[14] Very roughly, the idea is that, given just background institutions and given for each person a fair index of primary goods (as required by the principles of justice), citizens are thought to be capable of adjusting their aims and aspirations in the light of what they can reasonably expect to provide for. Moreover, they are regarded as capable of restricting their claims in matters of justice to the kinds of things the principles of justice allow. Thus, citizens are to recognize that the weight of their claims is not given by the strength and psychological intensity of their wants and desires (as opposed to their needs and requirements as citizens), even when their wants and desires are rational from their point of view. I cannot pursue these matters here. But the procedure is the same as before: we start with the basic intuitive idea of society as a system of social cooperation. When this idea is developed into a conception of political justice, it implies that, viewing ourselves as persons who can engage in social cooperation over a complete life, we can also take responsibility for our ends, that is, that we can adjust our ends so that they can be pursued by the means we can reasonably expect to acquire given our prospects and situation in society. The idea of responsibility for ends is implicit in the public political culture and discernible in its practices. A political conception of the person articulates this idea and fits it into the idea of society as a system of social cooperation over a complete life.

To sum up, I recapitulate three main points of this and the preceding two sections: First, in section III persons were regarded as free and equal in virtue of their possessing to the requisite degree the two powers of moral personality (and the powers of reason, thought, and judgment connected with these powers), namely, the capacity for a sense of justice and the capacity for a conception of the good. These powers we associated with two main elements of the idea of cooperation, the idea of fair terms of cooperation and the idea of each participant's rational advantage, or good.

Second, in this section (section V), we have briefly surveyed three respects in which persons are regarded as free, and we have noted that in the public political culture of a constitutional democratic regime citizens conceive of themselves as free in these respects.

Third, since the question of which conception of political justice is most appropriate for realizing in basic institutions the values of liberty and equality has long been deeply controversial within the very democratic tradition in which citizens are regarded as free and equal persons, the aim of justice as fairness is to try to resolve this question by starting from the basic intuitive idea of society as a fair system of social cooperation in which the fair terms of cooperation are agreed upon by citizens themselves so conceived. In section IV, we saw why this approach leads to the idea of the original position as a device of representation.

## VI

I now take up a point essential to thinking of justice as fairness as a liberal view. Although this conception is a moral conception, it is not, as I have said, intended as a comprehensive moral doctrine. The conception of the citizen as a free and equal person is not a moral ideal to govern all of life, but is rather an ideal belonging to a conception of political justice which is to apply to the basic structure. I emphasize this point because to think otherwise would be incompatible with liberalism as a political doctrine. Recall that as such a doctrine, liberalism assumes that in a constitutional democratic state under modern conditions there are bound to exist conflicting and incommensurable conceptions of the good. This feature characterizes modern culture since the Reformation. Any viable political conception of justice that is not to rely on the autocratic use of state power must recognize this fundamental social fact. This does not mean, of course, that such a conception cannot impose constraints on individuals and associations, but that when it does so, these constraints are accounted for, directly or in-directly, by the requirements of political justice for the basic structure.[15]

Given this fact, we adopt a conception of the person framed as part of, and restricted to, an explicitly political conception of justice. In this sense, the conception of the person is a political one. As I stressed in the previous section, persons can accept this conception of themselves as citizens and use it in discussing questions of political justice without being committed in other parts of their life to comprehensive moral ideals often associated with liberalism, for example, the ideals of autonomy and individ-uality. The absence of commitment to these ideals, and indeed to any par-ticular comprehensive ideal, is essential to liberalism as a political doctrine. The reason is that any such ideal, when it is pursued as a comprehensive ideal, is incompatible with other conceptions of the good, with forms of per-sonal, moral, and religious life consistent with justice and which, therefore, have a proper place in a democratic society. As comprehensive moral ideals, autonomy and individuality are unsuited for a political conception of jus-tice. As found in Kant and J. S. Mill, these comprehensive ideals, despite their very great importance in liberal thought, are extended too far when they are presented as the only appropriate foundation for a constitutional regime. So understood, liberalism becomes but another sectarian doctrine.

This conclusion requires comment: it does not mean, of course, that the liberalisms of Kant and Mill are not appropriate moral conceptions from which we can be led to affirm democratic institutions. But they are only two such conceptions among others, and so but two of the philosophical doctrines likely to persist and gain adherents in a reasonably just demo-cratic regime. In such a regime the comprehensive moral views which sup-port its basic institutions may include the liberalisms of individuality and autonomy; and possibly these liberalisms are among the more prominent doctrines in an overlapping consensus, that is, in a consensus in which, as noted earlier, different and even conflicting doctrines affirm the publicly shared basis of political arrangements. The liberalisms of Kant and Mill have a certain historical preeminence as among the first and most impor-tant philosophical views to espouse modern constitutional democracy and to develop its underlying ideas in an influential way; and it may even turn out that societies in which the ideals of autonomy and individuality are widely accepted are among the most well-governed and harmonious.[16]

By contrast with liberalism as a comprehensive moral doctrine, justice as fairness tries to present a conception of political justice rooted in the basic intuitive ideas found in the public culture of a constitutional democ-racy. We conjecture that these ideas are likely to be affirmed by each of the opposing comprehensive moral doctrines influential in a reasonably just democratic society. Thus justice as fairness seeks to identify the kernel of an overlapping consensus, that is, the shared intuitive ideas which, when they are worked up into a political conception of justice, turn out to be sufficient to underwrite a just constitutional regime. This is the most we can expect, nor do we need more. We must note, however, that when justice as fairness is fully realized in a well-ordered society, the value of full autonomy is likewise realized. In this way justice as fairness is indeed similar to the liberalisms of Kant and Mill; but in contrast with them, the value of full autonomy is here specified by a political conception of justice, and not by a comprehensive moral doctrine.

It may appear that, so understood, the public acceptance of justice as fairness is no more than prudential; that is, that those who affirm this conception do so simply as a modus vivendi which allows the groups in the overlapping consensus to pursue their own good subject to certain constraints which each thinks to be for its advantage given existing circumstances. The idea of an overlapping consensus may seem essentially Hobbesian. But against this, two remarks. First, justice as fairness is a moral conception: it has conceptions of person and society, and concepts of right and fairness, as well as principles of justice with their complement of the virtues through which those principles are embodied in human character and regulate political and social life. This conception of justice provides an account of the cooperative virtues suitable for a political doctrine in view of the conditions and requirements of a constitutional regime. It is no less a moral conception because it is restricted to the basic structure of society, since this restriction is what enables it to serve as a political conception of justice given our present circumstances. Thus, in an overlapping consensus (as understood here), the conception of justice as fairness is not regarded merely as a modus vivendi.

Second, in such a consensus each of the comprehensive philosophical, religious, and moral doctrines accepts justice as fairness in its own way; that is, each comprehensive doctrine, from within its own point of view, is led to accept the public reasons of justice specified by justice as fairness. We might say that they recognize its concepts, principles, and virtues as theorems, as it were, at which their several views coincide. But this does not make these points of coincidence any less moral or reduce them to mere means. For, in general, these concepts, principles, and virtues are accepted by each as belonging to a more comprehensive philosophical, religious, or moral doctrine. Some may even affirm justice as fairness as a natural moral conception that can stand on its own feet. They accept this conception of justice as a reasonable basis for political and social cooperation, and hold that it is as natural and fundamental as the concepts and principles of honesty and mutual trust, and the virtues of cooperation in everyday life. The doctrines in an overlapping consensus differ in how far they maintain a further foundation is necessary and on what that further foundation should be. These differences, however, are compatible with a consensus on justice as fairness as a political conception of justice.

## VII

I shall conclude by considering the way in which social unity and stability may be understood by liberalism as a political doctrine (as opposed to a comprehensive moral conception).[17]

One of the deepest distinctions between political conceptions of justice is between those that allow for a plurality of opposing and even incommensurable conceptions of the good and those that hold that there is but one conception of the good which is to be recognized by all persons, so far as they are fully rational. Conceptions of justice which fall on opposite sides of this divide are distinct in many fundamental ways. Plato and Aristotle, and the Christian tradition as represented by Augustine and Aquinas, fall on the side of the one rational good. Such views tend to be teleological and to hold that institutions are just to the extent that they effectively promote this good. Indeed, since classical times the dominant tradition seems to have been that there is but one rational conception of the good, and that the aim of moral philosophy, together with theology and metaphysics, is to determine its nature. Classical utilitarianism belongs to this dominant tradition. By contrast, liberalism as a political doctrine supposes that there are many conflicting and incommensurable conceptions of the good, each compatible with the full rationality of human persons, so far as we can ascertain within a workable political conception of justice. As a consequence of this supposition, liberalism assumes that it is a characteristic feature of a free democratic culture that a plurality of conflicting and incommensurable conceptions of the good are affirmed by its citizens. Liberalism as a political doctrine holds that the question the dominant tradition has tried to answer has no practicable answer; that is, it has no answer suitable for a political conception of justice for a democratic society. In such a society a teleological political conception is out of the question: public agreement on the requisite conception of the good cannot be obtained.

As I have remarked, the historical origin of this liberal supposition is the Reformation and its consequences. Until the Wars of Religion in the sixteenth and seventeenth centuries, the fair terms of social cooperation were narrowly drawn: social cooperation on the basis of mutual respect was regarded as impossible with persons of a different faith; or (in the terminology I have used) with persons who affirm a fundamentally different conception of the good. Thus one of the historical roots of liberalism was the development of various doctrines urging religious toleration. One theme in justice as fairness is to recognize the social conditions that give rise to these doctrines as among the so-called subjective circumstances of justice and then to spell out the implications of the principle of toleration.[18] As liberalism is stated by Constant, de Tocqueville, and Mill in the nineteenth century, it accepts the plurality of incommensurable conceptions of the good as a fact of modern democratic culture, provided, of course, that these conceptions respect the limits specified by the appropriate principles of justice. One task of liberalism as a political doctrine is to answer the question How is social unity to be understood, given that there can be no public agreement on the one rational good, and a plurality of opposing and incommensurable conceptions must be taken as given? And granted that social unity is conceivable in some definite way, under what conditions is it actually possible?

In justice as fairness, social unity is understood by starting with the conception of society as a system of cooperation between free and equal persons. Social unity and the allegiance of citizens to their common institutions are not founded on their all affirming the same conception of the good, but on their publicly accepting a political conception of justice to regulate the basic structure of society. The concept of justice is independent from and prior to the concept of goodness in the sense that its principles limit the conceptions of the good that are permissible. A just basic structure and its background institutions establish a framework within which permissible conceptions can be advanced. Elsewhere I have called this relation between a conception of justice and conceptions of the good the priority of right (since the just falls under the right). I believe this priority is characteristic of liberalism as a political doctrine, and something like it seems essential to any conception of justice reasonable for a democratic state. Thus to understand how social unity is possible given the historical conditions of a democratic society, we start with our basic intuitive idea of social cooperation, an idea present in the public culture of a democratic society, and proceed from there to a public conception of justice as the basis of social unity in the way I have sketched.

As for the question of whether this unity is stable, this importantly depends on the content of the religious, philosophical, and moral doctrines available to constitute an overlapping consensus. For example, assuming the public political conception to be justice as fairness, imagine citizens to affirm one of three views: the first view affirms justice as fairness because its religious beliefs and understanding of faith lead to a principle of toleration and underwrite the fundamental idea of society as a scheme of social cooperation between free and equal persons; the second view affirms it as a consequence of a comprehensive liberal moral conception such as those of Kant and Mill; while the third affirms justice as fairness not as a consequence of any wider doctrine but as in itself sufficient to express values that normally outweigh whatever other values might oppose them, at least under reasonably favorable conditions. This overlapping consensus appears far more stable than one founded on views that express skepticism and indifference to religious, philosophical, and moral values, or that regard the acceptance of the principles of justice simply as a prudent modus vivendi given the existing balance of social forces. Of course, there are many other possibilities.

The strength of a conception like justice as fairness may prove to be that the more comprehensive doctrines that persist and gain adherents in a democratic society regulated by its principles are likely to cohere together into a more or less stable overlapping consensus. But obviously all this is highly speculative and raises questions that are little understood, since doctrines that persist and gain adherents depend in part on social conditions, and in particular, on these conditions when regulated by the public conception of justice. Thus we are forced to consider at some point the effects of the social conditions required by a conception of political justice on the acceptance of that conception itself. Other things equal, a conception will be more or less stable depending on how far the conditions to which it leads support comprehensive religious, philosophical, and moral doctrines that can constitute a stable overlapping consensus. These questions of stability I cannot discuss here. It suffices to remark that in a society marked by deep divisions between opposing and incommensurable conceptions of the good, justice as fairness enables us at least to conceive how social unity can be both possible and stable.

## NOTES

1. John Rawls, *A Theory of Justice* (Cambridge, Mass.: Harvard University Press, 1971).

2. Rawls, *Theory of Justice,* sec. 2, and see index; also "The Basic Structure as Subject," in *Values and Morals,* ed. Alvin Goldman and Jaegwon Kim (Dordrecht: Reidel, 1978), pp. 47–71.

3. See "Basic Structure as Subject," ibid., pp. 48–50.

4. This idea was introduced in *Theory of Justice,* pp. 387f., as a way to weaken the conditions of the reasonableness of civil disobedience in a nearly just democratic society. Here and later in secs. VI and VII it is used in a wider context.

5. *Theory of Justice,* preface, p. viii.

6. Ibid., pp. 582f.

7. *Theory of Justice,* pp. 20f., 48–51, and 120f.

8. Ibid., p. 214f.

9. Although *Theory of Justice* uses this idea from the outset (it is introduced on p. 4), it does not emphasize, as I do here, that the basic ideas of justice as fairness are regarded as implicit or latent in the public culture of a democratic society.

10. It should be emphasized that a conception of the person, as I understand it here, is a normative conception, whether legal, political, or moral, or indeed also philosophical or religious, depending on the overall view to which it belongs. In this case the conception of the person is a moral conception, one that begins from our everyday conception of persons as the basic units of thought, deliberation, and responsibility, and adapted to a political conception of justice and not to a comprehensive moral doctrine. It is in effect a political conception of the person, and given the aims of justice as fairness, a conception of citizens. Thus, a conception of the person is to be distinguished from an account of human nature given by natural science or social theory.

11. *Theory of Justice,* sec. 77.

12. Ibid., sec. 4 ch. 3 and the index.

13. On the veil of ignorance, see ibid., sec. 24, and the index.

14. See "Social Unity and Primary Goods," in *Utilitarianism and Beyond,* ed. Amartya Sen and Bernard Williams (Cambridge: Cambridge University Press, 1982), sec. IV, pp. 167–70.

15. For example, churches are constrained by the principle of equal liberty of conscience and must conform to the principle of toleration, universities by what may be required to maintain fair equality of opportunity, and the rights of parents by what is necessary to maintain their children's physical well-being and to assure the adequate development of their intellectual and moral powers. Because churches, universities, and parents exercise their authority within the basic structure, they are to recognize the requirements this structure imposes to maintain background justice.

16. This point has been made with respect to the liberalisms of Kant and Mill, but for American culture one should mention the important conceptions of democratic individuality expressed in the works of Emerson, Thoreau, and Whitman. These are instructively discussed by George Kateb in his "Democratic Individuality and the Claims of Politics," *Political Theory* 12 (Aug. 1984).

17. This account of social unity is in "Social Unity and Primary Goods," pp. 160f., 170–73.

18. The distinction between the objective and the subjective circumstances of justice is made in *Theory of Justice,* p. 126ff.

# PART III
## THE COMMUNITARIAN CRITIQUE

# 5

## *Citizenship and Community:*
## *Civic Republicanism and the Modern World*
### ADRIAN OLDFIELD

### STATUS OR PRACTICE, RIGHTS OR DUTIES?

The political mind in Britain and the United States has, in recent years, been much exercised by talk of citizenship. The issue of citizenship has been addressed from a variety of perspectives and with different questions. For some, the issue has been citizenship as entitlement, where the question has been how the material benefits of prosperity can be more equitably distributed, in recognition of the dignity of human life. For others, the issue has been citizenship as need: how to provide people with the resources thought to be necessary for effective human agency. For yet others, the issue has been citizenship as admission: how can groups suffering the prejudice against some kind of social stigma have the stigma removed and be admitted to the human world that everyone else lives in? And for still others, the issue has been citizenship as self-government, where the question has been how to widen the opportunities for popular participation in political life. What all these perspectives share is the assumption that individuals are citizens, and that, as such, they have certain requirements. In both literature and rhetoric, these requirements are typically referred to as "rights."

Such an emphasis on rights is not surprising given the presence of a common element in the political and cultural traditions of American and

British society, namely, liberal individualism. Though liberal individualism is only one strain of liberal thought, it has, since the seventeenth century, roughly from Hobbes on, been a dominant one in Anglo-American political thinking. Liberal individualism accords the individual not only ontological and epistemological priority, but moral priority as well. Individuals as citizens are sovereign, not in the sense that they are sufficiently in control of their lives in significant and relevant ways, but in the sense that they ought to be. And the threat to their sovereignty comes just as much from society, and especially the state, as it does from other individuals. Thus to insist upon the rights of citizens is to endorse their claims to protection from threatening forces. As human beings, individuals require the freedom and security to pursue their lives unhindered. Hence the term *liberal individualism.*

Within this way of thinking, citizenship is a "status," a status to be sought and, once achieved, to be maintained. One major difference between the modern Western world and earlier times is in the definition of who may be legitimately accorded the status of citizen. There is some distance between the world of Hobbes and Locke (when, arguably, citizenship was confined to certain male property owners) and our world, where, at least in rhetoric, all human beings — men, women, and children — have the rights of citizenship, though the latter do not have the full exercise of their rights until they reach adulthood. Many of today's political debates and movements are directed towards fulfilling the promise of the rhetoric: that is, towards making the status of citizenship, and the possession of the rights which belong to that status, meaningful in terms of empowering individuals to exercise their rights, of creating opportunities for them to do so, and in terms of placing curbs on political authorities to prevent their encroaching on individual rights. In this discourse, political authorities are regarded with the same suspicion that Locke had for civil government — and that some of the framers of the United States Constitution had for a central executive — for it is human beings who act in the name of the political authorities, and human beings are not to be trusted, especially when they have power.

The function of the political realm is to render service to individual interests and purposes, to protect citizens in the exercise of their rights, and to leave them unhindered in the pursuit of whatever individual and collective interests and purposes they might have. Political arrangements are thus seen in utilitarian terms. To the extent that they afford the required protection for citizens and groups to exercise their rights and pursue their purposes, then citizens have little to do politically beyond choose who their leaders are to be. The duty of citizens is to abide by the authoritative decisions made by political leaders. When otherwise satisfactory political arrangements come under threat, the duty of citizens will extend to defending them. Should political arrangements fail, for whatever reason, to provide freedom and security, then citizens claim the right to change them, with the ultimate right of resistance being held in reserve. One of the rights of citizens within this framework is the right to be active politically: to participate, that is, in more substantial ways than merely by choosing political leaders. Because it is a right, however, citizens choose — on the assumption that they have the resources and the opportunity — when and whether to be active in this way. It is no derogation from their status of citizen if they choose not to be so active.

For its proponents, a major advantage of liberal individualism — a rights-based account of the relationship between individuals and the wider society — is that it does not postulate any one conception of the good life. It advocates the procedures and rules, and the maintenance of an institutional framework, within which individuals — with their given or chosen interests and purposes — pursue their own versions of the good life for themselves. Justice is required as a "remedial" value,[1] in order to ensure that each individual's pursuit of his or her own good life does not prejudice in certain unacceptable ways the pursuit by others of their own good lives.

Behind such an argument is a view of the individual as autonomous. Largely unaided, individuals choose their own life projects, and ask the state to be allowed to follow them and to be protected accordingly. This individual responsibility for both the choice and the pursuit contributes to the necessary moral development of individuals. Rights-based accounts of the relationship between individuals and society are predicated, therefore, upon the autonomous and responsible moral agent. Followed through consistently, they sustain that agent's autonomy and responsibility. But unless forms of collective life — for example, devotion to a neighborhood, a class, a nation — constitute a substantive part of the good life of the agent, then such forms are conceived by the agent as instruments assisting pursuit of whatever good life is chosen. Nothing is enjoined upon the individual beyond a respect for the autonomy of others and the minimal civic duties of keeping the state in being — voting, paying taxes and, when the state itself is under threat, a readiness to come to its aid in some form of military service. . . .

Any alternative account of the relationship between individuals and society must, if it is to be taken seriously, accommodate itself to the fact that, in the Western world, individuals do conceive of themselves as possessing rights and as being autonomous, in the sense that they are in some ways both independent of the society in which they live and responsible for their own lives. Autonomous individuals are the subject matter of any social and political theory, but they are not its only subject matter.

There are a number of reasons why some alternative account is required. The first and most obvious one is that the rights-based account does not exhaust all that can be said — and that is in fact true — of the relationship between individuals and society. Individuals do not only conceive of themselves as bearing rights, nor is their posture toward forms of collective life solely instrumental. In particular, individuals recognize that they have duties, duties which extend further than the minimally civic and respect for others, and which are associated with the fact that they identify themselves socially — as parents and children; as members of a class, a religion, or a race; as neighbors and friends; as carrying on a trade or profession; as acknowledging a common nationality. Some of these social identities are no doubt chosen by individuals, but many are the "givens" of their very existence: acknowledged certainly, but acquired involuntarily, and often imperishable. Apostasy is sometimes simply not an option to be considered without profound personal unease, as, for instance, in renouncing one's family, one's faith, or one's country. These social identities are expressive of many forms of collective life, and many carry explicit duties with them; thus, they make it impossible for individuals to regard collective life purely instrumentally.[2]

If one of the social identities to which duties are attached is that of citizen, then one of the forms of collective life is the political community. This is the second reason for an alternative account: the revival of interest in the idea of community. There is a lively debate between liberals and communitarians,[3] and there have at times been penetrating discussions of whether there is any meaningful conception of community in the modern world which is consistent with the continued autonomy of individuals.[4] The theme of community has been addressed in many and different ways, and often by the same people who have expressed concern about what they consider to be the relative emptiness of liberal individualism's conception of citizenship. One consistent thought in the literature has been the idea that the modern world lacks, or has lost, any sense of community. For some this lack is not loss at all, but palpable gain, especially when they have reflected on the closed, hierarchical communities of the preindustrial world. Escape from the stultifying deadness of such communities could only benefit the individual in terms of gain to his or her autonomy and freedom. Others, however, have regretted the decline in the social solidarity and cohesion which past communities were alleged to possess, such a decline being simply the corollary of the triumph of the individual. Still others have looked back, sometimes with sweet and undisguised nostalgia, to the political communities of the ancient world where life was lived "whole," as it were, and individual freedom coexisted with social solidarity. They have, however, quickly shaken themselves out of this nostalgia, dusted themselves down, and concluded that they were dreaming. Such reveries have nothing to do with the modern world. But they have been too precipitate, for if there is one place in Western political thought where one might expect the themes of citizenship and community to be considered together, then it is in the civic-republican tradition that has its beginnings in the ethical and political thought of Aristotle. This tradition, reinforced and modified by a succession of subsequent thinkers from Machiavelli to Rousseau and beyond, via seventeenth-century English and eighteenth-century American republican thought, is at least as resilient a strain in Western thinking as liberal individualism, and it addresses much more cogently the twin themes of citizenship and community.

It is [my] contention that the civic-republican tradition repays study in two important respects. The first is its test of full membership of the political community. This test, by which the individual becomes a citizen, is performance of the duties of the practice of citizenship. Within civic republicanism, citizenship is an activity or a practice, and not simply a status, so that not to engage in the practice is, in important senses, not to be a citizen. Second, civic republicanism recognizes that, unsupported, individuals cannot be expected to engage in the practice. This means more than that individuals need empowering and need to be afforded with opportunities to perform the duties of the practice: it means, further, that they have to be provided with a sufficiency of motivation. Civic republicanism is a hard school of thought. There is no cozy warmth in life in such a community. Citizens are called to stern and important tasks which have to do with the very sustaining of their identity. There may be, indeed there ought to be, a sense of belonging, but that sense of belonging may not be associated with inner peace and, even if it is, it is not the kind of peace that permits a relaxed and private leisure, still less a disdain for civic concerns.

. . . [My] argument will be, following in the civic-republican tradition, that . . . far from undermining the individual's autonomy, institutional supports that motivate individuals to engage in the practice of citizenship enable them to reach a degree of moral and political autonomy which a rights-based account cannot vouchsafe. . . . Civic republicanism . . . holds that political life — the life of a citizen — is not only the most inclusive, but also the highest, form of human living-together that most individuals can aspire to. . . .

The argument that follows does not depend upon a change in human nature. Citizenship may be an unnatural practice for human beings . . .

but it is not thereby one for which they are congenitally unfitted. Furthermore, and in case the following discussion appears fanciful if not hopelessly utopian, what is put forward here is more than an ideal to which we can aspire: it is a standard against which we can measure the institutions and practices of our societies, and with which we can guide our own political activity. In this, the concepts of "citizenship" and "community" share important characteristics with other terms of political discourse—like "justice" and "freedom," for instance. We aspire to be just and free, even though we know we shall never be perfectly just or free. But that knowledge neither prompts us to abandon the ideals nor disposes us to discard the concepts as inappropriate or irrelevant to the world in which we live. We judge that world in terms of how just and free it is. The suggestion advanced here is that we should also judge our world in terms of how far it realizes the ideals of citizenship and community.

In a political community what is shared is identity, born in part from self-determination and in part from a common history, or language, or continued occupancy of the same territory. Political solidarity and cohesion result from the equality of a shared identity, which is at least in part self-determined and chosen. In other words, political solidarity and cohesion do not follow from the sharing of a history or a language, and so on. When we describe ourselves as American, Canadian, or British, or as Lancastrian, Quebecois, or Texan, we do not necessarily identify ourselves politically. We may be expressing something about our roots, or about our cultural inheritance, but because roots are experienced differently, and cultural inheritances variously interpreted, we do not thereby say anything about the commitment which a political identity involves as it is self-consciously recognized, acknowledged, and taken on. It is this choosing of a political identity that gives rise to the solidarity and cohesion of a political community. And it is as "active citizens" that we choose.

Now of course it is true that we are all born into networks of social, economic, and political relationships that we do not choose. Therein lies a large part of the difficulty of any attempt to make the practice of citizenship in a political community meaningful in the modern world. Yet, over the past two hundred years or more, many peoples have—by revolutions, rebellions, wars of liberation or independence—sought to forge new identities for themselves, or to give political expression to identities that they already possessed. In almost no country in the Western world...has this not occurred. This is one of the subversive lessons of history for the project of a political community. It is not that revolution and war have always, or even often, resulted in the practice of citizenship. Clearly they have not. It is rather that war or revolution may be necessary to the very choosing of a political identity. This is also one of the subversive lessons of many writers in the civic-republican tradition: it is a point which is made forcefully by both Machiavelli and Rousseau, for instance.

We cannot expect a practice of citizenship to grow merely because politicians and political thinkers wish it, and exhort their populations to effort. It is not, as again the civic-republican tradition makes clear, a natural practice for human beings, or one that they would spontaneously choose. "Natural" human beings, or "noncivic" or "precivic" ones, have to be molded and shaped for their role as citizens. In part this is the task of education in its broadest sense, but education needs to be supported and reinforced by a prevalent set of mores and practices conducive to sustaining the civic ideal. This may entail a civil religion, a profession of faith in the community. The practice of citizenship means that much more of one's life is lived publicly than is the case in the modern world. It is not that one has no private life; it is rather that to be a citizen is to be politically active, and political activity takes place in the public domain.

It is important, further, to distinguish between the bonds which tie citizens to each other and altruism. There is no doubt a reservoir of altruism in many people which compels them to give blood, to donate to worthy causes, or to spend time, effort, and money in organizing the disadvantaged. But citizenship is not about altruism: it is about acknowledging the community's goals as one's own, choosing them, and committing oneself to them. Altruism is the response of one human being to another. Citizenship is exclusive: it is not a person's humanity that one is responding to, it is the fact that he or she is a fellow citizen, or a stranger. In choosing an identity for ourselves, we recognize both who our fellow citizens are, and those who are not members of our community, and thus who are potential enemies. Citizenship cuts across both religious and secular universalism and involves recognizing that one gives priority, when and where required, to one's political community. This does not entail an aggressive posture towards strangers. It simply means that to remain a citizen one cannot always treat everyone as a human being. Again, this is a thought which lies at the heart of the civic-republican tradition.

## THE CITIZEN IN THE POLITICAL COMMUNITY
### ...AUTONOMY

... "Is there some way," Raymond Plant asks, "of understanding community which will enable the freedom of the individual and the cooperation and fraternity of the community to be meaningfully held together?"[5] ...

His formulation can stand to indicate the parameters of this inquiry. We need first to say something about "autonomy." What does it mean?

The assumption is that autonomous individuals exist; the question is, what does their autonomy consist in? The concept of "action" is a starting point here—action, as distinct from "behavior," draws attention to reasons, to motive, purpose, and will.[6] It thus refers to two further, closely related concepts: self-determination and authenticity. To say that someone's actions are self-determined is to say that they are a product of his or her will. Following Rousseau and Kant, this means that the self's will is not subject to, or constrained by, that of another. To say that a person's actions are authentic is to say not only that the will which wills them belongs to the self, and not to somebody else, but that it belongs to the self in some special way because the self has chosen it, or has at least rationally assented to it. The autonomous individual's actions, therefore—to the extent that they are self-determined—are expressions of that individual's authentic self....

... If we grant that people can some of the time act autonomously, and not unreflectively in response to the injunctions of a social role—or blindly in accordance with an ideology, or submissively in terms of the hierarchical ascription of a status—and if we are trying to find a place for autonomy within some conception of community, then it matters not just that people act, but how they act. Not all forms of conduct will be compatible with community life. Autonomous conduct requires some kind of affective or moral dimension.

## FRIENDSHIP

I can find no other word than *friendship* for the relationship that must exist between individuals for community to work.... It is friendship—rather than some other characteristic such as "civic virtue" or "civility"—which must obtain if there is to be such a thing as community, for it is the bond between individuals that creates the community itself. It is not a matter of each individual being bound separately to the community. This latter type of bonding can all too easily lead to the community's having a life of its own, over and above the lives of those who are its members. It is friendship which moralizes the actions of the autonomous individual, and which creates citizens.

Here, the reference point is Aristotle's discussion of friendship in Books VIII and IX of the *Nicomachean Ethics*. In order to place this discussion in an appropriate context, however, it is necessary to examine briefly what kind of association the *polis* is, and what constitutes its unity. In the

Politics, Aristotle describes the *polis* as an association of men, but an association of different kinds of men. It is "by its nature . . . some sort of aggregation,"[7] and not a total unity. It requires different and complementary capacities among its members if both it and they are to attain a better and higher form of life: "A real unity, such as a polis, must be made up of elements which differ in kind."[8] And this "real unity" is founded on justice and friendship. It is justice and friendship which create the bonds between members of diverse capacities, and which thus constitute the unity of the *polis.* To be just, Aristotle comments in the *Ethics,* means to be "lawful and fair": lawful, "because the law directs us to live in accordance with every virtue, and refrain from every kind of wickedness."[9] "Fair" in this context refers to both distributive and rectificatory justice, and requires that we take no more than our share, and accord others their proper share. . . .

It is justice which constitutes the spirit of friendship. "Friendship," he remarks in Book VIII of the *Ethics,* "seems to be the bond that holds communities together, and lawgivers seem to attach more importance to it than justice, . . . but people who are just still need the quality of friendship; and indeed friendliness is considered to be justice in the fullest sense."[10] . . . For Aristotle, friendship also includes the relationship between fellow-citizens, which is not love or affection, but "concord." In Book IX of the *Ethics,* he distinguishes "goodwill" from friendship: "Goodwill resembles friendship but is not identical with it, because goodwill can be felt towards people that one does not know, and without their knowledge, but friendship cannot."[11] Between fellow-citizens, and thus as the basis of political association and action, friendship takes the form of concord — "homonoia":

> There is said to be concord in a state when the citizens agree
> about their interests, adopt the same policy, and put their common resolves into effect. Thus concord is concerned with practical ends, and among these only with such as are important,
> and can be achieved . . . by the whole body of citizens. . . . Thus
> concord is evidently . . . friendship between the citizens of a state,
> because it is concerned with their interests and living conditions.[12]

. . . Concord is, thus, that friendship which exists between citizens as members of a political community. It is a relationship between people who know each other; they are not strangers, between whom goodwill is possible, but not friendship. It is a relationship between people who differ in their talents and capacities. It is a relationship based on respect for such differences, and on concern for others' interests: each, thus, acknowledges the other's autonomy. It is above all a relationship based on recognition that living is a shared venture that can be successfully engaged in only if there is commitment. The commitment, however, is to the fellow citizens, who — in choosing amongst themselves how to conduct their shared lives in the spirit of justice — create and sustain a community.

The community is prevented from becoming an entity that is somehow outside, above, or other than the individuals who compose it — such that it could make demands on its members against their wills — by adopting democratic procedures. It is only in such procedures that the implications of community membership can be explored. Furthermore, and given that no set of public purposes may exist waiting to be discovered, democratic procedures are necessary for creating such purposes, which in part identify the community as this community rather than any other. It is the fellow citizens of the community who collectively, through democratic procedures, are the guardians of the community's identity and ethos, so that the only claims that are made upon the members are self-assumed. A spirit of "concord," thus, allied with such procedures, creates the possibility — though it does not guarantee — that the outcome from democratic procedures will be socially acceptable.

Aristotle, of course, was writing about the Greek *polis* — a political community, geographically defined. That the possibilities for autonomous action by individuals in a spirit of concord are not exhausted in such communities is indicated by Raymond Plant's analysis of community in the modern world. Plant's argument is that it no longer makes sense to think of community in geographical terms.

Any search for a community appropriate to the modern world cannot be bound up with nostalgia for a lost rural ethos, with its emphasis on fixity of place and role, for the simple reason that such an ethos has become progressively weaker with the passage of time. It is possible to think of community, however, in functional terms, and trade off the very division of labor thought by other theorists actually to be destructive of community. The professions, he suggests, can be seen as functional communities in which there is common identity, stable membership, shared values, a common language, and acknowledged authority: "These seem to be criteria enough for agreeing that the notion of functional community makes sense."[13] It makes sense, moreover, from "some overall liberal view of man," for it takes into account "the values of autonomy and freedom realized as a result of the decline of the traditional community."[14] Any coherent view of community must, however, Plant claims, recognize the notion of authority as a necessary condition. In the traditional community, authority was customary, but social mobility has destroyed this idea of authority. How then can authority be compatible with an idea of community which does justice to individualism?

. . . It is in Plant's argument that authority is a necessary condition of any form of social life, and thus of any community, that he directs attention to what it is that members of a community do when they contemplate their lives in friendship — in "concord" — as autonomous beings. They establish the rules that are for them going to be authoritative and, in this, they exercise their judgment. Together with the ideas of autonomy and friendship, judgment is the third term denoting what is constitutive of a political community. With the exercise of political judgment, we come to the major duty of the practice of citizenship.

## JUDGMENT

...As practical wisdom, judgment occupies that space (if that metaphor is appropriate) within autonomous individuals which allows them to distance themselves from their social roles, and to choose both within a specific role and between roles what conduct is appropriate and proper for them. . . .

Judgments in political communities entail an implied responsibility for the assumption of a shared way of life. . . . Judgments are needed, first, about the kind of conduct which is constitutive of that collective life in which members of a community undertake to share. It is not a question, here, of a community setting itself some overriding purpose, or of establishing one exclusive path towards the good life. The community, after all, is composed of diverse autonomous beings, different in their capacities, talents, and functions. The good life for one is not necessarily the good life for another, but the good life for each must include activity which sustains the political community. It is thus a question both of establishing rules or norms of conduct in accordance with which each citizen will pursue his or her own independently determined good life, and of specifying those activities which are necessary to make the individual pursuit of the good life possible.

The survival of a community depends both upon its ability to protect itself, and upon the education and training of the young. Citizens have duties and responsibilities in these areas, which are thus a proper object of political judgment. Further, the community would cease to be a community if its citizens did not also recognize duties and responsibilities to those who, in some way — from old age or sickness, for instance — were incapacitated.

It is not supposed that the practice of citizenship in the political community, as so far defined, is "natural" to individuals as autonomous — or, indeed, any other — beings, in the sense that they spontaneously and necessarily conduct their relationships with their fellow members in ways conducive to the community's survival. To live as a member of a political community is a highly artificial form of life. It is not so much that citizens would be malicious, as that they would be ignorant both of the conditions necessary to sustain that life, and of conduct inimical to its survival, until they had engaged with their fellow citizens in political judgment about such matters.

All such judgments identify a community, and authorize a way of life appropriate to it. The authority possessed both by the rules and norms of conduct, and by the substantive purposes of the community, derives from the public judgment of its citizens. Since they remain autonomous beings, it is open to them to reconsider the desirability of the rules and norms, and of the purposes they once established. . . .

What the community does is not the incidental, and mechanical, by-product of the discrete activities of individuals, but is consciously and intentionally done. Deliberation is necessary among citizens who, because they are different and autonomous, may genuinely disagree about the answer to the question "How are we to live together?" Coordination among autonomous beings who genuinely differ, but also hold each other in mutual respect, is achieved by their public judgment on matters of common concern. Political judgment, thus, is that capacity of autonomous beings exercised by them as members of a community. The principles which are constitutive of the concept of community, therefore, are also those active principles which are constitutive of the way of life — or "constitution," to use that term in its Greco-Roman sense[15] — of the community in question. . . . In acting, citizens use their judgment in deliberating on matters of common concern. The judgments that are crucial here, and that underlie all others, are those that provide the community of which they are members with its identity.

## IMPLICATIONS FOR POLITICAL PRACTICE

Citizenship in these terms is difficult to achieve in the modern world: potential citizens lack the resources for engaging in the practice of citizenship; they lack the opportunities; and they lack the appropriate attitudes of mind — in other words, motivation.

Resources can be seen as enabling or empowering individuals to be active agents in this world. For activity of any kind, including that involved in the practice of citizenship, people need certain resources. Some of these have to do with what liberal individualism identifies as civil, political, and legal rights. Others have to do with economic and social resources. Without health, education, and a reasonable income, for instance, individuals do not have the capacity to be effective agents in the world, and the possibilities of a practice of citizenship are thus foreclosed. Such rights and resources have to be secured for citizens, for citizenship is an egalitarian practice.

Merely to empower individuals in this way, though necessary, is not, of course, sufficient for the practice of citizenship. The institutional setting has to be appropriate. There have to be arenas where potentially everyone can take part, where everyone can do something. In the modern state, this means the decentralization of political tasks and functions. Not everything that needs doing to make life possible in the modern world can be decentralized, but much more can be than is usually thought possible or is usually permitted — just as much less can be done at the level of the nation-state than used to be possible. What is to be sought is the creation and widening of opportunities for responsible self-government by citizens. It is not necessary that such self-government be conceived in any narrow political sense, where by "political" is meant "that which has an effect on everyone within a community, and which is open to change by collective action on the part of members." Self-government can refer to any public tasks and activities that a community wishes to engage in. Local initiatives can thus respond and cater to particular "publics" that are narrower in scope and coverage than the entire community.

Yet even empowerment and opportunity together are not sufficient for the practice of citizenship. What is further required is that a particular attitude of mind be encouraged, an attitude which not only prompts individuals to recognize what their duties are as citizens, but which motivates them to perform them as well. The problem to be overcome is that of the "free-rider." The variety and diversity which give vitality to the political community cannot be carried so far that certain individuals, whether from inclination or eccentricity, may renege on their duties as citizens, for this is destructive of "concord." The solution is education. Here, civic republicanism has a much broader conception than liberal individualism. Citizens are learners all their lives, and education in the sense of the building of the appropriate character for willing engagement in the practice of citizenship never ceases....

... Civic republicanism depends on "habits of the heart" for its viability. This is the central teaching of the civic-republican tradition. The phrase "habits of the heart" belongs to Tocqueville, but it is what Machiavelli meant by good laws, good religion, and good examples; what Rousseau meant by *moeurs*; what Hegel meant by ethical understanding. No amount of political participation and economic democracy, no level of civic education or national service, will suffice for the practice of citizenship in a political community — unless and until the external covenant becomes an internal one. This much, civic republicanism recognizes.

## THE SENSE OF COMMUNITY

... It cannot be the case in the modern world that the nation-state can be a community like the ancient *polis* — a face-to-face society in which everyone knows everyone else, even if only by reputation. ... Size, complexity, and heterogeneity all argue against such a position. This does not mean, however, that in times of "clear and present danger," to use Oliver Wendell Holmes's words — as in Britain in 1940, or in the United States after Pearl Harbor — there cannot emerge a sense of community: the idea that everyone is in the same predicament, and that each owes every other his or her utmost in escaping what is common to them all. Such moments, at the level of the nation-state, are rare.

Size, complexity, and heterogeneity all militate against any national consensus except on isolated occasions; what they do mean, on the other hand, is that we have plural societies. Human beings may or may not be sociable animals; the fact is that they live in societies composed of diverse and various social groupings ranging from the semiformal, like the family, to the highly organized, like the trade union or the political party. No human being can live a fully satisfactory life, indeed a fully human life, without ties to some such groupings. In modern societies there are thus multiple points of entry for individuals. There may not be a sufficient number, or entry points of the right kind, but variety is what characterizes modern society, and greater variety is what modern societies make possible. In such societies as we live in, this is where community is found. Why?

The idea of community has less to do with formal organization than with a sense of belonging and commitment. The commitment is to others who share interests, or positions, or purposes, and it is also to those who, for whatever reason, are unable to look after their own interests or pursue their own purposes. It is to seek the good of others at the same time as, and sometimes in neglect of, one's own good. It is to approach social relationships in an Aristotelian spirit of "concord." It is this that creates the sense of community; and it is this that creates citizens.

The argument is therefore that if one creates citizens, one also, and at the same time, creates community. Citizenship, as conceived in civic republicanism, entails community. If the conditions for the practice of citizenship are met, then so, too, are those for the existence of community. There are certain duties that all citizens must perform, such as choosing political leaders and holding them to account, paying taxes, and, when called upon, defending political arrangements which, because they create order, make the achievement of other purposes and goals possible. But these do not exhaust the areas of public life where the duties of citizenship may be practiced. Because modern societies are plural and heterogeneous, citizens who are properly motivated will find that there is much else that they can do. To a large extent, they will choose where to be active and, when and where they are active, they will create a sense of community. Community is found, therefore, not in formal organization, but wherever there are individuals who take the practice of citizenship seriously. The problem is to generate the commitment, which is what this [essay] has been about.

## NOTES

1. See Michael J. Sandel, *Liberalism and the Limits of Justice* (Cambridge: Cambridge University Press, 1982), ch. 1, esp. pp. 31–33, for a discussion of justice as a "remedial" value.

2. For a discussion of the social dimension of individual identity, see Edward R. Portis, "Citizenship and Personal Identity," *Polity* 18, no. 3 (1986):457–72.

3. Two recent contributions are Amy Gutmann, "Communitarian Critics of Liberalism," *Philosophy and Public Affairs* 14, no. 3 (1985):308–22, and Robert B. Thigpen and Lyle A. Downing, "Liberalism and the Communitarian Critique," *American Journal of Political Science* 31 (1987):637–55.

4. See Raymond Plant, *Community and Ideology* (London: Routledge & Kegan Paul, 1974).

5. Ibid., p. 32.

6. Martin Hollis, *Models of Man* (Cambridge: Cambridge University Press, 1977), p. 15.

7. Aristotle, *The Politics,* ed. Ernest Barker (Oxford: Clarendon, 1961), p. 40 (1261a).

8. Ibid., p. 41 (1261a).

9. Aristotle, *The Ethics,* ed. Jonathan Barnes (Harmondsworth: Penguin, 1976), pp. 172 (1129a), 176 (1130b).

10. Ibid., pp. 258–59 (1155a).

11. Ibid., p. 296 (1166b).

12. Ibid., p. 297 (1167a-b).

13. Plant, *Community and Ideology,* pp. 40–44.

14. Ibid., p. 47.

15. This sense refers not just to a body of laws assigning political offices, but to a way of life, or system of social ethics. (See Ernest Barker's introduction to Aristotle, *The Politics* [Oxford: Clarendon, 1961], p. lxvi.)

# PART IV
## THE SOCIAL DEMOCRATIC CRITIQUE

# 6

## *Citizenship and Social Class*

### T. H. MARSHALL

...Is it...true that basic equality, when it is enriched in substance and embodied in the formal rights of citizenship, is consistent with the inequalities of social class? I shall suggest that our society today assumes that the two are still compatible, so much so that citizenship has itself become, in certain respects, the architect of legitimate social inequality. Is it still true that the basic equality can be created and preserved without invading the freedom of the competitive market? Obviously it is not true.... But it is equally obvious that the market still functions — within limits. Here is a...possible conflict of principles which demands examination. And thirdly, what is the effect of the marked shift of emphasis from duties to rights? Is this an inevitable feature of modern citizenship — inevitable and irreversible? Finally...I shall ask whether there appear to be limits beyond which the modern drive towards social equality cannot, or is unlikely to, pass, and I shall be thinking not of the economic cost (I leave that vital question to the economists), but of the limits inherent in the principles that inspire the drive. But the modern drive towards social equality is, I believe, the latest phase of an evolution of citizenship which has been in continuous progress for some two hundred and fifty years. My first task, therefore, must be to prepare the ground for an attack on the problems of today by digging for a while in the subsoil of [English] history.

## THE DEVELOPMENT OF CITIZENSHIP TO
## THE END OF THE NINETEENTH CENTURY

I shall be running true to type as a sociologist if I begin by saying that I propose to divide citizenship into three parts. But the analysis is, in this case, dictated by history even more clearly than by logic. I shall call these three parts, or elements, civil, political, and social. The civil element is composed of the rights necessary for individual freedom — liberty of the person; freedom of speech, thought, and faith; the right to own property and to conclude valid contracts; and the right to justice. The last is of a different order from the others, because it is the right to defend and assert all one's rights on terms of equality with others and by due process of law. This shows us that the institutions most directly associated with civil rights are the courts of justice. By the political element I mean the right to participate in the exercise of political power, as a member of a body invested with political authority or as an elector of the members of such a body. The corresponding institutions are parliament and councils of local government. By the social element I mean the whole range from the right to a modicum of economic welfare and security to the right to share to the full in the social heritage and to live the life of a civilized being according to the standards prevailing in the society. The institutions most closely connected with it are the educational system and the social services.[1]

In early times these three strands were wound into a single thread. The rights were blended because the institutions were amalgamated. As Maitland said, "The further back we trace our history the more impossible it is for us to draw strict lines of demarcation between the various functions of the State: the same institution is a legislative assembly, a governmental council and a court of law.... Everywhere, as we pass from the ancient to the modern, we see what the fashionable philosophy calls differentiation."[2] Maitland is speaking here of the fusion of political and civil institutions and rights. But a man's social rights, too, were part of the same amalgam, and derived from the status which also determined the kind of justice he could get and where he could get it, and the way in which he could take part in the administration of the affairs of the community of which he was a member. But this status was not one of citizenship in our modern sense. In feudal society status was the hallmark of class and the measure of inequality. There was no uniform collection of rights and duties with which all men — noble and common, free and serf — were endowed by virtue of their membership of the society. There was, in this sense, no principle of the equality of citizens to set against the principle of the inequality of classes.

In the medieval towns, on the other hand, examples of genuine and equal citizenship can be found. But its specific rights and duties were strictly local, whereas the citizenship whose history I wish to trace is, by definition, national.

Its evolution involved a double process, of fusion and of separation. The fusion was geographical, the separation functional. The first important step dates from the twelfth century, when royal justice was established with effective power to define and defend the civil rights of the individual — such as they then were — on the basis, not of local custom, but of the common law of the land. As institutions the courts were national, but specialized. Parliament followed, concentrating in itself the political powers of national government and shedding all but a small residue of the judicial functions which formerly belonged to the Curia Regis, that "sort of constitutional protoplasm out of which will in time be evolved the various councils of the crown, the houses of parliament, and the courts of law."[3] Finally, the social rights which had been rooted in membership of the village community, the town, and the guild, were gradually dissolved by economic change until nothing remained but the Poor Law, again a specialized institution which acquired a national foundation, although it continued to be locally administered.

Two important consequences followed. First, when the institutions on which the three elements of citizenship depended parted company, it became possible for each to go its separate way, traveling at its own speed under the direction of its own peculiar principles. Before long they were spread far out along the course, and it is only in the present century... that the three runners have come abreast of one another.

Secondly, institutions that were national and specialized could not belong so intimately to the life of the social groups they served as those that were local and of a general character. The remoteness of parliament was due to the mere size of its constituency; the remoteness of the courts, to the technicalities of their law and their procedure, which made it necessary for the citizen to employ legal experts to advise him as to the nature of his rights and to help him to obtain them. It has been pointed out again and again that, in the Middle Ages, participation in public affairs was more a duty than a right. Men owed suit and service to the court appropriate to their class and neighborhood. The court belonged to them and they to it, and they had access to it because it needed them and because they had knowledge of its affairs. But the result of the twin process of fusion and separation was that the machinery giving access to the institutions on which the rights of citizenship depended had to be shaped afresh. In the case of political rights, the story is the familiar one of the franchise and the qualifications for membership of parliament. In the case of civil rights, the issue hangs on the jurisdiction of the various courts, on the privileges of the legal profession, and above all on the liability to meet the costs of litigation. In the case of social rights, the center of the stage is occupied by the Law of Settlement and Removal and the various forms of means test. All this apparatus combined to decide, not merely what rights were recognized in principle, but also to what extent rights recognized in principle could be enjoyed in practice.

When the three elements of citizenship parted company, they were soon barely on speaking terms. So complete was the divorce between them that it is possible, without doing too much violence to historical accuracy, to assign the formative period in the life of each to a different century — civil rights to the eighteenth, political to the nineteenth, and social to the twentieth. These periods must, of course, be treated with reasonable elasticity, and there is some evident overlap, especially between the last two.

To make the eighteenth century cover the formative period of civil rights it must be stretched backwards to include Habeas Corpus, the Toleration Act, and the abolition of the censorship of the press; and it must be extended forwards to include Catholic Emancipation, the repeal of the Combination Acts, and the successful end of the battle for the freedom of the press associated with the names of Cobbett and Richard Carlile. It could then be more accurately, but less briefly, described as the period between the Revolution and the first Reform Act. By the end of that period, when political rights made their first infantile attempt to walk in 1832, civil rights had come to man's estate and bore, in most essentials, the appearance that they have today. "The specific work of the earlier Hanoverian epoch," writes Trevelyan, "was the establishment of the rule of law; and that law, with all its grave faults, was at least a law of freedom. On that solid foundation all our subsequent reforms were built."[4] This eighteenth-century achievement, interrupted by the French Revolution and completed after it, was in large measure the work of the courts, both in their daily practice and also in a series of famous cases in some of which they were fighting against parliament in defense of individual liberty. The most celebrated actor in this drama was, I suppose, John Wilkes, and, although we may deplore the absence in him of those noble and saintly qualities which we should like to find in our national heroes, we cannot complain if the cause of liberty is sometimes championed by a libertine.

In the economic field the basic civil right is the right to work, that is to say, the right to follow the occupation of one's choice in the place of one's choice, subject only to legitimate demands for preliminary technical training. This right had been denied by both statute and custom: on the one hand by the Elizabethan Statute of Artificers, which confined certain occupations to certain social classes, and on the other by local regulations reserving employment in a town to its own members and by the use of apprenticeship as an instrument of exclusion rather than recruitment. The recognition of the right involved the formal acceptance of a fundamental change of attitude. The old assumption that local and group monopolies were in the public interest, because "trade and traffic cannot be maintained or increased without order and government,"[5] was replaced by the new assumption that such restrictions were an offense against the liberty of the subject and a menace to the prosperity of the nation. As in the case of the other civil rights, the courts of law played a decisive part in promoting and registering the advance of the new principle. The Common Law was elastic enough for the judges to apply it in a manner which, almost imperceptibly, took account of gradual changes in circumstances and opinion and eventually installed the heresy of the past as the orthodoxy of the present. . . .

By the beginning of the nineteenth century this principle of individual economic freedom was accepted as axiomatic. You are probably familiar with the passage quoted by the Webbs from the report of the Select Committee of 1811, which states that

> no interference of the legislature with the freedom of trade, or with the perfect liberty of every individual to dispose of his time and of his labor in the way and on the terms which he may judge most conducive to his own interest, can take place without violating general principles of the first importance to the prosperity and happiness of the community.[6]

The repeal of the Elizabethan statutes followed quickly, as the belated recognition of a revolution which had already taken place.

The story of civil rights in their formative period is one of the gradual addition of new rights to a status that already existed and was held to appertain to all adult members of the community — or perhaps one should say to all male members, since the status of women, or at least of married women, was in some important respects peculiar. This democratic, or universal, character of the status arose naturally from the fact that it was essentially the status of freedom, and in seventeenth-century England all men were free. Servile status, or villeinage by blood, had lingered on as a patent anachronism in the days of Elizabeth, but vanished soon afterwards. This change from servile to free labor has been described by Professor Tawney as "a high landmark in the development both of economic and political society," and as "'the final triumph of the common law" in regions from which had been excluded for four centuries. Henceforth the English peasant "is a member of a society in which there is, nominally at least, one law for all men."[7] The liberty which his predecessors had won by fleeing into the free towns had become his by right. In the towns the terms *freedom* and *citizenship* were interchangeable. When freedom became universal, citizenship grew from a local into a national institution.

The story of political rights is different both in time and in character. The formative period began, as I have said, in the early nineteenth century, when the civil rights attached to the status of freedom had already acquired sufficient substance to justify us in speaking of a general status of citizenship. And, when it began, it consisted, not in the creation of new rights to enrich a status already enjoyed by all, but in the granting of old rights to new sections of the population. In the eighteenth century political rights were defective, not in content, but in distribution — defective, that is to say, by the standards of democratic citizenship. The Act of 1832 did little, in a purely quantitative sense, to remedy that defect. After it was passed, the voters still amounted to less than one-fifth of the adult male population. The franchise was still a group monopoly, but it had taken the first step towards becoming a monopoly of a kind acceptable to the ideas of nineteenth-century capitalism — a monopoly which could, with some degree of plausibility, be described as open and not closed. A closed group monopoly is one into which no man can force his way by his own efforts; admission is at the pleasure of the existing members of the group. The description fits a considerable part of the borough franchise before 1832, and it is not too wide of the mark when applied to the franchise based on freehold ownership of land. Freeholds are not always to be had for the asking, even if one has the money to buy them, especially in an age in which families look on their lands as the social, as well as the economic, foundation of their existence. Therefore the Act of 1832, by abolishing rotten boroughs and by extending the franchise to leaseholders and occupying tenants of sufficient economic substance, opened the monopoly by recognizing the political claims of those who could produce the normal evidence of success in the economic struggle.

It is clear that, if we maintain that in the nineteenth century citizenship in the form of civil rights was universal, the political franchise was not one of the rights of citizenship. It was the privilege of a limited economic class, whose limits were extended by each successive Reform Act. It can nevertheless be argued that citizenship in this period was not politically meaningless. It did not confer a right, but it recognized a capacity. No sane and law-abiding citizen was debarred by personal status from acquiring and recording a vote. He was free to earn, to save, to buy property or to rent a house, and to enjoy whatever political rights were attached to these economic achievements. His civil rights entitled him, and electoral reform increasingly enabled him, to do this.

It was, as we shall see, appropriate that nineteenth-century capitalist society should treat political rights as a secondary product of civil rights. It was equally appropriate that the twentieth century should abandon this position and attach political rights directly and independently to citizenship as such. This vital change of principle was put into effect when the Act of 1918, by adopting manhood suffrage, shifted the basis of political rights from economic substance to personal status. I say "manhood" deliberately in order to emphasize the great significance of this reform quite apart from the second, and no less important, reform introduced at the same time—namely, the enfranchisement of women. But the Act of 1918 did not fully establish the political equality of all in terms of the rights of citizenship. Remnants of an inequality based on differences of economic substance lingered on until, [in 1948], plural voting (which had already been reduced to dual voting) was finally abolished.

When I assigned the formative periods of the three elements of citizenship each to a separate century—civil rights to the eighteenth, political to the nineteenth, and social to the twentieth—I said that there was a considerable overlap between the last two. I propose to confine what I have to say now about social rights to this overlap, in order that I may complete my historical survey to the end of the nineteenth century, and draw my conclusions from it, before turning my attention to the second half of my subject, a study of our present experiences and their immediate antecedents. In this second act of the drama social rights will occupy the center of the stage.

The original source of social rights was membership of local communities and functional associations. This source was supplemented and progressively replaced by a Poor Law and a system of wage regulation which were nationally conceived and locally administered. The system of wage regulation was rapidly decaying in the eighteenth century, not only because industrial change made it administratively impossible, but also because it was incompatible with the new conception of civil rights in the economic sphere, with its emphasis on the right to work where and at what you pleased under a contract of your own making. Wage regulation infringed on this individualist principle of the free contract of employment.

The Poor Law was in a somewhat ambiguous position. . . . For the Poor Law was the last remains of a system which tried to adjust real income to the social needs and status of the citizen and not solely to the market value of his labor. . . . [But] by the Act of 1834 the [new] Poor Law renounced all claim to trespass on the territory of the wages system, or to interfere with the forces of the free market. It offered relief only to those who, through age or sickness, were incapable of continuing the battle, and to those other weaklings who gave up the struggle, admitted defeat, and cried for mercy. . . . The minimal social rights that remained were detached from the status of citizenship. The Poor Law treated the claims of the poor, not as an integral part of the rights of the citizen, but as an alternative to them — as claims which could be met only if the claimants ceased to be citizens in any true sense of the word. For paupers forfeited in practice the civil right of personal liberty, by internment in the workhouse, and they forfeited by law any political rights they might possess. This disability of defranchisement remained until 1918, and the significance of its final removal has, perhaps, not been fully appreciated. The stigma which clung to poor relief expressed the deep feelings of a people who understood that those who accepted relief must cross the road that separated the community of citizens from the outcast company of the destitute.

The Poor Law is not an isolated example of this divorce of social rights from the status of citizenship. The early Factory Acts show the same tendency. Although in fact they led to an improvement of working conditions and a reduction of working hours to the benefit of all employed in the industries to which they applied, they meticulously refrained from giving this protection directly to the adult male — the citizen par excellence. And they did so out of respect for his status as a citizen, on the grounds that enforced protective measures curtailed the civil right to conclude a free contract of employment. Protection was confined to women and children, and champions of women's rights were quick to detect the implied insult. Women were protected because they were not citizens. If they wished to enjoy full and responsible citizenship, they must forgo protection. By the end of the nineteenth century such arguments had become obsolete, and the factory code had become one of the pillars in the edifice of social rights. . . .

The education of children has a direct bearing on citizenship, and, when the state guarantees that all children shall be educated, it has the requirements and the nature of citizenship definitely in mind. It is trying to stimulate the growth of citizens in the making. The right to education is a genuine social right of citizenship, because the aim of education during childhood is to shape the future adult. Fundamentally, it should be regarded, not as the right of the child to go to school, but as the right of the adult citizen to have been educated. And there is here no conflict with civil rights as interpreted in an age of individualism. For civil rights are designed for use by reasonable and intelligent persons, who have learned to read and write. Education is a necessary prerequisite of civil freedom.

By the end of the nineteenth century, elementary education was not only free, it was compulsory. . . . It was increasingly recognized, as the nineteenth century wore on, that political democracy needed an educated electorate, and that scientific manufacture needed educated workers and technicians. The duty to improve and civilize oneself is therefore a social duty, and not merely a personal one, because the social health of a society depends upon the civilization of its members. And a community that enforces this duty has begun to realize that its culture is an organic unity and its civilization a national heritage. It follows that the growth of public elementary education during the nineteenth century was the first decisive step on the road to the reestablishment of the social rights of citizenship in the twentieth. . . .

## THE EARLY IMPACT OF CITIZENSHIP ON SOCIAL CLASS

So far my aim has been to trace in outline the development of citizenship in England to the end of the nineteenth century. For this purpose I have divided citizenship into three elements, civil, political, and social. I have tried to show that civil rights came first, and were established in something like their modern form before the first Reform Act was passed in 1832. Political rights came next, and their extension was one of the main features of the nineteenth century, although the principle of universal political citizen was not recognized until 1918. Social rights, on the other hand, sank to the vanishing point in the eighteenth and early nineteenth centuries. Their revival began with the development of public elementary education, but it was not until the twentieth century that they attained equal partnership with the other two elements in citizenship.

I have as yet said nothing about social class, and I should explain here that social class occupies a secondary position in my theme. . . . Time would not allow me to do justice to so formidable a subject. My primary concern is with citizenship, and my special interest is in its impact on social inequality. I shall discuss the nature of social class only so far as is necessary for the pursuit of this special interest. I have paused in the narrative at the end of the nineteenth century because I believe that the impact of citizenship on social inequality after that date was fundamentally different from what it had been before it. That statement is not likely to be disputed. It is the exact nature of the difference that is worth exploring. Before going any further, therefore, I shall try to draw some general conclusions about the impact of citizenship on social inequality in the earlier of the two periods.

Citizenship is a status bestowed on those who are full members of a community. All who possess the status are equal with respect to the rights and duties with which the status is endowed. There is no universal principle that determines what those rights and duties shall be, but societies in which citizenship is a developing institution create an image of an ideal citizenship against which achievement can be measured and towards which aspiration can be directed. The urge forward along the path thus plotted is an urge towards a fuller measure of equality, an enrichment of the stuff of which the status is made and an increase in the number of those on whom the status is bestowed. Social class, on the other hand, is a system of inequality. And it too, like citizenship, can be based on a set of ideals, beliefs, and values. It is therefore reasonable to expect that the impact of citizenship on social class should take the form of a conflict between opposing principles. If I am right in my contention that citizenship has been a developing institution in England at least since the latter part of the seventeenth century, then it is clear that its growth coincides with the rise of capitalism, which is a system, not of equality, but of inequality. Here is something that needs explaining. How is it that these two opposing principles could grow and flourish side by side in the same soil? What made it possible for them to be reconciled with one another and to become, for a time at least, allies instead of antagonists? The question is a pertinent one, for it is clear that, in the twentieth century, citizenship and the capitalist class system have been at war.

It is at this point that a closer scrutiny of social class becomes necessary. I cannot attempt to examine all its many and varied forms, but there is one broad distinction between two different types of class which is particularly relevant to my argument. In the first of these, class is based on a hierarchy of status, and the difference between one class and another is expressed in terms of legal rights and of established customs which have the essential binding character of law. In its extreme form such a system divides a society into a number of distinct, hereditary human species — patricians, plebeians, serfs, slaves, and so forth. Class is, as it were, an institution in its own right, and the whole structure has the quality of a plan, in the sense that it is endowed with meaning and purpose and accepted as a natural order. The civilization at each level is an expression of this meaning and of this natural order, and differences between social levels are not differences in standard of living, because there is no common standard by which they can be measured. Nor are there any rights — at least none of any significance — which all share in common.[8] The impact of citizenship on such a system was bound to be profoundly disturbing, and even destructive. The rights with which the general status of citizenship was invested were extracted from the hierarchical status system of social class, robbing it of its essential substance. The equality implicit in the concept of citizenship, even though limited in content, undermined the inequality of the class system, which was in principle a total inequality. National justice and a law common to all must inevitably weaken and eventually destroy class justice, and personal freedom, as a universal birthright, must drive out serfdom. No subtle argument is needed to show that citizenship is incompatible with medieval feudalism.

Social class of the second type is not so much an institution in its own right as a by-product of other institutions. Although we may still refer to "social status," we are stretching the term beyond its strict technical meaning when we do so. Class differences are not established and defined by the laws and customs of the society (in the medieval sense of that phrase), but emerge from the interplay of a variety of factors related to the institutions of property and education and the structure of the national economy. Class cultures dwindle to a minimum, so that it becomes possible, though admittedly not wholly satisfactory, to measure the different levels of economic welfare by reference to a common standard of living. The working classes, instead of inheriting a distinctive though simple culture, are provided with a cheap and shoddy imitation of a civilization that has become national.

It is true that class still functions. Social inequality is regarded as necessary and purposeful. It provides the incentive to effort and designs the distribution of power. But there is no overall pattern of inequality, in which an appropriate value is attached, a priori, to each social level. Inequality therefore, though necessary, may become excessive. As Patrick Colquhoun said, in a much quoted passage, "Without a large proportion of poverty there could be no riches, since riches are the offspring of labor, while labor can result only from a state of poverty.... Poverty therefore is a most necessary and indispensable ingredient in society, without which nations and communities could not exist in a state of civilization."[9] But Colquhoun, while accepting poverty, deplored "indigence," or, as we should say, destitution. By "poverty" he meant the situation of a man who, owing to lack of any economic reserves, is obliged to work, and to work hard, in order to live. By "indigence" he meant the situation of a family which lacks the minimum necessary for decent living. The system of inequality which allowed the former to exist as a driving force inevitably produced a certain amount of the latter as well. Colquhoun, and other humanitarians, regretted this and sought means to alleviate the suffering it caused. But they did not question the justice of the system of inequality as a whole. It could be argued, in defense of its justice, that, although poverty might be necessary, it was not necessary that any particular family should remain poor, or quite as poor as it was. The more you look on wealth as conclusive proof of merit, the more you incline to regard poverty as evidence of failure — but the penalty for failure may seem to be greater than the offense warrants. In such circumstances it is natural that the more unpleasant features of inequality should be treated, rather irresponsibly, as a nuisance, like the black smoke that used to pour unchecked from our factory chimneys. And so in time, as the social conscience stirs to life, class-abatement, like smoke-abatement, becomes a desirable aim to be pursued as far as is compatible with the continued efficiency of the social machine.

But class-abatement in this form was not an attack on the class system. On the contrary, it aimed, often quite consciously, at making the class system less vulnerable to attack by alleviating its less defensible consequences. It raised the floor-level in the basement of the social edifice, and perhaps made it rather more hygienic than it was before. But it remained a basement, and the upper stories of the building were unaffected. And the benefits received by the unfortunate did not flow from an enrichment of the status of citizenship. Where they were given officially by the state, this was done by measures which, as I have said, offered alternatives to the rights of citizenship, rather than additions to them. But the major part of the task was left to private charity, and it was the general, though not universal, view of charitable bodies that those who received their help had no personal right to claim it.

Nevertheless it is true that citizenship, even in its early forms, was a principle of equality, and that during this period it was a developing institution. Starting at the point where all men were free and, in theory, capable of enjoying rights, it grew by enriching the body of rights which they were capable of enjoying. But these rights did not conflict with the inequalities of capitalist society; they were, on the contrary, necessary to the maintenance of that particular form of inequality. The explanation lies in the fact that the core of citizenship at this stage was composed of civil rights. And civil rights were indispensable to a competitive market economy. They gave to each man, as part of his individual status, the power to engage as an independent unit in the economic struggle and made it possible to deny to him social protection on the ground that he was equipped with the means to protect himself. . . . Status was not eliminated from the social system. Differential status, associated with class, function, and family, was replaced by the single uniform status of citizenship, which provided the foundation of equality on which the structure of inequality could be built.

... This status was clearly an aid, and not a menace, to capitalism and the free-market economy, because it was dominated by civil rights, which confer the legal capacity to strive for the things one would like to possess but do not guarantee the possession of any of them. A property right is not a right to possess property, but a right to acquire it, if you can, and to protect it, if you can get it.... Similarly, the right to freedom of speech has little real substance if, from lack of education, you have nothing to say that is worth saying, and no means of making yourself heard if you say it. But these blatant inequalities are not due to defects in civil rights, but to lack of social rights, and social rights in the mid-nineteenth century were in the doldrums. The Poor Law was an aid, not a menace, to capitalism, because it relieved industry of all social responsibility outside the contract of employment, while sharpening the edge of competition in the labor market. Elementary schooling was also an aid, because it increased the value of the worker without educating him above his station.... Thus although citizenship, even by the end of the nineteenth century, had done little to reduce social inequality, it had helped to guide progress into the path which led directly to the egalitarian policies of the twentieth century.

It also had an integrating effect, or, at least, was an important ingredient in an integrating process.... Prefeudal societies [were] bound together by a sentiment and recruited by [the] fiction... [of] kinship, or the fiction of common descent. Citizenship requires a bond of a different kind, a direct sense of community membership based on loyalty to a civilization which is a common possession. It is a loyalty of free men endowed with rights and protected by a common law. Its growth is stimulated both by the struggle to win those rights and by enjoyment of them when they are won. We see this clearly in the eighteenth century, which saw the birth, not only of modern civil rights, but also of modern national consciousness. The familiar instruments of modern democracy were fashioned by the upper classes and then handed down, step by step, to the lower: political journalism for the intelligentsia was followed by newspapers for all who could read, public meetings, propaganda campaigns and associations for the furtherance of public causes. Repressive measures and taxes were quite unable to stop the flood. And with it came a patriotic nationalism, expressing the unity underlying these controversial outbursts....

This growing national consciousness, this awakening public opinion, and these first stirrings of a sense of community membership and common heritage did not have any material effect on class structure and social inequality for the simple and obvious reason that, even at the end of the nineteenth century, the mass of the working people did not wield effective political power. By that time franchise was fairly wide, but those who had recently received the vote had not yet learned how to use it. The political rights of citizenship, unlike the civil rights, were full of potential danger to the capitalist system, although those who were cautiously extending them down the social scale probably did not realize quite how great the danger was. They could hardly be expected to foresee what vast changes could be brought about by the peaceful use of political power, without a violent and bloody revolution. The planned society and the welfare state had not yet risen over the horizon or come within the view of the practical politician. The foundations of the market economy and the contractual system seemed strong enough to stand against any probable assault. In fact, there were some grounds for expecting that the working classes, as they became educated, would accept the basic principles of the system and be content to rely for their protection and progress on the civil rights of citizenship, which contained no obvious menace to competitive capitalism. Such a view was encouraged by the fact that one of the main achievements of political power in the later nineteenth century was the recognition of the right of collective bargaining. This meant that social progress was being sought by strengthening civil rights, not by creating social rights; through the use of contract in the open market, not through a minimum wage and social security.

... Civil rights became, for the workers, an instrument for raising their social and economic status, that is to say, for establishing the claim that they, as citizens, were entitled to certain social rights. But the normal method of establishing social rights is by the exercise of political power, for social rights imply an absolute right to a certain standard of civilization which is conditional only on the discharge of the general duties of citizenship. Their content does not depend on the economic value of the individual claimant. There is therefore a significant difference between a genuine collective bargain through which economic forces in a free market seek to achieve equilibrium and the use of collective civil rights to assert basic claims to the elements of social justice. Thus the acceptance of collective bargaining was not simply a natural extension of civil rights; it represented the transfer of an important process from the political to the civil sphere of citizenship. But *transfer* is, perhaps, a misleading term, for at the time when this happened the workers either did not possess, or had not yet learned to use, the political right of the franchise. Since then they have obtained and made full use of that right. Trade unionism has, therefore, created a secondary system of industrial citizenship parallel with and supplementary to the system of political citizenship. . . .

## SOCIAL RIGHTS IN THE TWENTIETH CENTURY

The period of which I have hitherto been speaking was one during which the growth of citizenship, substantial and impressive though it was, had little direct effect on social inequality. Civil rights gave legal powers whose use was drastically curtailed by class prejudice and lack of economic opportunity. Political rights gave potential power whose exercise demanded experience, organization, and a change of ideas as to the proper functions of government. All these took time to develop. Social rights were at a minimum and were not woven into the fabric of citizenship. The common purpose of statutory and voluntary effort was to abate the nuisance of poverty without disturbing the pattern of inequality of which poverty was the most obviously unpleasant consequence.

A new period opened at the end of the nineteenth century. . . . A rise of money incomes unevenly distributed over the social classes altered the economic distance which separated these classes from one another, diminishing the gap between skilled and unskilled labor and between skilled labor and nonmanual workers, while the steady increase in small savings blurred the class distinction between the capitalist and the propertyless proletarian. Secondly, a system of direct taxation, ever more steeply graduated, compressed the whole scale of disposable incomes. Thirdly, mass production for the home market and a growing interest on the part of industry in the needs and tastes of the common people enabled the less well-to-do to enjoy a material civilization which differed less markedly in quality from that of the rich than it had ever done before. All this profoundly altered the setting in which the progress of citizenship took place. Social integration spread from the sphere of sentiment and patriotism into that of material enjoyment. The components of a civilized and cultured life, formerly the monopoly of the few, were brought progressively within reach of the many, who were encouraged thereby to stretch out their hands towards those that still eluded their grasp. The diminution of inequality strengthened the demand for its abolition, at least with regard to the essentials of social welfare.

These aspirations have in part been met by incorporating social rights in the status of citizenship and thus creating a universal right to real income which is not proportionate to the market value of the claimant. Class-abatement is still the aim of social rights, but it has acquired a new meaning. It is no longer merely an attempt to abate the obvious nuisance of destitution in the lowest ranks of society. It has assumed the guise of action modifying the whole pattern of social inequality. It is no longer content to raise the floor-level in the basement of the social edifice, leaving the super-structure as it was. It has begun to remodel the whole building, and it might even end by converting a skyscraper into a bungalow. It is therefore impor-tant to consider whether any such ultimate aim is implicit in the nature of this development, or whether, as I put it at the outset, there are natural limits to the contemporary drive towards greater social and economic equality. . . .

The most familiar principle in use is . . . the guaranteed minimum. The state guarantees a minimum supply of certain essential goods and ser-vices (such as medical attention and supplies, shelter, and education) or a minimum money income available to be spent on essentials — as in the case of old age pensions, insurance benefits, and family allowances. Anyone able to exceed the guaranteed minimum out of his own resources is at lib-erty to do so. Such a system looks, on the face of it, like a more generous version of class-abatement in its original form [of scaled prices]. It raises the floor-level at the bottom, but does not automatically flatten the super-structure. . . . Flat-rate benefits do not reduce the gaps between different in-comes. Their equalizing effect depends on the fact that they make a bigger percentage addition to small incomes than to large. . . . When a free service, as in the case of health, is extended from a limited income group to the whole population, the direct effect is in part to increase the inequality of disposable incomes, again subject to modification by the incidence of taxes. For mem-bers of the middle classes, who used to pay their doctors, find this part of their income released for expenditure on other things. [A total scheme is less specifically class-abating in a purely economic sense than a limited one.]

. . . The extension of the social services is not primarily a means of equalizing incomes. In some cases it may be, in others it may not. . . . What matters is that there is a general enrichment of the concrete substance of civilized life, a general reduction of risk and insecurity, an equalization be-tween the more and the less fortunate at all levels — between the healthy and the sick, the employed and the unemployed, the old and the active, the bachelor and the father of a large family. Equalization is not so much between classes as between individuals within a population which is now treated for this purpose as though it were one class. Equality of status is more impor-tant than equality of income. . . .

The common experience offered by a general health service em-braces all but a small minority at the top and spreads across the important class barriers in the middle ranks of the hierarchy. At the same time the guaranteed minimum has been raised to such a height that the term *mini-mum* becomes a misnomer. The intention, at least, is to make it approximate so nearly the reasonable maximum that the extras which the rich are still able to buy will be no more than frills and luxuries. The provided service, not the purchased service, becomes the norm of social welfare. . . .

Benefits in the form of a service have this further characteristic that the rights of the citizen cannot be precisely defined. The qualitative element is too great. A modicum of legally enforceable rights may be granted, but what matters to the citizen is the superstructure of legitimate expectations. It may be fairly easy to enable every child below a certain age to spend the required number of hours in school. It is much harder to satisfy the legitimate expectation that the education should be given by trained teachers in classes of moderate size. . . . The rate of progress depends on the magnitude of the national resources and their distribution between competing claims. Nor can the state easily foresee what it will cost to fulfill its obligations, for, as the standard expected of the service rises — as it inevitably must in a progressive society — the obligations automatically get heavier. The target is perpetually moving forward, and the state may never be able to get quite within range of it. It follows that individual rights must be subordinated to national plans. . . .

I see no signs of any relaxation of the bonds that tie education to occupation. On the contrary, they appear to be growing stronger. Great and increasing respect is paid to certificates, matriculation, degrees, and diplomas as qualifications for employment, and their freshness does not fade with the passage of the years. A man of forty may be judged by his performance in an examination taken at the age of fifteen. The ticket obtained on leaving school or college is for a life journey. The man with a third-class ticket who later feels entitled to claim a seat in a first-class carriage will not be admitted, even if he is prepared to pay the difference. . . . The right of the citizen in this process of selection and mobility is the right to equality of opportunity. Its aim is to eliminate hereditary privilege. In essence it is the equal right to display and develop differences, or inequalities; the equal right to be recognized as unequal. In the early stages of the establishment of such a system the major effect is, of course, to reveal hidden equalities — to enable the poor boy to show that he is as good as the rich boy. But the final outcome is a structure of unequal status fairly apportioned to unequal abilities. . . .

The conclusion of importance to my argument is that, through education in its relations with occupational structure, citizenship operates as an instrument of social stratification. There is no reason to deplore this, but we should be aware of its consequences. The status acquired by education is carried out into the world bearing the stamp of legitimacy, because it has been conferred by an institution designed to give the citizen his just rights.

That which the market offers can be measured against that which the status claims. If a large discrepancy appears, the ensuing attempts to eliminate it will take the form not of a bargain about economic value, but of a debate about social rights. . . .

I said earlier that in the twentieth century citizenship and the capitalist class system have been at war. Perhaps the phrase is rather too strong, but it is quite clear that the former has imposed modifications on the latter. . . . Social rights in their modern form imply an invasion of contract by status, the subordination of market price to social justice, the replacement of the free bargain by the declaration of rights. . . .

## CONCLUSIONS

I have tried to show how citizenship, and other forces outside it, have been altering the pattern of social inequality. To complete the picture I ought now to survey the results as a whole on the structure of social class. They have undoubtedly been profound, and it may be that the inequalities permitted, and even molded, by citizenship do not any longer constitute class distinctions in the sense in which that term is used for past societies. . . .

We have to look for the combined effects of three factors. First, the compression, at both ends, of the scale of income distribution. Second, the great extension of the area of common culture and common experience. And third, the enrichment of the universal status of citizenship, combined with the recognition and stabilization of certain status differences chiefly through the linked systems of education and occupation. The first two have made the third possible. Status differences can receive the stamp of legitimacy in terms of democratic citizenship provided they do not cut too deep, but occur within a population united in a single civilization; and provided they are not an expression of hereditary privilege. This means that inequalities can be tolerated within a fundamentally egalitarian society provided they . . . do not create incentives which spring from dissatisfaction and the feeling that "this kind of life is not good enough for me." . . .

## NOTES

1. By this terminology, what economists sometimes call "income from civil rights" would be called "income from social rights." Cf. H. Dalton, *Some Aspects of the Inequality of Incomes in Modern Communities* (London: Routledge, 1920), part 3, chapters 3 and 4.

2. F. Maitland, *Constitutional History of England* (Cambridge: Cambridge University Press, 1908), p. 105.

3. A. F. Pollard, *Evolution of Parliament* (London: Longmans, 1920), p. 25.

4. G. M. Trevelyan, *English Social History* (London: Longmans, 1943), p. 351.

5. City of London Case, 1610. See E. F. Heckscher, *Mercantilism,* vol.1 (London: Allen & Unwin, 1935), pp. 269–325, where the whole story is told in considerable detail.

6. Sidney and Beatrice Webb, *History of Trade Unionism* (London: Longmans, 1920), p. 60.

7. R. H. Tawney, *Agrarian Problem in the Sixteenth Century* (London: Longmans, 1912), pp. 43–44.

8. See the admirable characterization given by R. H. Tawney in *Equality* (New York: Harcourt Brace, 1931), pp. 121–22.

9. Colquhoun, *A Treatise on Indigence* (London: Hatchard, 1806), pp. 7–8.

# 7

## Contract versus Charity: Why Is There No Social Citizenship in the United States?

### NANCY FRASER AND LINDA GORDON

*Citizen* and *citizenship* are powerful words. They speak of respect, of rights, of dignity. Consider the meaning and emotion packed into the French *citoyen* of 1789, a word that condemned tyranny and social hierarchy while affirming self-government and status equality; that was a moment when even women succeeded in claiming address as *citoyenne* rather than as *madame* or *mademoiselle*. Since then the word appears often as a prefix to another term, always adding dignity to the original, as in *citizen-soldier, citizen-worker, citizen-mother*. The word has so much dignity it rarely appears in slang. In a few informal phrases it continues to carry approval and respect, as in *a citizen of the world* or *citizens' committee*. We find no pejorative uses. It's a weighty, monumental, humanist word.

It is telling, therefore, that people in the United States rarely speak of "social citizenship." That expression, if it were used, would convey the idea that in a welfare state citizenship includes an entitlement to social provision—the guarantee of a decent standard of living. It would bring such social provision within the aura of dignity surrounding "citizenship" and "rights." People who enjoy "social citizenship" get "social rights," not "handouts." They receive aid while maintaining their status as full members of society entitled to "equal respect." And they share a common set of institutions and services designed for *all* citizens, the use of which constitutes the *practice of* social citizenship: for example, public schools, public parks, universal social insurance, public health services. Thus, the expression "social citizenship" evokes themes from three major traditions of political theory: liberal themes of rights and equal respect; communitarian norms of solidarity and shared responsibility; and republican ideals of participation in public life (through use of "public goods" and "public services").

But the expression "social citizenship" is almost never heard in public debate in the United States today. Receipt of "welfare" is usually considered grounds for disrespect, a threat to, rather than a realization of, citizenship. And in the area of social services, the word *public* is often pejorative. Public hospitals are institutions of last resort, sites of stigma, not solidarity. Public schools, once considered "cradles of citizenship," are often so inferior to their "private" (commodified) counterparts as to fit the expression "private wealth, public squalor." And public parks are often too dangerous to enter. In general, the idea of social citizenship in a welfare state is out of phase with powerful currents in contemporary U.S. political culture. The connotations of *citizenship* are positive, powerful, and proud, while those of *welfare* are so negative, weak, and degraded that "social citizenship" here sounds almost oxymoronic.

No wonder, then, that neither the phrase nor the idea figured in the 1992 presidential campaign. Although Bill Clinton defended public schools, he joined the campaign against "entitlements," attacking the notion that people have a right to help. No major-party politician in the United States today seems willing to defend this principle. Virtually all prefer the demeaning rhetoric of "dependency," accepting without question that public assistance must reduce people's independence and that public provision should be minimized, its recipients moved off the welfare rolls as quickly as possible. In this climate, social citizenship finds no foothold.

If "social citizenship" designates an absence in U.S. political discourse, civil citizenship is emphatically a presence. People in the United States pride themselves on a commitment to civil liberties and civil rights, even when they do not always respect them in practice. Phrases like "individual liberties" and "freedom of speech" are central to the country's rhetorical traditions, despite frequent efforts to curtail them. So resonant and powerful are these themes that collective movements have sometimes sought to harness their prestige to social-egalitarian aims—witness the "civil rights movement" for racial equality.

U.S. political culture thus combines a richly elaborated discourse of "civil citizenship" with a near-total silence about "social citizenship." Consequently, U.S. thinking about social provision has been shaped largely by images drawn from civil citizenship, especially images of contract. The result has been a tendency to focus on two rather extreme forms of human relationship: discrete contractual exchanges of equivalents, juxtaposed against unreciprocated, unilateral charity. Most debates over welfare state policy have been framed in terms of this contract-versus-charity opposition. Invidious distinctions are drawn, for example, between "contributory" programs and "noncontributory" ones, between social insurance (or "Social Security"), where beneficiaries have a right to what they receive, since they merely "get back what they put in," and public assistance, where they have no such right, since they are thought to "get something for nothing." These extremes, perversely, appear to exhaust all social possibilities.

As long as we remain trapped in a contract-versus-charity opposition we will not solve the "welfare problem." Full employment *simpliciter* is no solution, since it would not erase the needs of single parents, the old, or the infirm. No decent welfare policy can emerge without a vision of honorable entitlement for those who require help. "Social citizenship" is a conceptual resource for developing such a vision. It assumes there can be relations among members of society that are neither contractual nor charitable. This idea thus provides some leverage for a critique of U.S. political culture, which is what we attempt in this essay. It is not, however, without difficulties of its own. Not only does it presuppose the increasingly problematic unit of the nation-state — a *major* difficulty we shall not discuss here — but standard conceptions of social citizenship are pervaded by androcentrism and ethnocentrism. Thus our discussion proceeds simultaneously on two fronts. We use a concept derived largely from English sociological theory to critique U.S. political culture, while at the same time we use aspects of U.S. history and culture to reveal some limitations of the English concept.

## THE LEGACY OF T. H. MARSHALL

Our touchstone is T. H. Marshall's brilliant 1949 essay "Citizenship and Social Class," the source of all discussions of "social citizenship." Marshall was the first to conceptualize and defend social citizenship as the crowning stage in the historical development of modern citizenship. In his conception, it was the last of three stages. The first stage, civil citizenship, he held to have been constructed primarily in the eighteenth century and to have established the rights necessary for individual freedom: rights to property and personal liberty, and especially the right to justice. The second stage, political citizenship, was built primarily in the nineteenth century, in his view, and encompassed the right to participate in the exercise of political power, whether by holding office or by voting. The third and final stage, social citizenship, was to be constructed in the twentieth century; for Marshall, it would encompass not only the guarantee of economic security, but also the more far-reaching right to "a share in the full social heritage and to live the life of a civilized being according to the standards prevailing in the society."[1]

Marshall wrote at a moment of hopefulness about social citizenship. The British electorate after World War II "ungratefully" overthrew Churchill and installed a Labour Party committed to building a welfare state. Marshall envisaged a state that would not only smooth the roughest edges off the sharp inequalities of class society, but actually erode some class-based status differences altogether. He saw universal provision as a way to create status equality and social solidarity. . . .

Marshall expected universal educational and health services to help dissolve divergent class cultures into a "unified civilization." He envisioned a progressive decoupling of money income from a larger "social wage," which would include many tax-funded services provided publicly. The "minimum standard" established by public provision, he hoped, would in time be raised so high as to approach the maximum, so that the extras the rich could buy would be mere frills. The public service, not the purchased service, would become the norm.

Marshall's utopianism did not derive from a simple Whiggish view of progress. He was sensitive to the contradictions between the three evolving dimensions of citizenship as well as to differences of interest among citizens. He noted those excluded from citizenship and understood that citizenship itself had functioned as an architect of social inequality. He also grappled with the question of whether a uniform status of citizenship could be achieved while respecting the inviolability of market mechanisms and private property. But he remained convinced that the further development of social citizenship could renovate social relations toward greater equality.

T. H. Marshall's essay is tonic reading in this period of widespread pessimism about public life, but it should not be appropriated uncritically. When questions about gender and race are put at the center of the inquiry, key elements of Marshall's analysis become problematic. His periodization of the three stages of citizenship, for example, fits the experience of white workingmen only, a minority of the population. His conceptual distinctions between civil, political, and social citizenship tend to take for granted, rather than problematize, gender and racial hierarchies. Finally, his assumption, continued in later social-democratic thought and practice, that the chief aims of social citizenship are erosion of *class* inequality and protection from *market* forces slights other key axes of inequality and other mechanisms and arenas of domination.

Most questionable for our purposes here, however, is Marshall's optimism about the ease with which social citizenship could be built upon a foundation laid in terms of civil citizenship. This faith seems misplaced from the standpoint of the contemporary United States, where we find not only new depths of immiseration and inequality, but also new levels of hostility to a welfare state. Moreover, this hostility is often expressed in terms of the contractual norms of civil citizenship — in the idea that welfare recipients are getting something for nothing while others must work, hence that they are violating standards of equal exchange. Such formulations prompt us to consider whether the cultural mythology of civil citizenship may not stunt the capacity to envision social citizenship.

In what follows, we reexamine the relationship between civil citizenship and social citizenship. (We leave aside questions about the relationship between political citizenship and social citizenship, although they, too, would repay reexamination in the light of gender and race.) Our focus is the historical construction of the opposition between contract and charity. We trace the genealogy of this opposition — from its origins in the cultural mythology of contract surrounding civil citizenship to its current role in the United States in stunting the development of social citizenship. In so doing, we take special care to reveal the important but neglected role of gender and race in structuring these cultural conceptions.

Let us not be misunderstood. We do not claim that civil rights are inherently antithetical to social rights. Current ideological antitheses between work and welfare, entitlement and charity, are historically constructed and contingent, not conceptually necessary. The civil rights of citizenship need not be cloaked in commercial metaphors of contractual exchange. Reimagining these rights in better, more solidaristic ways remains a crucial task — both for political theorists and for social movements. What follows is a critical prelude to such reimagination.

## COMMERCIAL MYTHS/CIVIL WRONGS

The first stage of citizenship in Marshall's analysis — civil citizenship — by no means spelled progress for everyone affected. Rather, in raising the status of some it simultaneously lowered the relative status of others. Nor can the development of civil citizenship be understood in isolation from the question of entitlements to social provision. All societies contain people who cannot obtain their subsistence in the socially normative way: people who are disabled or who lack family help, for example. The new individual property rights that emerged with civil citizenship frequently undercut the traditional claims of such persons for community support. The result was a gendered, ideological opposition between contract and charity that still structures state provision of welfare today. (In this essay we use "social citizenship" to refer to Marshall's, and others', vision of an ideal "welfare state." Where we refer to the actually existing welfare, we speak of "social provision" or the like.)

In its earliest English meaning, "citizenship" was residence in a city. Since city dwellers were among the first groups to separate themselves from feudal relations of servitude, the term also carried connotations of freedom. Marshall placed the beginnings of citizenship in early modern England, where by the eighteenth century permanent and hereditary servility had been legally abolished. "Citizenship" at this time meant free status, and the rights attaching to that status were called "civic rights" or "civil rights." These included the right to own property and to make valid contracts, the right to sue in court, the liberty of one's person, and, after the English Revolution, freedom of speech, thought, and religious faith.

Thus, civil citizenship brought important new "civil" rights to many people. These rights did not arrive in the form of thin, abstract moral norms, however, but came laden with cultural meanings and images. Liberal social contract theory supplied many of the cultural trappings. It justified modern constitutional government by tracing the origin of legitimate political power to a voluntary, conventional agreement among free, rational "men" in "the state of nature." The result of their "original pact" was government by law and, simultaneously, its other face: the legal constitution of a "civil" sphere within society, in which independent individuals could contract freely with one another, secure in their persons and in their property. These individuals thus acquired legal personalities and civil rights; they became "citizens" of "civil society."

The constitution of "civil society," both in contract theory and in contract law, was tantamount to a revolution in social ontology. The subjects of civil society were "individuals," existing prior to their relationships. Relationships were cast as voluntary, temporary, and limited arrangements, entered into out of individual self-interest. The prototype was the contractual agreement, defined as an exchange of equivalents. This presupposed the liberty and independence of the contractors, neutral mechanisms to enforce their agreements, and individual ownership of the items exchanged, be they commodities, labor power, or opinions. In C. B. Macpherson's memorable phrase, civil society was premised on a "possessive individualism."[2]

"Possessive individualism" was prototypically the basis of economic exchange, but its conceptual reach was far wider. It underlay the whole of modern civil society, itself broader than, albeit modeled on, commerce.

The ability to enter freely into agreements or relationships of any kind presupposed freedom from subjection to a master, a condition understood to mean self-ownership. Because of this, "individuals" were proprietors not only of the tangible goods in their possession but of their "persons" as well. Their guarantees of civil citizenship exceeded economic property rights to include the ability to sell one's labor power, principles of personal liberty — freedom from arbitrary imprisonment and from unreasonable search and seizure; liberty of movement and bodily integrity; freedom of speech, thought, and religion — and the right to sue in a court of law in order to enforce all one's other rights.

Certainly, this property-centered contract model is not the only way of conceiving civil society. In the eighteenth and nineteenth centuries, another model, less economistic, more "associational," was developed — by Montesquieu and Tocqueville, among others. But the contract model has predominated in the United States, supplying the images and interpretations that have colored cultural understandings of civil citizenship.

Commonsensical as it has since become, the contract-centered ontology of civil society represented a revolutionary departure from earlier views of personhood and social relations. Previous legal understandings did not recognize "individuals" as bearing rights that were prior to, and independent of, their place in a status hierarchy. Nor were social relations treated as freely chosen, limited agreements between parties of equal status. Rather, relationally defined statuses were cast as conceptually prior to individuals and constitutive of their entitlements and obligations. Relationships, moreover, were characteristically quasi-permanent, nonvoluntary, hierarchical arrangements obligating subordinates to obey and superordinates to protect. This earlier ontology recognized masters and subjects but had no place for citizens.

Contract-centered civil citizenship was not meant to replace traditional subjectship wholesale. Even for the most radical early proponents of "civil society," not all human beings were "individuals." Women, of course, were excluded from independent civil (and political) citizenship for centuries, and there was no agreement on what degree of citizenship should be accorded the poor, servile, and "racially" different. Consequently, civil society was viewed as but one subsector within society, standing in a complex, symbiotic relation to others.

We can highlight the apparent paradoxes here by considering two modern forms of subjection, coverture and slavery. In the legal fiction of coverture, married women were subsumed into the legal personalities of their husbands. This looks at first like a continuation of traditional subjectship, which is how T. H. Marshall apparently saw it. But coverture is better understood as a modern phenomenon that helped *constitute civil* citizenship. Coverture was a stage in the decline of patriarchy. (By "patriarchy" we mean not just relations between men and women but societies pervaded by hierarchical relations, in which nearly everyone was subordinate to some superior, whether king, lord, landlord, father, or husband.)

With the construction of modern civil society, married men who would earlier have been "dependents" within larger patriarchal units became family "heads" and "individuals." Family headship became a newly salient and honorific status rivaling rank, caste, and property ownership. By granting independent legal standing to most (white) male heads of families, coverture democratized relations and undercut patriarchy among adult free (that is, in the United States, white) men, for whom marriage conferred "independence" and full civil, if not yet electoral, rights. Contrary to Marshall's assumption, the exclusion of married women from civil citizenship was no mere archaic vestige destined to fade as citizenship evolved. Rather, women's subsumption in coverture was the other face and enabling ground of modern civil citizenship. The two mutually defined one another.

The same is true for the brutal new forms of slavery that emerged in the New World in tandem with the elaboration of civil citizenship. In the United States, for example, the world's most extensive civil rights for white men coexisted with history's most totalitarian, rights-depriving system of chattel slavery for black men and women. The modern "scientific" concept of "race" justified the subjection of blacks at the very moment when the discourse of "citizenship" proclaimed liberty the natural birthright of "man." The centerpiece of civil citizenship in "the white republic" was a property conception of rights. In the slave states, free white men were "persons," while black slaves were "property," and civil citizenship guaranteed the property rights of one to possess the other. In one of the great ironies in the history of civil citizenship, the first U.S. Married Women's Property Act, passed in Mississippi in 1839, was aimed at securing slaveholders' wives rights over slaves.[3] Meanwhile, the citizenship claims of white male wage workers rested in part on their ability to claim their labor power as a form of personal property. "Free labor" found its meaning and honor largely in contrast to the degraded condition of the slave, who labored but did not earn.[4] Again, arrangements treated by Marshall as peripheral exceptions helped construct core cultural meanings of civil citizenship.

Since civil citizenship often made property rights the model for all other rights, it is hardly surprising that those excluded from civil citizenship were usually those who did not own property, either because they were unable to get their resources defined as property (for example women, tenants, workers) or because they *were* property (slaves). Similarly, some civil rights functioned to the disadvantage of the propertyless. Rights accorded to heads of households against intruders and the state, for example, often deprived slaves, workers, women, and children of outside protection to stop abuse by their masters.

Notwithstanding the rhetoric of liberal contract theory, then, civil rights were not at first rights of "individuals." They belonged instead to male property owners and family heads, often by virtue of their responsibility for "dependents." "Having dependents," in fact, became in some jurisdictions a qualification for full civil citizenship. The legal subsumption of wives in coverture, and the legal classification of slaves as property, were no simple matters of exclusion. They actually helped instead to define civil citizenship, for it was by protecting, subsuming, and even owning others that white male property owners and family heads became citizens.

The construction of civil citizenship did not simply elevate those men freed from the bonds of dependency; those women, men, and children who did not acquire independent legal personalities suffered a comparative demotion in status. Previously, to lack civil "independence" had been the normal majority condition; it was not particularly stigmatized or demeaning. But when white married men, small freeholders, and family heads achieved independent legal status, subsumption into the legal personality of another became increasingly anomalous — and stigmatizing. By the mid-nineteenth century, both coverture and slavery had come to seem abhorrent to many people. Some white women and black slaves responded by appropriating the rhetoric of social contract theory and claiming to be "individuals." But in so doing, they were not simply demanding admission to a preexisting status. Rather, they were challenging the grounds on which claims to social resources were made, a fundamental aspect of the social order.

## THE EROSION OF COMMUNAL RESPONSIBILITY

The construction of modern civil citizenship also transformed the basis of entitlements to social resources, which had implications for "social welfare." In traditional, precapitalist societies, claims to resources were often grounded in some variation of a "moral economy" that curbed individual self-interest. Ownership was usually a matter of divided, overlapping rights to various kinds of use. As a result, most property was not entirely liquid, its disposition being constrained by tradition. Similarly, the traditional extended family gave a wide range of kinfolk, and at times neighbors and villagers, some economic responsibilities for each other. No single relationship defined anyone's whole entitlement to support; every particular relationship formed a link in a longer chain of dependency. These arrangements were patriarchal, to be sure, but they differed markedly from coverture. Women figured as centrally as men, though without as much power, in the full range of community- and kin-based relationships. Instead of depending exclusively on husbands, wives usually had a variety of bases from which to claim needed resources.

The rise of civil citizenship eroded these arrangements, in part by creating a new form of property right that trumped customary obligations and entitlements. When land became a commodity, rural populations lost their age-old rights of tenancy and use. Later, "reforms" of traditional poor relief weakened established patterns of community support, facilitating the creation of a "free" market in labor—free, that is, from the moral-economic strictures of the "just wage." For the majority, consequently, the property right enshrined by civil citizenship spelled dispossession.

It was just such new forms of property right and labor contract that T. H. Marshall had in mind when he claimed that the rise of civil citizenship at first set back social citizenship. Yet he failed to notice the gender and family meanings of civil citizenship, which helped create the norm of the family wage and undercut earlier, kin-based claims on social resources. These arrangements signaled the contraction of kinship to one "sphere" of society; from being a model for all social relations it shrank to a counterpoint to, and support for, "civil society."[5] Starting in the late eighteenth century, the "kinship sphere" became hegemonically defined as the realm of "the feminine" and "the domestic," a "private sphere" of familial intimacy and affect.

The result was the appearance—especially among the urban bourgeoisie and those who aspired to "middle class" status—of a new ideological disjuncture between two different kinds of claims to social resources, associated with two different "spheres" of society. In civil society, the "male sphere," contractual relations dominated: resources were exchanged for exact equivalents in discrete, monetarized transactions between self-interested independent individuals. In the domestic sphere of the intimate family, in contrast, resources appeared to flow with sentiment wholly outside the circuit of exchange.

This gender division between two "spheres" was ideological in several respects. The norms it propounded were constantly violated in practice, and different social groups sought to refashion them to serve different political agendas. For example, working-class men and women used ideas of womanly "domesticity" in their struggles for better living and working conditions and in the development of working-class standards of discipline and respectability. Likewise, women's-rights activists used domesticity ideas to argue for the importance of women's influence as mothers.

The "male" side of the divide, contractual exchange, was increasingly represented as the basic form of human interaction. Contract became a metaphor for the presupposition of rational choice in which the motive was self-advantage. It was applied even to nonmarket spheres, such as politics, as well as to commercial relations. Within commerce, moreover, the contract metaphor reconstructed the meaning of paid labor as "wage labor," a supposedly free and equal contractual exchange of labor power for wages. This extension of the contract model rebounded to influence representations of the "female sphere," making kinship and intimate relations appear to be "natural," and hence outside the province of social theory.

As contract gained ascendance over a progressively larger share of human relations, the range of alternatives narrowed. Noncontractual forms of reciprocity were increasingly assimilated to contractual exchange, except for those "inside" the nuclear family. Any interactions that seemed neither contractual nor familial now appeared to be unilateral and entirely voluntary, entailing neither entitlements nor responsibilities. Thus, the hegemony of contract helped to generate a specifically modern conception of "charity" as its complementary other. Charity came to appear a pure, unilateral gift, on which the recipient had no claim and for which the donor had no obligation. Thus, whereas contract connoted equal exchange, mutual benefit, self-interest, rationality, and masculinity, charity took on contrasting connotations of inequality, unilateral gift-giving, altruism, sentiment, and, at times, femininity. The contrast, moreover, assumed the guise of a stable, conceptually exhaustive dichotomy: all extrafamilial relations had to be either contractual or charitable; there appeared to be no other possibilities.

The binary opposition between contract and charity had still further ideological consequences. First, in the modern conception of charity, the giver got moral credit while the taker was increasingly stigmatized. This distribution of value was inherently unstable, since the devaluation of recipients naturally spawned doubts about the merits of giving. In the nineteenth-century United States, such doubts fueled repeated waves of "reform" that sought to counter the "degenerative" effects of "indiscriminate giving" both on recipients and on society as a whole. Thus the contract side of the opposition repeatedly menaced the charity side; what had appeared to be a stable dichotomy was always in danger of dissolving.

Second, the contract-versus-charity dichotomy shrouded the very possibility of noncontractual reciprocity, rendering invisible a whole range of popular practices that defied the official binary categorization. Kinship, neighborly, and community obligations continued strong, despite the ideology of the independent nuclear family; and informal mutual aid persisted in a variety of guises and forms. Yet these practices lost public recognition and official political legitimacy. In time, the lack of a language to validate their existence contributed to their decline and decay. Throughout the nineteenth century, moreover, while charity was under constant attack, the definition of kinship was becoming more nuclear. Economic responsibilities for members of extended families were growing weaker in the United States, thus further constricting the experience of interpersonal help that was neither contractual nor charitable.

## CONTRACT, CHARITY, AND WELFARE

The contract-versus-charity dichotomy thus to some extent remade reality in its image, crowding out other types of relations. It impressed its stamp strongly on state provision of welfare, which developed along dichotomous lines. In the United States, government programs from early in the twentieth century divided into two streams. Those with the most legitimacy took on some of the trappings of civil exchange, guaranteeing secure entitlements to some citizens by mimicking private contracts. Other programs, in contrast, were cast as proffering unreciprocated aid to the "innocent" and "deserving" poor, with the state assuming the role of previously private charity. These two streams, moreover, were strongly gendered. The contract stream had its first U.S. prototype in workman's compensation (industrial accident insurance), while the charity stream was exemplified by mothers' pensions.[6]

The gender-coded contract/charity dichotomy persists today in many countries in the opposition between social insurance and public assistance programs. The first were designed by reformers to appear "contributory," seemingly embodying the principle of exchange; recipients, originally intended to be exclusively white, male, and relatively privileged members of the working class, are defined as "entitled." Public assistance, in contrast, continued the "noncontributory" charity tradition, so that its recipients appear to get something for nothing, in violation of contractual norms.

The reality is considerably more complicated. Numerous social insurance advocates of the early twentieth century deliberately used the term *contributory* as a rhetorical selling device for the new programs, fully aware that all welfare programs are financed through "contributions," differing only as to where and how these are collected—through sales taxes or wage deductions, for example. Despite their official image as contractual, Social Security "insurance" programs depart significantly from actuarial principles, and benefits do not actually reflect financial contributions. And while the legitimacy of Social Security retirement pensions derives in part from the view that they compensate previous service, one might with equal plausibility claim that seemingly "noncontributory" programs like Aid to Families with Dependent Children (AFDC, the successor to mother's pensions) compensate the child-rearing "service" of single mothers. Far from accurately representing the two tiers of U.S. state provision, then, the contract-versus-charity dichotomy merely rationalizes their differential legitimacy. But that differential ultimately rests on the privileging of waged labor and the derogation of women's unpaid care work.

As the cultural mythology of civil citizenship affected the design of welfare programs, so too has the stratified, gendered construction of social welfare shaped the terms of civil citizenship. Recipients of public assistance have often found their civil rights curtailed. For example, AFDC claimants in the United States have been denied the right to interstate travel (abridged by state residency requirements); the right to due process (abridged by administrative procedures for determining eligibility and terminating benefits); the right to protection from unreasonable search and seizure (abridged by unannounced home visits); the right to privacy (abridged by "morals testing"); and the right to equal protection under the law (abridged by all of the above). In the 1960s and 1970s U.S courts overturned many of these practices, but the 1970s and 1980s brought a rash of new restrictions. By contrast, receipt of "social insurance" entailed no comparable loss of civil rights.

. . . The contract norm continues to hamper attempts to expand social provision today. Since the wage appears as an exchange in return for labor, it is argued that all resources should be apportioned in terms of exchange. The widespread fear that "welfare" recipients are "getting something for nothing" is an understandably embittered response from those who work hard and get little; their own paltry remuneration becomes their norm and they see themselves cheated by welfare clients rather than by their employers. Such responses are of course exacerbated when the poor are represented as female, sexually immoral, and/or racially "other." The result is that, particularly under the impact of economic recession, the claims of the poor in the United States today are being weakened by a resurgence of the rhetoric of contract.

In sum, the cultural mythology of civil citizenship stands in a tense, often obstructing relationship to social citizenship. This is nowhere more true than in the United States, where the dominant understanding of civil citizenship remains strongly inflected by notions of "contract" and "independence," while social provision has been constructed to connote "charity" and "dependence." What is missing is a public language capable of expressing ideas that escape those dichotomous oppositions: especially the ideas of solidarity, noncontractual reciprocity, and interdependence that are central to any humane social citizenship.

## A New Rhetoric of Citizenship?

Our analysis reveals considerable tension between the cultural mythology of civil citizenship and T. H. Marshall's conception of social citizenship. The chief obstacles to social citizenship in the United States are, of course, political and economic — international as well as domestic. Nevertheless, ideological conceptions, such as contract, make it more difficult to develop public support for a welfare state, especially where the cultural mythology of civil citizenship is highly developed. Marshall underestimated these ideological difficulties. Should we conclude, then, that civil rights and social rights are incompatible with one another? Our analysis does not support that conclusion. On the contrary, we maintain that reconciliation of the two forms of citizenship represents an urgent task, for political theorists and social movements.

What would it take to revivify social citizenship in the face of the new contractarianism? One beginning is to reimagine civil citizenship in a less property-centered, more solidaristic form. This would permit us to reclaim some of the moral and conceptual ground for social rights that has been colonized by property and contract. We might try to reconceive personal liberties in terms that nurture rather than choke off social solidarity. Certainly we need to contest conservative and liberal claims that the preservation of civil and political rights requires jettisoning rights to social support. Today, when rhetoric about the "triumph of democracy" accompanies social and economic devastation, it is time to insist that there can be no democratic citizenship without social rights.

## Notes

1. T. H. Marshall, "Citizenship and Social Class," in *Class, Citizenship, and Social Development: Essays by T. H. Marshall,* ed. Seymour Martin Lipset (Chicago: University of Chicago Press, 1964), p. 78.

2. C. B. Macpherson, *The Political Theory of Possessive Individualism: Hobbes to Locke* (Oxford: Oxford University Press, 1974).

3. Rogers M. Smith, "One United People: Second-Class Female Citizenship and the American Quest for Community," *Yale Journal of Law and the Humanities* 1, no. 2 (May 1989): 229–93.

4. Judith Shklar, *American Citizenship: The Quest for Inclusion* (Cambridge, Mass.: Harvard University Press, 1991).

5. Linda J. Nicholson, *Gender and History: The Limits of Social Theory in the Age of the Family* (New York: Columbia University Press, 1986).

6. See the essays in *Women, the State and Welfare,* ed. Linda Gordon (Madison: University of Wisconsin Press, 1991), especially the papers by Barbara J. Nelson and Diana Pearce; and Linda Gordon, "Social Insurance and Public Assistance: The Influence of Gender in Welfare Thought in the United States, 1890–1935," *American Historical Review* 97, no. 1 (Feb. 1992).

# PART V
## THE NATIONALIST CRITIQUE

# 8

## Immigration, Citizenship, and the Nation-State in France and Germany

### ROGERS BRUBAKER

Citizenship and nationhood have recently become intensely contested issues in European politics.[1] The reactivation of these long dormant issues reflects the sharply increased volume and ethnocultural diversity of immigration during the last quarter century. The demographic legacy of Europe's "new immigration" is the large and unprecedentedly diverse population of immigrant origin;[2] its political legacy is the intensifying debate about citizenship and nationhood.

This essay addresses the emerging European politics of citizenship and nationhood in historical and comparative perspective. It begins by evoking in general terms the challenge posed by immigration to the nation-state. Constructing an ideal-typical model of nation-state membership, it highlights the several respects in which the membership status of today's immigrants is politically anomalous. Next, focusing on the problem of admission to citizenship, the essay analyzes the wide variation in European citizenship law and naturalization practice. It then examines in detail one striking instance of this variation — French readiness and West German reluctance to transform immigrants into citizens. The expansive French politics of citizenship vis-à-vis immigrants, it argues, reflects a state-centered, assimilationist, essentially political national self-understanding, while the restrictive German politics reflects an ethnocultural understanding of nationhood as prior to and independent of the state. The essay analyzes the genesis and development of these distinctive traditions of nationhood and concludes by showing how they shaped the development of citizenship law—and thereby the citizenship status and chances of immigrants—in France and Germany.

## Citizenship in the Nation-State:
## A Model of Membership

Debates about citizenship, in the age of the nation-state, are debates about nationhood—about what it means, and what it ought to mean, to belong to a nation-state.[3] As an institutional and social-psychological reality, the nation-state is a distinctive way of organizing and experiencing political and social membership. But the nation-state is also an idea—and an ideal: it is a distinctive way of characterizing and evaluating political and social membership. As an ideal-typical model of membership, the nation-state can be characterized in terms of six membership norms. According to this model, membership of the nation-state should be *egalitarian, sacred, national, democratic, unique, and socially consequential.*[4] Inherited from the classical age of the European nation-state, these norms continue to inform political talk about nationality, citizenship, immigration, military service, the welfare state, patriotism, national identity, and other subjects bearing on membership. In sketching these norms, I do not mean to endorse them. I want simply to characterize the backdrop of taken-for-granted ideas and ideals against which the politics of immigration and citizenship unfolds today.

Membership of the nation-state, according to the ideal-typical model, should be *egalitarian.* There should be a status of full membership, and no other (except in the transitional cases of children and persons awaiting naturalization). Basic and enduring gradations of membership status are inadmissible. This norm derives, most immediately, from the French Revolution, which opposed a unitary, unmediated, undifferentiated, and therefore (formally) egalitarian conception of state-membership to the plural, differentiated, essentially inegalitarian ancien-régime notion of state-membership as mediated by corporate bodies.[5]

Second, membership should be *sacred.* Citizens must make sacrifices—etymologically, perform "sacred acts"—for the state. They must be prepared to die for it if need be (Walzer 1970a; Contamine 1986). Profane attitudes toward membership, involving calculations of personal advantage, are profoundly inappropriate. The sacralization of social and political membership, to be sure, long antedates the French Revolution. But the modern democratic, national, and (paradoxical though it may sound) secular understanding of the sacredness of social and political membership, like the modern understanding of state-membership as essentially egalitarian, dates from the French Revolution.[6]

Third, state-membership should be *based on nation-membership*. The political community should be simultaneously a cultural community, a community of language, mores, and character.[7] Only thus can a nation-state be a nation's state, the legitimate representative and the authentic expression of the nation. Those aspiring to membership of the state must be or become members of the nation. If not (presumptively) acquired through birth and upbringing, such nation-membership must be earned through assimilation.[8] This norm, unlike the egalitarian and sacralizing components of the nation-state model, derives not directly from the French Revolution but from the nineteenth-century national movements it helped set in motion.

Fourth, membership should be *democratic*. Full membership should carry with it significant participation in the business of rule. And membership itself should be open: since a population of long-term resident nonmembers violates democratic understandings of membership, the state must provide some means for resident nonmembers to become members. Over the long run, residence and membership must coincide. Like the national idea, the democratic idea derives indirectly from the French Revolution and directly from the democratic movements of the nineteenth century.

Fifth, state-membership should be *unique*, that is, exhaustive and mutually exclusive. Every person should belong to one and only one state. The orderliness of interstate relations requires that this norm be at least approximately realized in a world that is "filled up" with states, each of which claims a fraction of the human population as its own, for which it has special responsibility and on which it can make special demands. Statelessness, as Hannah Arendt (1973:290–302) has shown with particular poignancy, can be catastrophic in a world in which even so-called human rights are enforceable for the most part only by particular states. And dual (or multiple) citizenship has long been considered undesirable for states and individuals alike. There are legal techniques for regulating and mitigating the conflicts, inconveniences, and ambiguities it occasions. But these techniques cannot solve the central political problem of dual citizenship—the problem of divided allegiance.

Lastly, membership should be socially *consequential*; it should be expressed in a community of well-being. Membership should entail important privileges. Together with the sacralized duties mentioned above, these should define a status clearly and significantly distinguishable from that of nonmembers.[9] Membership should be objectively valuable and subjectively valued—it should be prizeworthy and actually prized.

IMMIGRATION AND ANOMALIES OF MEMBERSHIP

This model of membership is largely vestigial. As such, it is significantly out of phase with contemporary realities of state-membership. Conspicuous deviations from the model occur quite independently of immigration. The desacralization of state-membership, for example, has more to do with the emotional remoteness of the bureaucratic welfare state (Walzer 1970b:204; Kelly 1979:22) and the obsolescence of the citizen army in the nuclear age (Doorn 1975) than it does with immigration and occasional naturalizations of convenience. And if citizenship today is not very robustly democratic, this has more to do with the highly attenuated participation of most citizens in the exercise of sovereignty than it does with the exclusion of noncitizens from the franchise.

Still, postwar immigration has accentuated existing deviations from the nation-state model and generated new ones. These include the proliferation of statuses of partial membership (Brubaker 1989b:16–20, 1989d:160–62; Hammar 1990); the declining value of citizenship (Schuck 1989); the desacralization of membership through the calculating exploitation of the material advantages it confers (Sayad 1982:28ff.; Brubaker 1992; Schuck and Smith 1985:95, 109–12); the increasing demands for, and instances of, full membership of the state without membership of the cultural nation (Minces 1985; Centre de Relations Internationales 1984; Griotteray 1984); the soaring numbers of persons with dual citizenship (Hammar 1989; Brubaker 1989c:115–17; Costa-Lascoux 1988:108–16); and the exclusion of large numbers of long-term residents from the franchise (Oriol 1985:138–43, 149–51; Balibar 1984). These trends in the organization of membership deviate from every component of the nation-state model; and all arise from unexpected development of postwar immigration to northwestern Europe.[10]

Unexpected: for the settlers of today were the sojourners of yesterday—temporary labor migrants, segregated from and invisible to the surrounding society, existing (for the host society) only in the sphere of work. By definition, neither strictly temporary labor migration nor unambiguous and accepted immigration for purposes of permanent settlement poses insuperable problems of membership. But the gradual transformation of sojourners into settlers, only partially and belatedly acknowledged by both immigrants and the receiving country, generates complex and delicate problems of membership.[11]

The membership status of these migrants-turned-immigrants has developed in an ad hoc fashion with the piecemeal administrative, legislative, and judicial acknowledgment of their potentially permanent status (Miller 1986). This process of piecemeal inclusion contrasts with the "total" transformation effected by naturalization. Paradoxically, the further this process of piecemeal inclusion has gone, the weaker the incentive to naturalize. Ad hoc enlargements of migrants' rights may thus obstruct rather than clear the path to full membership, trapping large numbers of migrants-turned-immigrants in an intermediate status, carrying with it many of the privileges and obligations of full membership but excluding two of the most important, symbolically and practically: the right to vote and the duty of military service.

The immigration was unexpected, too, in its volume, which peaked at very high rates in 1968–72, and in its provenance, with the 1950s immigrants from neighboring countries giving way to their geographically and culturally more distant successors of the late 1960s and early 1970s (and to the Third World refugees of the late 1970s and the 1980s). Against the backdrop of the norms of membership sketched above, the triply unexpected quality of the postwar immigration — unexpected in its permanence, volume, and ethnocultural heterogeneity — helps to explain Europe's profound political uncertainty in the face of today's increasingly settled and increasingly assertive immigrant population.

Not everyone shares this uncertainty, of course. Nationalists defend the integral validity of the classical model of the nation-state, stressing that state-membership presupposes nation-membership. Postnational pluralists, on the other hand, deny any validity to this model, arguing for new forms of political membership that would mirror an emerging multicultural, postnational society. The former demand of immigrants either naturalization, stringently conditioned upon assimilation, or departure; the latter demand for immigrants a full citizenship stripped of its sacred character and divorced from nationality. Neither position is particularly nuanced. Neonationalists treat the nation-state as something frozen in social and political time; theirs is a profoundly anachronistic interpretation, neglecting the specific contexts in which the membership norms emerged and to which they responded. Postnational pluralists, in their haste to condemn the nation-state to the dustbin of history, underestimated the richness and complexity of a normative tradition that, reinterpreted to take account of the changing economic, military, and demographic contexts of membership, may have life in it yet.

## ADMISSION TO CITIZENSHIP

This, then, is the ideological backdrop against which the contemporary politics of citizenship and social membership is played out. The ideas and ideals sketched above, however, are riddled with internal tensions and contradictions. And there are marked variations over historical time and political space in the normative and institutional construction of nation-statehood. These tensions, contradictions, and variations will be the focus of the rest of the essay.

So long as one talks about the nation-state in abstraction from concrete problems of nation-statehood, one can gloss over these internal tensions, these historical and national variations. But the tensions and variations are inescapable when one addresses concrete questions of membership. Consider the question of admission to citizenship. It is immediately evident that the norms of membership sketched above point in different directions. The norms of egalitarian and democratic membership require the admission of long-term residents to full citizenship. But the norms of unique, sacred, and national membership can be used to justify a series of more or less restrictive preconditions for admission.[12] At the limit, these may be sufficiently dissuasive to block the large-scale incorporation of immigrants as citizens.

The model of membership developed above, then, provides a matrix of arguments bearing on the question of admission to membership, but no univocal answer to this question. This normative ambivalence is mirrored by institutional variety. This is evident, first, in the special provisions — or lack thereof — for the admission of second-generation immigrants to citizenship. At one pole, traditional countries of immigration like the United States, Canada, and most Latin American countries attribute citizenship unconditionally to all persons born in the territory. At the other pole, Germany and Switzerland have no special provisions for second-generation immigrants. In intermediate cases, some combination of birth and residence suffices for the quasi-automatic or declarative acquisition of citizenship. In France and the Netherlands, for example, persons born in the territory and residing there for a certain length of time can opt for citizenship at majority. In Sweden and Belgium, persons brought up in the territory, even if not born there, can acquire citizenship through simple declaration.

Immigrants and their descendants not benefiting from these and certain other special provisions[13] can accede to citizenship only through naturalization. Here too, the range of variation is wide. At one pole, naturalization is a purely discretionary decision of the state. The candidate must fulfill certain conditions that are often only vaguely specified; in addition, the state must judge whether or not the granting of citizenship is in its own interest. A negative decision need not be justified, and cannot be appealed against. In such a purely discretionary system, geared to a low volume of immigration, naturalization is an anomalous and infrequent event, a privilege bestowed by the state, after careful scrutiny, on certain deserving individuals. The state does not promote naturalization, and may indeed discourage it by imposing a high fee and a bafflingly complex procedure.

At the other pole, all candidates meeting certain clearly specified conditions are naturalized. In this system, adapted to mass immigration, naturalization is expected, while the failure to naturalize is anomalous. Naturalization is actively promoted by the state. The procedure is simple, the scrutiny of most applications is perfunctory, and the fees are low.

Roughly speaking, the systems of naturalization in place in the United States, to a greater extent in Canada, and to a surprising extent also in Sweden, approach the latter pole, while those in Switzerland and especially in Germany approach the former. This is indicated by their results. Taking Germany as a base, foreign residents naturalize at a rate four times higher in France, ten times higher in the United States, fifteen times higher in Sweden, and over twenty times higher in Canada (Brubaker 1989c:117–20).

There are major differences, then, in the extent to which Europe's postwar immigrants have been incorporated as citizens. These differences have been largely neglected in the literature on immigration.[14] In the socioeconomic perspective that prevails in this literature, citizenship is of minor importance. What really matters as a determinant of life chances, it is argued — and here I am in full agreement — is immigrants' social, economic, and cultural marginalization, determined by their weak position in the labor market, the housing market, and the educational system, a position that results in part from their status as ethnocultural minorities but is largely independent of formal citizenship status. It is clear from the experience of the United States and Britain that the possession of full formal citizenship does not impede the development of multiply disadvantaged ethnocultural minorities.

Even in the "life chances" perspective, however, formal membership status is important, indeed increasingly important. As a result of the widening demographic and economic rift between the First and the Third World and the simultaneous eclipse of distance between the two through the mutually reinforcing links of transportation, communication, and migration, the demand for entry into the more prosperous and peaceful territories of the earth is greater than ever before (Zolberg 1983). In these circumstances, the state's control, imperfect though it remains, over admission to and residence in its territory (and thus, indirectly, over admission to its labor markets and to its welfare institutions) has never been more important. The crucial status in this respect, however, is not citizenship but the status of "privileged," "established," or "permanent" resident, which confers an ordinarily irrevocable right of residence as well as civil and socioeconomic rights virtually identical to those of citizens (Schuck 1989; Brubaker 1989d). In terms of life chances, then, the decisive gap is between privileged noncitizen residents and persons, inside or outside the territory, without long-term residence rights. Full citizenship adds complete protection against expulsion and complete access to public service employment, but its marginal contribution to life chances is seldom decisive.

But if citizenship status is not a decisive determinant of immigrants' life chances, it remains a crucial determinant of their place in the polity and, more broadly, of the general character of politics in the countries of postwar immigration. This is not to imply that noncitizen immigrants are politically mute (Miller 1989). Nor is it to attribute miraculous virtues to universal suffrage: the possession of full political rights does not guarantee their effective exercise, particularly by a group singularly lacking in political resources. It is simply to recall the obvious: the fact that the exclusion or self-exclusion of immigrants from formal citizenship is tantamount to the disfranchisement of a significant fraction of the population, and of a much higher fraction of the manual working class; and that the interests of disfranchised groups do not count for much in the political process. The substantial cross-national variation in the civic incorporation of postwar immigrants thus deserves more attention than it has to date received.

## TRADITIONS OF NATIONHOOD AND POLITICS OF CITIZENSHIP

The model of nation-state membership sketched above, then, is ambivalent with respect to the admission of immigrants to citizenship. But the model in its general form corresponds to no sociopolitical reality. "The" nation-state is a figment of the sociological imagination. What exists are particular nation-states, formed under particular historical circumstances, bearing even today the stamp of these distinctive historical origins, and, in consequence, unequally disposed to accept immigrants as citizens.

This is an argument that I want to develop with respect to the exemplary pair of France and Germany.[15] French conceptions of nationhood and citizenship bear the stamp of their monarchical gestation, Revolutionary birth, and Republican apotheosis. The nation, in this tradition, has been conceived in relation to the institutional and territorial frame of the state: political unity, not shared culture, has been understood to constitute nationhood. Revolutionary and Republican definitions of nationhood and citizenship — militantly unitarist, universalist, and secular — reinforced what was already in the ancien régime an essentially political understanding of nationhood. But if nationhood is constituted by political unity, it is centrally *expressed* in the striving for cultural unity. Political inclusion has ideally entailed cultural assimilation, for ethnic peripheries and immigrants alike; the universalist theory and practice of citizenship have depended on confidence in the assimilatory workings of school, army, and centralized administration.

If the French conception of nationhood has been universalist, rationalist, assimilationist, and state-centered, the German conception has been particularist, organic, differentialist, and *Volk*-centered. Because national feeling developed before the nation-state, the German idea of the nation was not, originally, a political one, nor was it linked with the abstract idea of citizenship. This prepolitical German nation, this nation in search of a state, was conceived not as the bearer of universal political values, but as an organic, cultural, linguistic, or racial community — as an irreducibly particular *Volksgemeinschaft*. On this understanding, nationhood is constituted by ethnocultural unity and expressed in political unity. While this ethnocultural self-understanding was overlaid by a more state-centered self-understanding under Bismarck, it has remained influential and is expressed even in certain provisions of the Basic Law of the Federal Republic.[16]

As one would expect, citizenship is more accessible to immigrants in France (where it is defined in political terms) than in Germany (where membership is defined in ethnocultural terms).[17] Immigrants naturalize (or are automatically defined as citizens) at a rate ten times higher in France than in Germany.[18] The policies and politics of citizenship in France and Germany have been strikingly different since the late nineteenth century and remain so despite converging immigration policies and comparable immigrant populations.

The postwar migrations, to be sure, have placed considerable strain on both French and German self-understandings. The French tradition of assimilation has been challenged both by the multiculturalist left, arguing that immigrants *should not* be assimilated, and by the exclusionary right, arguing that they *cannot* be assimilated. In Germany, on the other hand, even the present conservative government has had to acknowledge that large numbers of Turkish migrants have become permanent immigrants, and has proclaimed a public interest in the naturalization of second-generation immigrants. . . .

The next four sections offer what Clifford Geertz (1971:19) has called a "condensed and generalized" history of these traditions, considering successively: (1) their roots in the political and cultural geography of early modern Europe; (2) the crystallization of the French national self-understanding during the Revolutionary period; (3) the development of German national self-understanding in reaction to the Revolution and Napoleonic domination; and (4) the consolidation of the French nation-state and the founding of a German nation-state in the nineteenth century. The final sections sketch the bearing of these traditions on the development of sharply differing citizenship law in France and Germany.[19]

## STATE-BUILDING AND THE GEOGRAPHY OF NATIONHOOD

The nation-state that was invented during the French Revolution was heir to centuries of state-building, and to the gradual development of national consciousness *within* the spatial and institutional frame of the developing territorial state. The Bismarckian quasi nation-state also succeeded to long traditions of state-building and national consciousness, but the two traditions — one Prussian, one German — were radically distinct, even incompatible, in territorial frame, social base, and political inspiration. The Prussian tradition of state-building was not only subnational and, after the partitions of Poland, supranational: it was also, in principle, antinational, while German national consciousness developed *outside* and — when national consciousness became politicized — *against* the territorial and institutional frame of existing states.

This is not to say that national consciousness had no political-institutional mooring in Germany. The medieval and early modern Empire — the Holy Roman Empire of the German Nation, as it came to be called, not without ambiguity, in the sixteenth century — was the institutional incubator of German national consciousness, analogous in this respect to the Capetian monarchy in France. But to the progressive conceptual fusion of nation and kingdom in France corresponds the conceptual differentiation of nation and supranational Empire in Germany; and to the early consolidation and progressively increasing stateness of the French monarchy, with its integrative workings on national consciousness, corresponds the thirteenth-century disintegration and subsequent "nonstateness" of the Empire. The Empire with its increasingly rickety institutions survived into the nineteenth century but, lacking the integrative power of a centralizing bureaucratic administration, failed to shape a firmly state-anchored national consciousness.

German national consciousness was never purely cultural, purely apolitical: but while it was linked to the memory and to the anticipation of effective political organization, it was for six centuries divorced from the reality. In France, then, a political-territorial conception of nationhood reflected the early nationwide reach of the monarchy, while in Germany, an ethnocultural conception of nationhood developed in the space between the supranational Empire and the subnational profusion of sovereign and semisovereign political units.

I am not suggesting that the sense of membership or "identity" was primarily ethnocultural in medieval or early modern Germany. To the extent that anachronistic talk of "identity" makes sense at all, the subjective "identity" of the vast majority of the population throughout Europe was no doubt largely local, on the one hand, and religious, on the other, until at least the end of the eighteenth century. The point is a structural, not a social-psychological, one. The political and cultural geography of central Europe made it possible to conceive of an ethnocultural Germany whose roughly imagined extent coincided neither with the supranational pretensions of the Empire nor with the subnational reach of effective political authority. As a result of the triangular relation between supranational Empire, subnational *Kleinstaaterei,*[20] and ethnocultural nation, consciousness of political and cultural membership — among the strata that were carriers of such supralocal group consciousness — was distributed across and differentiated with respect to a greater variety of units in Germany than in France, each with its own distinctive coordinates of reference. Without denying the complexity of patterns of state-building in France, it may nonetheless be said that a structural space for the differentiation of nation and state, and thus a space for the development of an ethnocultural understanding of nationhood, existed in Germany but not in France.

Even before the French Revolution, then, the nation was conceived in a different manner in France and Germany. This difference was brought into sharper focus in the second half of the eighteenth century, when the idea of nationhood was first given self-conscious theoretical elaboration. In France, writings of reformist philosophes and discussions of the urban public conceived the nation in polemical opposition to the variously privileged orders and corporations of ancien régime society, giving the concept a critical edge and a new, dynamic political significance. The *cahiers de doléance,* moreover, suggest that a high political charge was attached to the idea of the nation by the population at large in the immediately pre-Revolutionary period (Godechot 1971:494). Coinciding with the politicization of nationhood in pre-Revolutionary France, however, was its unprecedented depoliticization in late-eighteenth-century Germany. In the writings of the flourishing *Bildungsbürgertum*[21] of the epoch, the German nation was conceived less and less frequently in the traditional political context of the Empire and more and more frequently as an apolitical, ethnocultural entity — as an "inward Empire," as Schiller put it in 1801, when the old Empire had entered its final phase of disintegration (Conze 1985:29–30) or as a *Kulturnation*, in the later formulation of Friedrich Meinecke. If this *bildungsbürgerlich* understanding of nationhood was never exclusively cultural, its political dimension was nonetheless in deep recess during the late eighteenth century and the first years of the nineteenth (Meinecke 1919: ch. 2). Elaboration of the idea of nationhood in the second half of the eighteenth century in France and Germany, then, was the work of a broad bourgeois stratum in France and of a narrower, purely literary, stratum in Germany; more important, it was oriented to the reform of an existing nationwide state in France but was identified with a purely cultural, indeed a specifically literary, national spirit (*Nationalgeist*) in Germany.

## THE REVOLUTIONARY CRYSTALLIZATION

It was the Revolutionary era that decisively fixed the contrast between the French political and the German ethnocultural construction of nationhood. Theorists of the nation in late-eighteenth-century France had called for the reform of an existing state. When reform failed, the radicalized third estate constituted itself as the National Assembly and proclaimed the sovereignty of the nation.[22] Membership of this sovereign nation was conceived and institutionalized in the political-legal form of citizenship; nationality, as an ethnoculturally or even a legally defined quality distinct from citizenship, is absent from the Revolutionary constitutions. The dominance of citizenship over nationality, of political over ethnocultural conceptions of nationhood, is perhaps best expressed in Tallien's remark of the spring of 1795: "the only foreigners in France are the bad citizens."[23] Qualifications for membership were of course disputed during the Revolutionary epoch, but such disputes turned on a political rather than an ethnocultural axis.

So too did the question of the territorial boundaries of the new nation-state. The principle of self-determination, pregnant with immense disruptive potential for a dynastically organized and ethnoculturally intermixed Europe (Kedourie 1985), was invoked to justify the territorial gains of 1791–93, and even to reinterpret retrospectively the terms of the accession of Alsace to France in the seventeenth century (Soboul 1960:63; Godechot 1983:69). But the collective "self" entitled by revolutionary doctrine to self-determination was conceived in the cosmopolitan, rationalistic terms characteristic of the eighteenth, not in the Romantic terms characteristic of the nineteenth century.[24] The point of self-determination as understood by the Revolutionaries was to give expression to the universal desire for liberty and thus — how could it be otherwise? — for incorporation into France; it was emphatically not to permit the projection of ethnocultural identity onto the political plane.

Even the briefly if radically assimilationist linguistic politics of the Revolution was determined by political considerations rather than by any conception of the nation as an ethnolinguistic entity. Linguistic variety was denounced as conducive to reaction, linguistic unity advocated as indispensable to Republican citizenship.[25] This short-lived assimilationist politics was not of great consequence. Such linguistic unification as in fact occurred during the Revolutionary and Napoleonic period was due rather to the indirectly assimilationist workings of the army, the schools, and the Napoleonic administrative machine (Kohn 1967:90–93). Yet the ideological and practical importance of assimilation in the French tradition and the bad name that assimilation has acquired in the last two decades justify a more general observation. Assimilation — that is, a deliberate policy of making similar — is incompatible with all consistently "organic" conceptions of membership, according to which "natural" ethnolinguistic boundaries are prior to and determinative of national and (ideally) state boundaries. It is one thing to want to make all citizens of Utopia speak Utopian, and quite another to want to make all Utopiphones citizens of Utopia. Crudely put, the former represents the French, the latter the German model of nationhood. Whether juridical (as in naturalization) or cultural, assimilation presupposes a political conception of membership and the belief, which France took over from the Roman tradition, that the state can turn strangers into citizens, peasants — or immigrant workers — into Frenchmen.[26]

If the French nation-state was invented in 1789, French nationalism was a product of war.[27] Before the outbreak of war, nationalism existed neither as a "blind and exclusive preference for all that belongs to the nation" nor as a "demand in favor of subject nationalities."[28] Only from 1792 on, when the new order felt itself besieged by enemies within and enemies without, did there develop, superseding the ostentatious fraternal cosmopolitanism and pacifism of 1789–91,[29] and justified by the doctrine of the "patrie en danger," elements of an exclusivistic nationalism directed against foreigners inside the territory (Azimi 1988) and an expansive, aggressive nationalism directed abroad, originally missionary and crusading, later simply imperialist and triumphalist.[30] This emergent internal and external nationalism had throughout a political-ideological, not an ethnocultural, character. But it contributed to the later emergence, during the Napoleonic period, of a German counternationalism in which ethnocultural motifs came to play an important role. Revolutionary expansion, itself driven by political nationalism, thus engendered ethnocultural nationalism; the "crusade for liberty" elicited in response the myth, if not the reality, of a "holy war" of ethnonational resistance.

## ROMANTICISM AND REFORM IN GERMANY

The German tradition of nationhood was crucially formed during the Revolutionary era by the Romantic movement, on the one hand, and the Prussian reform movement, on the other, both occurring in the shadow of French occupation of Germany (Kohn 1967). The Romantic movement, though not itself centrally concerned with nationhood, supplied patterns of thought and appraisal for the consolidation, celebration, and eventual repoliticization of the ethnocultural understanding of nationhood; while the Prussian reformers, appealing to a radically different conception of nationhood, aimed to "nationalize" the Prussian state from above and thus to regenerate the state after the catastrophic defeat of 1806.

The aesthetic and sociohistorical idiom of German Romanticism was perfectly suited to the elaboration of the ethnocultural conception of nationhood. The celebration of individuality as *Einzigkeit* or uniqueness as over against *Einzelheit* or mere oneness; of depth and inwardness as over against surface polish; of feeling as over against desiccated rationality; of unconscious, organic growth as over against conscious, artificial construction; of the vitality and integrity of traditional, rooted folk cultures as over against the soullessness and artificiality of cosmopolitan culture — all of these themes were easily transposed from the domain of aesthetics and cultural criticism to that of social philosophy. In the social and political thought of Romanticism, and in the larger and more enduring body of social and political thought permeated by its fundamental categories and values, nations are conceived as historically rooted, organically developed individualities, united by a distinctive *Volksgeist* and by its infinitely ramifying expression in language, custom, law, culture, and the state. Despite the emphasis placed on the state,[31] the Romantic understanding of nationhood is fundamentally ethnocultural. The *Volksgeist* is constitutive, the state merely expressive, of nationhood.

The social and political thought of Romanticism was completely divorced from the realities of practical politics. The Prussian reformers, conversely, were untouched by the incipient ethnocultural nationalism of the period. Awed by French triumph and Prussian collapse, they wished to create a Prussian nation in order to regenerate the Prussian state. Thus Hardenberg wrote to Friedrich Wilhelm III in 1807, "We must do from above what the French have done from below" (Pinson 1966:33). Romantics and reformers understood the relation between nation and state in completely different terms: the former in quasi-aesthetic terms, with the state as the expression of the nation and of its constitutive *Volksgeist,* the latter in strictly political terms, with the nation — the mobilized and united *Staatsvolk* — as the deliberate and artificial creation of the state.

Thus was engendered the characteristic dualism and tension between ethnonational and state-national ideologies and programs — a dualism that has haunted German politics ever since. This suggests a way of reformulating the rough contrast that supplied the point of departure for these reflections: the contrast between the French political and the German ethnocultural conception of nationhood. In fact, traditions of nationhood have political and cultural components in both countries. These components have been closely integrated in France, where political unity has been understood as constitutive, cultural unity as expressive, of nationhood. In the German tradition, in contrast, political and ethnocultural aspects of nationhood have stood in tension with one another, serving as the basis for competing conceptions of nationhood. One such conception is sharply opposed to the French conception: on this view, ethnocultural unity is constitutive, political unity expressive, of nationhood. While this ethnocultural understanding of nationhood has never had the field to itself, it took root in early-nineteenth-century Germany and has remained widely available for political exploitation ever since. No such essentially ethnocultural conception of nationhood has ever taken root in France, where cultural nationhood has been conceived as an ingredient, not a competitor, of political nationhood.

## NATIONHOOD AND NATIONALISM
## IN THE NINETEENTH CENTURY

The nineteenth century saw the consolidation of the French and the construction of a German nation-state.[32] By the end of the century, there were noticeable similarities in the social structure and in the political style of the two nation-states. Nonetheless, the deeply rooted differences in the political and cultural construction of nationhood that I have sketched above remained significant, and were in certain respects reinforced.

For a hundred years from the end of the ancien régime, France experienced a succession of new regimes, the last of which, during the Boulangist crisis in the centennial year of the Revolution, seemed to be on the verge of collapsing like its predecessors before its twentieth anniversary. Chronic regime instability, however, did not impede the consolidation of the French nation-state from 1830 on. If the Bourbon regime, like the general European settlement imposed by the Congress of Vienna, was antinational, the July Monarchy was based implicitly, and all subsequent regimes explicitly, on the principle, if not the reality, of the sovereignty of the nation. Yet this formal-constitutional development represents only one aspect of the consolidation of French nation-statehood. More important was the consolidation of national memory effected in the works of historians such as Augustin Thierry, Michelet, and Ernest Lavisse; the pedagogic consolidation carried out by the schools of the Third Republic; the linguistic consolidation furthered by school and army; and the sociogeographical consolidation consequent on the development of new means of interlocal communication and transportation (Nora 1986; Weber 1976).

Nationalism, a contradictory mix of chauvinism and messianic humanism, heir to the tradition of revolutionary and Napoleonic expansion and to the principle of national self-determination, was located on the left for most of the century. After the defeat of 1870–71, it migrated to the right, with the Boulangist crisis of 1889 serving as a crucial pivot and the Dreyfus affair marking its definitive arrival (Rémond 1969:208f.; Girardet 1958). More precisely, Continental nationalism migrated to the right, while the left under Jules Ferry discovered in the 1880s a new field for the projection and reconstruction of national grandeur: a revitalized and expanded overseas empire (Girardet 1978). Ideologically and institutionally, this overseas imperialism was the heir to the Continental imperialism of the Revolutionary and Napoleonic period and, more remotely, to the Roman imperial tradition. Ideologically, it was conceived as a *mission libératrice et civilisatrice*; institutionally, it went much further than its British or German counterparts in the legal and political assimilation of metropolitan and overseas regimes, aiming at the construction of "la plus grande France." French Republicans pursued an assimilationist, civilizing, nationalizing mission inside France as well (Weber 1976:486f.); in the late 1880s, this assimilationist internal nationalism, linked to reforms of primary education and military conscription, formed the backdrop to an expansive, assimilationist reform of citizenship law whose central provisions have endured to this day (Brubaker 1992).

The newly nationalist right, despite its antiparliamentarism, shared with the old nationalist left (and with the new imperialist left) the sense of a privileged mission or vocation for France, a concern for national "grandeur," and a reverence for the army as the incarnation and instrument of this grandeur (Girardet 1958). Despite the rise of anti-Semitism toward the end of the century, the new nationalism did not abandon the traditional, essentially political, conception of nationhood for an ethnocultural conception.[33] Indeed, the question of Alsace-Lorraine led to the ideological accentuation of the subjectivist-voluntarist components of French as over against the objective-ethnocultural components of German nationhood.

The German ethnocultural conception of nationhood was a product of the distinctive political and cultural geography of central Europe. Yet a feature of that geography — the inextricable intermixture of Germans and other nationalities — made it impossible to found a German state precisely on the ethnocultural nation (Conze 1983:95; Lepsius 1985:48). None of the proposed solutions to the problem of national unification — including the "classical" Prussian-*kleindeutsch* and Austrian-*grossdeutsch* solutions — could bring into being a "perfect" nation-state: either Germans would be excluded, or non-Germans included, or both. Political considerations were dominant both in the programs of 1848 and in the later practice of Bismarck.

Unification under Bismarck, while conditioned, was not inspired by nationalism, still less by ethnocultural nationalism.[34] Nor was the constitutional structure of the unified Reich that of a nation-state. The constitution did not invoke popular sovereignty, and the imperial crown was offered to William I in Versailles by the princes, not by representatives of the people. There was no unified German citizenship: *Reichsangehörigkeit* (citizenship of the Empire) was derivative of *Landesangehörigkeit* (citizenship of the individual constituent states), and its limited political significance reflected the limited political significance of the Reichstag. The French nation-state had been constructed in polemical opposition not only to dynastic sovereignty but also to corporate and provincial privilege.[35] The German quasi nation-state challenged neither principle, even incorporating particular rights — *Reservatrechte* — into the treaties of accession of the South German states.

The Reich was nonetheless understood as a nation-state, both by those who welcomed it and by those who feared it.[36] As a nation-state, however, it was imperfect not only in its internal constitution but also in its external boundaries — indeed, doubly imperfect. As a *kleindeutsches* Reich, it was underinclusive, excluding above all millions of Austrian Germans. But it was at the same time overinclusive, including French in Alsace-Lorraine, Danes in North Schleswig, and Poles in Prussia. These were not simply linguistic but rather — especially in the last case — self-conscious national minorities. In spite of this dual imperfection, the Reich made significant

progress toward consolidated nation-statehood between 1871 and 1914—
chiefly through the development of new nationwide institutions and processes and through the integrative working of the state on national consciousness. At the outbreak of war, the Reich was no longer the conspicuously
*unvollendete* (unfinished) nation-state of 1871 (Schieder 1961; Kocka 1985).

The Reich was heir to secular traditions of Prussian statehood and
German nationhood. To a remarkable extent, it succeeded in integrating
these differing, even antagonistic traditions. Yet the old dualism survived,
the old tension between statist and ethnocultural components in the German tradition of nationhood. In the context of this persisting dualism, two
generations were not sufficient to create a consolidated, *selbstverständlich*
(taken-for-granted), national consciousness within the frame of the new state.
*Reichsnational* did not completely displace *volksnational* consciousness in
Imperial Germany: the ethnocultural conception of nationhood, though in
recess during the decades after the *Reichsgründung*, remained available for
subsequent political exploitation. This is shown by the pan-Germanist agi-
tation around the turn of the century (Arendt 1973:222f.), by the assumption that union with Austria would and should follow the breakup of the
Habsburg Empire, and by the development of *völkisch* thought and of a
*Deutschtum*-oriented politics during the Weimar Republic—to say nothing
of the subsequent exploitation of *völkisch* thought by Nazi propagandists.

## MIGRANTS INTO CITIZENS IN
## LATE-NINETEENTH-CENTURY FRANCE

The vicissitudes of French and German traditions of nationhood in the twentieth century cannot be analyzed here. I argue elsewhere that the deeply
rooted styles of national self-understanding sketched here survived the tur-
moil of the first half of the twentieth century, and that they continue to inform the politics of immigration and citizenship today (Brubaker 1992). But
the point I want to make here is a historical one. I want to sketch in conclusion the connection between the traditions of nationhood that I have out-
lined and the legal definitions of citizenship in which they were embodied.
For this purpose, it is unnecessary to carry the historical analysis into the
twentieth century, for the rules governing the attribution of citizenship in
France and Germany were fixed in very nearly their present form in 1889
and 1913 respectively. It is these rules—expansive in France, restrictive in
Germany—that govern the citizenship status and chances of today's immigrants. And parliamentary debates and reports confirm the bearing of distinctive French and German traditions of nationhood on the development
of these rules.

Under the 1889 law, French citizenship was attributed to all persons born in France of foreign-born parents and domiciled in France at their majority. This system, with minor modifications, remains in place today. Its effect is to automatically transform second-generation immigrants into citizens, much as happens in classical countries of immigration such as the United States and Canada.[37] Most commentators have explained the expansiveness of the law by appealing to the demographic and military interests of the French state. They suggest that French demographic stagnation, in the face of German demographic and military robustness, required the civic incorporation of second-generation immigrants. In fact, the civic incorporation of immigrants was not a military necessity (Brubaker 1992). But it did come to be defined as a *political* necessity. It was a response, first, to the "shocking inequality" that exempted even French-born foreigners from military service while Frenchmen had to serve up to five years (CD 3904; C2:594b). This exemption was especially galling now that military service had become, in theory if not yet in fact, a personal obligation of every Frenchman. By the mid-1880s, when the reform of citizenship law was being debated, it was evident that the new conscription law then in preparation would move decisively towards universal, although shorter, service. In this context, the exemption of second-generation immigrants was of scant military import; indeed, the new conscription law would saddle the military with too many, not too few, recruits. But in the context of universal service for citizens, the exemption of persons born and raised in France, yet choosing to retain their foreign citizenship, was ideologically scandalous and politically intolerable. Secondly, the civic incorporation of second-generation immigrants was a response to the incipient development of "different nations within the French nation" (C2:595a). Fears of solidary Italian ethnic communities in Southern France joined fears of "foreign" domination in Algeria, where the French barely outnumbered "foreigners" (Italians and Spaniards, for example, the vastly larger indigenous population being left out of account). Such solidary ethnic communities, real or imagined, challenged the unitarist French political formula at its core.[38]

But what made the civic incorporation of second-generation immigrants an effective and acceptable solution? Might it not be dangerous, after all, to incorporate immigrants into the army, especially now that military service was conceived in specifically national rather than statist terms, as the expression of the "nation in arms" and no longer as a "tribute exacted by an oppressive and alien state" (Monteilhet 1926:ch. 5; Challener 1965; Weber 1976:295)? How, moreover, could a formal legal transformation solve the sociopolitical problem of the nation within the nation? Would not the formal "nationalization" of the foreign population leave underlying social realities untouched? A stroke of the pen might make foreigners French from the point of view of the law — but would they be truly French?

If parliament was not susceptible to such doubts, if it did not hesitate to transform foreigners into French soldiers and French citizens, it was because of its robust confidence in the assimilatory virtues of France. Thus A. Dubost, reporting on the bill in the Chambre des Députés, called for the extension of French nationality to persons who, "having lived long on the soil on which they were born, have acquired its mores, habits and character, and are presumed to have a natural attachment for the country of their birth" (CD 2083:232b). Others echoed his sentiments. The assimilationist motif is an old one in France. But there was a new and specifically Republican tinge to the assimilationism of the 1880s. It was not mere residence or work in France that was credited with assimilatory virtue; it was participation in the newly Republicanized and nationalized institutions of the school and the army. To assimilate means to make similar: and school and army, in their Republican reincarnations, entrusted with "the mission of retempering the French soul" (Azéma and Winock 1976:149), were powerfully equipped to do just that. Their assimilatory virtues worked on persons long juridically French, reshaping their habits of thought and feeling to make them fit the wider frame of the nation. But they worked on foreigners and the newly naturalized as well. School attendance was obligatory for foreign and French children alike. And military service, after 1889, would be obligatory not only for old-stock French but for those newly defined as French by the reform of nationality law. Internal and external assimilation were sociologically identical: if school and army could turn peasants into Frenchmen,[39] they could turn native-born foreigners into Frenchmen in the same way.

## GERMANY: THE CITIZENRY AS COMMUNITY OF DESCENT

Unlike French citizenship law, German citizenship law assigns no significance to birth in the territory. It thus has no mechanism for automatically transforming second- or even third-generation immigrants into citizens. Citizenship is based solely on descent.[40] When German citizenship laws were first formulated, in 1870, it was only natural that citizenship should be based on descent.[41] This was the age of nationalism, and defining the citizenry as a community of descent, following the principle of *jus sanguinis,* was self-evidently preferable to defining the citizenry as a territorial community following the principle of *jus soli. Jus soli* was rejected as a feudal principle that based membership on ties to the soil, *jus sanguinis* preferred as a specifically national principle, which would found the nation on ties of kinship that were more substantial and more enduring than the superficial and external ties of common birthplace (Grawert 1973:190–91, 203). There was nothing unusual about this nationalist preference for *jus sanguinis*. Similar arguments were made in France. What is unusual in the German case is that citizenship was based *exclusively* on descent. In most Continental states, the principle of descent is complemented and tempered by the principles of birthplace and prolonged residence, so as to encourage or compel second- or third-generation immigrants to join the community of citizens. Few Continental states go as far as France in imposing citizenship automatically on second-generation immigrants. But they do at least make some provision for the incorporation of second- and third-generation immigrants. German law makes none.

Why was *jus sanguinis* untempered by *jus soli* in Germany? In some respects the situation in late-nineteenth- and early-twentieth-century Germany was like that in late-nineteenth-century France. Both countries were experiencing substantial immigration, and in both countries this was a period of heightened nationalism. But the nationalisms were of different kinds. French nationalism of the 1880s, state-centered and confidently assimilationist vis-à-vis non-Francophone citizens (Weber 1976:chs. 6 and 8) and vis-à-vis immigrants permitted, even required the transformation of second-generation immigrants into citizens (Brubaker 1992). Turn-of-the-century German nationalism, on the other hand, was ethnoculturally oriented and "dissimilationist" vis-à-vis its own ethnically Polish citizens in Eastern Prussia and vis-à-vis immigrants, or rather one crucial class of immigrants: Poles and Jews in the Prussian East. That nationalism required the civic exclusion rather than the civic incorporation of these unwanted immigrants (Brubaker 1992).

Immigration was an economic necessity in the eastern provinces of Prussia in the quarter century preceding the outbreak of the First World War. But the available immigrants — Poles in particular — were undesirable from a national point of view. To a surprising extent, given the traditional distance between Prussian statism and ethnocultural nationalism, the Prussian state had made this point of view its own. The state feared that Polish immigrants would strengthen the ethnically Polish at the expense of the ethnically German element in the Prussian East. A strict naturalization policy, coupled with an immigration policy requiring migrant workers to leave the country each winter, enabled the state to prevent the settlement of ethnoculturally "unwanted elements" in its eastern borderlands. Citizenship served here as an instrument of territorial closure (Brubaker 1992). By excluding immigrants from citizenship, the state retained its freedom of action. This meant, above all, the freedom to expel immigrants from the territory. Today, long-settled immigrants in Western Europe enjoy substantial legal as well as political protection against expulsion. They enjoyed no such protection in the late nineteenth and early twentieth century. In the 1880s, Prussia had expelled 30,000 Polish and Jewish immigrants, many of them long-term residents. There had been no further mass expulsions. But in the absence of restraints on the expulsion of resident noncitizens, citizenship status mattered to the state in a way that it no longer matters today: consequently, the state retained a stronger interest in a restrictive naturalization policy than it has today. Given the strong westward migratory currents in the German-Slav borderlands of Central Europe, the labor shortages in the Prussian East that compelled the employment of migrant workers, and the cultural and political definition of Slavs and Jews as "unwanted elements," the state interest in a restrictive naturalization policy was a compelling one.

Yet if there was a compelling state interest in a restrictive naturalization policy, there was none in a system of pure *jus sanguinis*. The state had a strong interest in controlling access to citizenship (and therefore to permanent settlement) on the part of recently arrived immigrants. But it had only a highly attenuated interest in preventing the access to citizenship of someone born and raised in the territory. Such persons, in effect, had *already* been allowed to settle in the territory. The state could have prevented their settlement, but it did not. As foreigners, to be sure, such persons would remain vulnerable to future expulsion; the state would retain more leverage over them than over citizens. Having already allowed their settlement, however, the state had very little to gain from this additional leverage.

Like the French extension of *jus soli* in 1889, the German insistence on pure *jus sanguinis* in 1913 must be understood in the context of habits of national self-understanding that were deeply rooted in the national past and powerfully reinforced at a particular historical conjuncture. In France, the legal transformation of second-generation immigrants into citizens presupposed confidence in their social, cultural, and political transformation into "real" Frenchmen. The French elite possessed that confidence. Their traditionally assimilationist understanding of nationhood was reinforced by the assimilationist theory and practice of the new national institutions of universal schooling and universal military service. This made the extension of *jus soli* possible and plausible. In Germany, the vehement repudiation of every trace of *jus soli* reflected the lack of elite confidence in the social, cultural, and political transformation of immigrants into Germans. In part, this was the legacy of a traditionally less state-centered and assimilationist, more ethnocultural understanding of nationhood in Germany than in France.

But this was powerfully reinforced in late Bismarckian and Wilhelmine Germany by the increasingly evident failure of attempts to assimilate ethno-culturally Polish German citizens in the Prussian East (Broszat 1972:143, 157; Blanke 1981:60; Wehler 1971:118). Having failed to win the political loyalty of Poles to the German nation-state, and having failed to assimilate them to German language and culture, Prussian-German *Polenpolitik* was increasingly "dissimilationist," treating ethnically German and ethnically Polish citizens differently in an effort to "strengthen Germandom" in frontier districts. Since the state had failed to assimilate *indigenous* Poles in the Prussian East, who had been citizens of Prussia since the late eighteenth century, there was no basis for believing that it would succeed in assimilating *immigrant* Poles. An assimilationist citizenship law, like that of France, automatically transforming second-generation immigrants into citizens, was therefore out of the question in Germany.

The French law of 1889 and the German law of 1913 established the principles that govern the attribution of citizenship even today. As a result, a substantial fraction of French postwar immigrants has (or will have) French citizenship, while only a negligible fraction of non-German immigrants to Germany has German citizenship. The French, of course, have not solved all of their problems by formally transforming immigrants into citizens. In many respects, the social, cultural, and economic situation of immigrants in the two countries is similar. Yet by transforming second-generation immigrants into citizens, France has formally recognized and guaranteed their permanent membership of state and society, and has granted them full civil, political, and social rights. When and whether the new German state will do the same is likely to be an increasingly salient question in the years to come.

## NOTES

1. An extended treatment of the issues discussed in this paper is in Rogers Brubaker, *Citizenship and Nationhood in France and Germany* (Cambridge, Mass: Harvard University Press, 1992).

2. Industrialization in Europe as elsewhere was accompanied by massive migrations, in many instances across state boundaries. Thus, while no European country is a "classical" country of immigration, Europe has considerable historical experience with international labor migration, much of it leading to settlement. I have borrowed the expression "new immigration" — used to describe the surge in Southern and Eastern European immigration to the United States in the late nineteenth century — to suggest that it is the magnitude and sources, not the mere existence, of immigration that is new in the European setting. A large and increasing proportion of European immigrants stems from Third World countries (often from ex-colonies): the Indian subcontinent and the Caribbean displaced

Ireland in the 1960s as the leading source of immigration to Britain; half of the foreign population in France is now from Africa or Asia (mainly from North Africa); and Turks surpassed Italians during the 1970s as the largest group of foreign workers in Germany.

3. This section and the next draw on and amplify material that has appeared in Brubaker 1989b.

4. This schema corresponds in certain respects to T. H. Marshall's (1950:10f.) distinction of civil, political, and social components of citizenship. The norm of egalitarian membership corresponds to the civil element, that of democratic membership to the political element, and that of socially consequential membership to the social element in Marshall's model. Yet the substantive overlap is only partial. In Marshall's schema nothing corresponds to the norms of sacred, national, and unique membership.

This partial correspondence is explained by historical considerations. Marshall analyzed the specifically English form of a general European (and later global) process—the development of the civil, political, and social rights constitutive of nationwide citizenship. While his analysis was tailored in detail to English peculiarity—and has recently been criticized for its Anglocentrism (Mann 1987)—his basic threefold distinction was modeled on the general European experience; hence the fruitful use of his schema outside the English setting (Bendix 1977; Schmid 1986; Schmitter 1979; Parsons 1965; Turner 1986). Given the integral connection, in Europe and elsewhere, between the development and institutionalization of civil, political, and social rights, and the construction of nation-statehood, the overlap between Marshall's model of citizenship and the model of nation-state membership sketched here should come as no surprise.

Nor should the incompleteness of the overlap. For the construction of citizenship in England, the basis for Marshall's model, took a peculiar form—peculiarity grounded in the geopolitical position of England, in the early coincidence of state authority and national community, in the celebrated gradualism of political development, in a continuous imperial tradition, and in the supranational character of Great Britain. England may have been the first national state, but France was the first and has remained the paradigmatic nation-state; neither England nor Britain ever became a nation-state *à la française*. The construction of citizenship in England occurred in the context of a taken-for-granted national community and thus was not bound up, as it was on the Continent, with the ideologically charged, contestatory construction of nation-statehood. Norms of membership linked specifically to the contestatory construction of nation-statehood—i.e., the principles of sacredness, uniqueness, and nationality—did not figure in the British experience and do not figure in Marshall's model.

For other general discussions of citizenship and membership, see Gallissot 1986; Balibar 1988; Leca 1983; Riedel 1972; Salmond 1901/1902; Walzer 1983:ch. 2; Walzer 1970b; Lochak 1988. And for general discussions of the nation-state with some bearing on questions of citizenship and membership, see Sayad 1984; Zolberg 1981; Young 1976:70–73; Gellner 1983:1–7, 53–58.

5. The principle of unitary citizenship, to be sure, far outstripped revolutionary practice, to which distinctions of class and gender were crucial. This does not vitiate the significance of the principle, the central place of which in the myth and mystique of the Revolution helped later to undermine the legitimacy of such distinctions.

6. The Revolution inaugurated a new style of political sacralization. The nation-state that was invented during the Revolution (and thereafter universalized as a mode of political and social organization) simultaneously *emancipated* itself from and *incorporated* the sacred. Asserting full autonomy from the sacred as a *transcendent,* external source of legitimation, it nonetheless appropriated religious emotion, transforming sacredness into an *immanent* source of legitimation.

7. To be sure, this cultural community is conceived and constructed differently in France than in Germany or — to take a very different example — in the United States.

8. The requirement of assimilation to the ethnocultural community, of course, is open to widely differing interpretations. The relevant *areas* of assimilation, as well as the *threshold* of assimilation required in a given arena, may vary considerably.

9. This principle is clearly enunciated by Rousseau. How, he asks rhetorically, can citizens be expected to love their country, "if their country is no more to them than it is to foreigners, if it grants to citizens only what it can refuse to nobody"? (1755:252). The principle takes on special importance, however, only with the development of the welfare state and the proliferation of state-provided benefits that can be withheld from resident nonmembers. In principle, welfare states are closed systems, presupposing "boundaries that distinguish those who are members of a community from those who are not" (Freeman 1986:52; see also Walzer 1983:31). In the theory of the welfare state, these boundaries are drawn between citizens and noncitizens; in practice, however, they are drawn elsewhere (Brubaker 1989d:155f).

10. For an alternative approach to internal migration as a "deviance from the prevailing norm of social organization at the world level," a norm expressed in "the model of society as a territorially based, self-reproducing cultural and political system, whose human population is assumed, tacitly or explicitly, to renew itself endogenously," see Zolberg 1981:6. For an overstated yet suggestive argument that immigration contradicts the constitutive categories of the modern social and political world, see Sayad 1984:190.

11. On the settlement process, see Piore 1979:59ff. On problems of membership, see Walzer 1983:ch. 2; Brubaker 1989b:14–22; Carens 1989.

12. These may include the renunciation of one's previous citizenship; the performance of a sacred act such as an oath of allegiance; the accomplishment

of the sacred duty of military service; the manifestation of "good character," and the more or less complete assimilation to the language and customs of the national community.

13. These include special provisions for spouses of citizens or for citizens of former colonies (Brubaker 1989c:113–15).

14. Exceptions include Brubaker 1989a; Hammar 1990; Schmitter 1979; Noiriel 1988; Wenden 1987, 1988. The following paragraphs draw on material that has appeared in Brubaker 1989d:146–47.

15. Exemplary for a number of reasons — not least because of the comparable magnitude and composition of the immigrant population in the two countries and because of their fateful position at the historic center of state- and nation-building in Europe.

16. The preamble to the Grundgesetz or Basic Law, in effect the constitution of the Federal Republic, invokes the "whole German people" (*das gesamte deutsche Volk*), while Article 116 defines the legal status of "German" as follows: "everyone is a German in the eyes of the Grundgesetz ... who holds German citizenship or who, as a refugee or expellee of German *Volkszugehörigkeit,* or as a spouse or descendant of such a person, has been admitted to the territory of the German Reich as it existed on December 31, 1937." (The criteria of German *Volkszugehörigkeit* [belonging to the German *Volk*], as specified in the 1953 Law on Expelled Persons and Refugees, include "descent, speech, upbringing, and culture.") The Germans thus defined have rights and duties virtually indistinguishable from those of German citizens. And the definition of German citizenship is itself vastly overinclusive, measured against West German territory, for it includes almost all citizens of the German Democratic Republic. There has never been a separate West German citizenship: in its citizenship law, the Federal Republic has always maintained the legal fiction of the continued existence of the German Reich, and thus of a single German citizenship. This insistence on a single German citizenship was central to the exodus of summer and autumn 1989 that set in motion the process of German unification (Brubaker 1990b).

17. By "immigrants" I mean labor migrants and their descendants, not resettlers from the German Democratic Republic or ethnic German immigrants from Eastern Europe and the Soviet Union. As one would expect, given the ethnocultural understanding of membership, these *German* immigrants to West Germany are legally defined as citizens (in the case of the East German resettlers) or quasi citizens (in the case of the ethnic German immigrants from Eastern Europe and the Soviet Union) (Brubaker 1990:359–64).

18. It is not simply that France has more liberal naturalization rules and a political culture of naturalization that Germany lacks. For French naturalization rates, despite being four to five times higher than those of the Federal Republic of Germany, are low compared to those of the United States, Canada, or Sweden (Brubaker 1989c:117–20; 1989d:154–60). More important is the fact that there

are, besides naturalization, other modes of access to French, but not to German, citizenship. Thus French citizenship is attributed at birth to a child born in France if at least one parent was also born in France — including Algeria and other colonies and territories before their independence. This means that the large majority of the roughly 400,000 children born in France since 1963 of Algerian parents are French citizens. Moreover, citizenship is acquired automatically at the age of eighteen by *all* children born in France of foreign parents, provided they have resided in France for the last five years and have not been the object of certain criminal condemnations. By this means roughly 250,000 persons have become French since 1973; and of the 1.2 million foreign residents under the age of eighteen, roughly two-thirds were born in France and are thus programmed to become French at the age of eighteen. There are no comparable provisions in the Federal Republic of Germany. Thus, while the large majority of the former *Gastarbeiter* and their families were born in the Federal Republic or have lived there for over ten years, only a minute fraction have acquired German citizenship. Of the 1.4 million Turks living in Germany, only about 1,000 are naturalized each year. Even if this number increased tenfold, to 10,000 per year, it would still be more than offset by the 25,000 to 30,000 new Turkish citizens born every year in Germany.

19. An earlier version of the next four sections appeared in Brubaker 1989a:15–27. The comparison of German and French understandings of nationhood and forms of nationalism developed here is, in its basic lines, a traditional one, going back to the early nineteenth century (Brubaker 1992:43n; Kohn 1944, 1967; Rothfels 1956; Schieder 1985; Szücs 1981). Recently, however, bipolar contrasts involving Germany, especially those pointing to a German *Sonderweg* (special road) to the modern world, have been subjected to criticism on a broad front. Such accounts, it is argued, measure German developments, minutely scrutinized for faults (in the geological and the moral sense) that might help explain the catastrophe of 1933–45, against an idealized version of "Western" — i.e., British, French, or American — developments (see especially Blackbourn and Eley 1984). Only through the doubly distorting lens of such culpabilization on the one hand, and idealization on the other, the argument continues, does the nineteenth-century German bourgeoisie appear "supine" next to its "heroic" French counterpart, the German party system deeply flawed by English standards, the "German conception of freedom" dangerously illiberal by comparison with the Anglo-American, German political culture fatally authoritarian in comparison with that of the "West" in general.

Comparisons of German and French conceptions of nationhood and forms of nationalism have not escaped indictment on this count (Berdahl 1972; Breuilly 1982:65–83). To characterize French and German traditions of citizenship and nationhood in terms of such ready-made conceptual pairs as universalism and particularism, cosmopolitanism and ethnocentrism, Enlightenment rationalism and romantic irrationalism is to pass from characterization to caricature. My use here of the simplifying opposition between the French political and the German ethnocultural definitions of nationhood is intended as a pointer to, and not a substitute for, a more nuanced analysis. I have tried to recover the analytical and explanatory potency of what remains, after all, an indispensable distinction, by rescuing it from the status of the routine and complacent formula, ripe for criticism, that it had become.

20. A pejorative expression emphasizing the fragmentation of political authority in Germany.

21. The word refers to the cultivated middle classes, the bourgeoisie constituted by *Bildung* (education or cultivation) and conscious of its *ständisch* [status-based] unity.

22. Article 3 of the Declaration of Rights of August 26, 1789, located "the principle of all sovereignty" in the nation, while the Constitution of 1791 was even more categorical: "Sovereignty is one [and] indivisible. . . . It belongs to the Nation" (Title III, Article I). The "nationalization" of political authority, however, was not limited to the constitutional domain. In effect, "all that was 'royal' became . . . national: national assembly, national gendarmerie, national guard, national army, national education . . . national domains . . . national debt" (Godechot 1971:495).

23. "Il n'y d'étranger en France que les mauvais citoyens" [the only foreigners in France are the bad citizens] (quoted by Azimi 1988:702). While Tallien's remark, as Azimi notes, cannot be taken as representative of the Revolution's attitude toward *étrangers*, it can be taken as illustrative of its strictly political definition of nationhood.

24. As Meinecke notes, the right of national self-determination could be applied to nations understood in a historical-political sense, which may have a strong ethnic component, with the emphasis on the "historically developed personality of the nation," or in a rational-political sense, with the nation understood as "a subdivision of Humanity, an abstractly constructed frame without [distinctive] individual content." Meinecke registers his clear preference for the former and his criticism of the "deep weaknesses and errors" of the latter, "entirely formalistic doctrine of national sovereignty" (1919:34). This corresponds roughly to Simmel's (1950:81) distinction between the nineteenth-century conception of individuality as *Einzigkeit* (uniqueness) and the eighteenth-century conception of individuality as *Einzelheit* (oneness).

25. Thus Barère's report to the Committee of Public Safety in January 1794: "Federalism and superstition speak low Breton; emigration and hatred of the Republic speak German; the counterrevolution speaks Italian, and fanaticism speaks Basque." Only when all citizens speak the same language, according to Abbé Grégoire's "Rapport sur la nécessité et les moyens d'anéantir les patois et d'universaliser l'usage de la langue française," can all citizens "communicate their thought without hindrance" and enjoy equal access to state offices. Both reports are reprinted in de Certeau et al. 1975:291–317; the quotations are from pp. 295 and 302.

26. Weber (1976) contains a wealth of material on assimilation, but focuses on the period 1870 to 1914. On the historical roots of the stronger assimilatory tendency of French than German society, see von Thadden (1987).

27. On September 20, 1792, at Valmy, under fire from the Prussian infantry, the best-trained troops in Europe, the ragtag French army held its ground to the cry of "Vive la Nation!" Valmy itself was of no great military significance, but thanks to the celebrated phrase of Goethe, who was present at the battle— "d'aujourd'hui et de ce lieu date une ère nouvelle dans l'histoire du monde" [here and today a new era of world history begins]=mthe episode has come to symbolize the transformation of war through the appeal to the nation in arms (Furet and Richet 1965:175; Soboul 1960:58).

28. Godechot concludes that "it is therefore absurd to speak of French *nationalism* during the first years of the Revolution: *patriotism* is an entirely different thing" (1971:498).

29. "The French nation renounces all wars of conquest, and will never employ her force against the liberty of any people.... Foreigners ... can receive successions from their parents, whether they be foreign or French. They can make contracts, acquire and receive goods in France, and dispose of them, in the same way as any French citizen.... Their person, their goods, their industry, their religious observances are also protected by law" (Title VI, Constitution of 1791).

30. The contradictions involved in this missionary nationalism are evident: "the Grande Nation is not only the nation that, in 1789, triumphed over the monarchy; it is the nation that has triumphed over its internal and external enemies and that will deliver the oppressed patriots of all Europe.... The expression Grande Nation applies to the liberating, emancipating nation, the nation that propagates the 'great principles' of 1789, the nation that must aid oppressed peoples to conquer their liberty... [but also to] the nation that, despite these loudly proclaimed principles, dominates, oppresses, annexes, without regard for the will of other peoples" (Godechot 1971:499–500). On the internal nationalism, see Azimi 1988; Nora 1988; Brubaker 1992.

31. The exaltation of the state found in Romantic political thought— Adam Müller's claim, for example, that "man cannot be imagined outside the state.... The state is the totality of all human concerns" (quoted by Kohn 1967:188)—reflects, on the one hand, an amorphous, globalizing conception of the state and, on the other, the teleological notion that the *Volksgeist* can reach its final and perfect expression only in the state.

32. In this context, "the nineteenth century" means roughly 1830 to 1914 in France, and 1815 to 1914 in Germany.

33. Even the traditionalist "nationalisme intégrale" of Charles Maurras, it may be argued, turned, despite its anti-Semitism, on a political and not on an ethnocultural principle. Anti-Semitism, propagated by Edouard Drumont from the mid-1880s on, and uniting anticapitalist and conservative-Catholic motifs, reached a paroxysmal peak in the Dreyfus affair. Yet the affair turned not on an ethno-

cultural or an ethnoreligious conception of nationhood but on the ancient themes of the place of church and army in the life of the nation — themes given a new urgency by the anticlericalism of the Third Republic and by the emergence of an internationalist and pacifist left.

34. On Bismarck's distance from nationalism, see Schieder 1961:22–26. The annexation of Alsace-Lorraine, while demanded and justified in terms of the ethnocultural principle of nationhood, was in fact determined by strategic considerations (Gall 1970).

35. Thus the preamble to the Constitution of 1791: "Il n'y a plus, pour aucune partie de la Nation, ni pour aucun individu, aucun privilège, ni exception au droit commun de tous les Français."

36. In the case of Poles in the Prussian East provinces, it was not the Reich, but already the Norddeutsche Bund, that had the ominous character of a nation-state. Poles accepted membership of the nonnational Prussian state, but protested against the incorporation of the East Prussian provinces into this newly national entity. In 1871 they renewed their protest: "We want to remain under Prussian authority, but we do not want to be incorporated into the German Reich" (Polish deputies quoted in Schieder 1961:19–20).

37. There are of course important differences between French and North American citizenship law. The North American system is based on unconditional *jus soli*: citizenship is attributed to all persons born in the territory. Thus even children of undocumented immigrants are assigned U.S. citizenship if they are born in the United States. French citizenship law, by contrast, is based on *jus sanguinis*: all persons born of French parents are French citizens, regardless of birthplace. But in addition — and this is where the similarity with North American citizenship law arises — France follows the principle of conditional *jus soli*. As a result, almost all persons born in France and residing there at majority have French citizenship.

38. Since the Revolution, the self-styled "nation une et indivisible" has been violently intolerant of anything that could be interpreted as a "nation within the nation." This unitarist attitude, at once intolerant of constituted groups and inclusive of their constituent members as individuals, is epitomized by the famous formula of the Comte de Clermont Tonnère during the Revolution: "One must refuse everything to Jews as a nation and grant everything to the Jews as individuals.... They must be citizens as individuals" (quoted in Schnapper and Leveau 1987:3). In the late nineteenth century, similarly, it was felt to be better that established immigrants become individually citizens than that they remain collectively foreigners, a foreign nation within the French nation and, as such, a "true peril" (CD 2083:34).

39. Weber (1976:494) stresses the "making similar": result of improved communications caused by roads and railroads, a generation of Republican schooling and universal military service, "variations in language and behavior were significantly less... [and] the regions of France were vastly more alike in 1910 than they had been before Jules Ferry."

40. Naturalization is of course possible, but only under severely restrictive conditions (Hailbronner 1989:67–70; Brubaker 1989c:110–11).

41. The 1870 law was enacted for the North German Confederation; it was extended the following year to the German Empire.

## BIBLIOGRAPHY

### I. French Parliamentary Materials

References are to the *Journal officiel de la République Française.* Abbreviations (CD, C) indicate the document; the page number follows.

CD 3904. Chambre des Députés, Documents Parlementaires, Session Ordinaire de 1885, Annexe no. 3904. "Proposition de loi relative à la nationalité des fils d'étrangers nés en France," présentée par M. Maxime Lecomte et al.

CD 2083. Chambre des Députés, Documents Parlementaires, Session Ordinaire de 1887, Annexe no. 2083. "Rapport fait au nom de la commission chargée d'examiner la proposition de loi, adoptée par le Sénat, sur la nationalité," par M. Antonin Dubost.

C2. Chambre des Députés, Compte Rendu, Séance du 16 mars 1889, 2e délibération sur la proposition de loi, adopté par le Sénat, relative à la nationalité.

### II. Other Sources

Arendt, H. 1973. *The Origins of Totalitarianism.* New York: Harcourt Brace Jovanovich.

Azema, J.-P., and M. Winock. 1976. *La IIIe République (1870–1940).* Paris: Calmann-Lévy.

Azimi, V. 1988. "L'étranger sous la Révolution." *Actes du Colloque d'Orléans, 11–13 Septembre 1986: La Révolution et l'ordre juridique privé: Rationalité ou scandale?* Paris: Presses Universitaires de France.

Balibar, E. 1984. "Sujets ou citoyens?" *Les temps modernes* 452–453–454:1726–53.

———. 1988. "Propositions sur la citoyenneté." In Wenden 1987.

Bendix, R. 1977. *Nation-Building and Citizenship.* Berkeley: University of California Press.

Berdahl, R. 1972. "New Thoughts on German Nationalism." *American Historical Review* 77:65–80.

Blackbourn, D., and G. Eley. 1984. *The Peculiarities of German History.* Oxford: Oxford University Press.

Blanke, R. 1981. *Prussian Poland in the German Empire.* Boulder, Colo.: East European Monographs.

Breuilly, J. 1982. *Nationalism and the State.* Chicago: University of Chicago Press.

Broszat, M. 1972. *Zweihundert Jahre deutsche Polenpolitik.* Frankfurt: Suhrkamp.

Brubaker, W. R., ed. 1989a. *Immigration and the Politics of Citizenship in Europe and North America.* Lanham, Md.: German Marshall Fund of the United States and University Press of America.

Brubaker, Rogers. 1992. *Citizenship and Nationhood in France and Germany.* Cambridge, Mass: Harvard University Press.

Brubaker, W. R. 1989b. Introduction to Brubaker 1989a.

———. 1989c. "Citizenship and Naturalization: Policies and Politics." In Brubaker 1989a.

———. 1989d. "Membership without Citizenship: The Economic and Social Rights of Non-Citizens." In Brubaker 1989a.

———. 1990. "Frontier Theses: Exit, Voice, and Loyalty in East Germany." *Migration World Magazine.*

Carens, J. 1989. "Membership and Morality: Admission to Citizenship in Liberal Democratic States." In Brubaker 1989a.

Centre de Relations Internationales et de Sciences Politiques d'Amiens and Revue Pluriel-Débat. 1984. *La France au pluriel?* Paris: L'Harmattan.

Challener, R. D. 1965. *The French Theory of the Nation in Arms 1866–1939.* New York: Russell and Russell.

Commission de la Nationalité. 1988. *Etre français aujourd'hui et demain.* 2 vols. Paris: La Documentation Française.

Contamine, P. 1986. "Mourir pour la patrie." In *La Nation* vol. 3, ed. P. Nora. Paris: Gallimard.

Conze, W. 1983. "Nationsbildung durch Trennung." In *Innenpolitische Probleme des Bismarkreichs,* ed. O. Pflanze. Munich: Oldenbourg.

———. 1985. "'Deutschland' und 'deutsche Nation' als historische Begriffe." In *Die Rolle der Nation in der deutschen Geschichte und Gegenwart,* ed. O. Büsch and J. Sheehan. Berlin: Colloquium Verlag.

Costa-Lascoux, J. 1988. "Intégration et nationalité." In Wenden 1987.

de Certeau, M., D. Julia, and J. Revel. 1975. *Une politique de la langue. La Révolution française et les patois: L'enquête de Gregoire.* Paris: Gallimard.

Doorn, J. van. 1975. "The Decline of the Mass Army in the West: General Reflections." *Armed Forces and Society* 1:147–57.

Freeman, G. 1986. "Migration and the Political Economy of the Welfare State." *Annals of the American Academy of Political and Social Science* 485:51–63.

Furet, F., and D. Richet. 1965. La Révolution française. Paris: Hachette. (Citations are to the paperback Pluriel edition, which does not give a publication date.)

Gall, L. 1970. "Das Problem Elsass-Lothringen." In *Reichsgründung 1870/71,* ed. T. Schieder and E. Deuerlein. Stuttgart: Seewald Verlag.

Gallissot, R. 1986. "Nationalité et citoyenneté: Aperçus sur cette contradiction à travers l'evolution du nationalisme français." *Après-demain* 286:8–15.

Geertz, C. 1971. *Islam Observed: Religious Development in Morocco and Indonesia.* Chicago: University of Chicago Press.

Gellner, E. 1983. *Nations and Nationalism.* Ithaca, N.Y.: Cornell University Press.

Girardet, R. 1978. *L'Idée coloniale en France de 1871 à 1962.* Paris: Pluriel.

Godechot, J. 1971. "Nation, patrie, nationalisme et patriotisme en France au XVIIIe siècle." *Annales historiques de la Révolution française,* no. 206.

———. 1983. *La Grande Nation: L'expansion révolutionnaire de la France dans le monde de 1789 à 1799.* Paris: Aubier.

Grawert, R. 1973. *Staat und Staatsangehörigkeit.* Berlin: Duncker and Humblot.

Griotteray, A. 1984. *Les immigrés: Le choc.* Paris: Plon.

Hailbronner, K. 1989. "Citizenship and Nationhood in Germany." In Brubaker 1989a.

Hammar, T. 1989. "State, Nation, and Dual Citizenship." In Brubaker 1989a.

———. 1990. *Democracy and the Nation-State: Aliens, Denizens, and Citizens in a World of International Migration.* Aldershot: Avebury.

Kedourie, E. 1985. *Nationalism.* London: Hutchinson.

Kelly, G. A. 1979. "Who Needs a Theory of Citizenship?" *Daedalus,* Fall:21–36.

Kocka, J. 1985. "Probleme der politischen Integration der Deutschen, 1867 bis 1945." In *Die Rolle der Nation in der deutschen Geschichte und Gegenwart,* ed. O. Büsch and J. Sheehan. Berlin: Colloquium Verlag.

Kohn, H. 1944. *The Idea of Nationalism.* New York: Collier.

———. 1967. *Prelude to Nation-States: The French and German Experience, 1789–1815.* Princeton, N.J.: Van Nostrand.

Leca, J. 1983. "Questions sur la citoyenneté." *Projet* 171–72:113–25.

Lepsius, R. 1985. "The Nation and Nationalism in Germany." *Social Research* 52(1):43–64.

Lochak, D. 1988. "Etrangers et citoyens au regard du droit." In Wenden 1987.

Mann, M. 1987. "Ruling Class Strategies and Citizenship." *Sociology* 21:339–54.

Marshall, T. H. 1950. *Citizenship and Social Class and Other Essays.* Cambridge: Cambridge University Press.

Meinecke, F. 1919. *Weltbürgertum und Nationalstaat.* Munich: Oldenbourg.

Miller, M. 1986. "Policy Ad-Hocracy." *Annals of the American Academy of Political and Social Science 485.*

———. 1989. "Political Participation and Representation of Noncitizens." In Brubaker 1989a.

Minces, J. 1985. "Le piège de la société pluriculturelle." *Esprit* 102:139–42.

Monteilhet, J. 1926. *Les institutions militaires de la France (1814–1924).* Paris: Félix Alcan.

Noiriel, G. 1988. *Le creuset français.* Paris: Seuil.

Nora, P., ed. 1986. *La nation,* 3 vols. Part 2 of *Les lieux de la mémoire.* Paris: Gallimard.

Nora, P. 1988. "Nation." In *Dictionnaire critique de la Révolution française,* ed. F. Furet and M. Ozouf. Paris: Flammarion.

Oriol, P. 1985. *Les immigrés: Métèques ou citoyens?* Paris: Syros.

Parsons, T. 1965. "Full Citizenship for the Negro American?" *Daedalus,* Fall:1009–54.

Pinson, K. 1966. *Modern Germany.* New York: Macmillan.

Piore, M. 1979. *Birds of Passage: Migrant Labor and Industrial Societies.* Cambridge: Cambridge University Press.

Rémond, R. 1969. *The Right Wing in France.* Philadelphia: University of Pennsylvania Press.

Renan, E. 1870. "Lettre à M. Strauss." *Oeuvres complètes,* vol.1. Paris: Calmann-Lévy (undated).

Riedel, M. 1972. "Bürger, Staatsbürger, Bürgertum." In *Geschichtliche Grundbegriffe,* vol. 1, ed. O. Brunner. Stuttgart.

Rothfels, H. 1956. "Die Nationsidee in westlicher und östlicher Sicht." *Osteuropa und der deutsche Osten* 1, no. 3:7–18. Cologne-Braunsfeld: Rudolf Müller.

Rousseau, J.-J. 1962 [1755]. "De l'économie politique." In *The Political Writings of Jean-Jacques Rousseau,* ed. C. E. Vaughan. Oxford: Basil Blackwell.

Salmond, J. 1901/1902. "Citizenship and Allegiance." *Law Quarterly Review* 17 (1901):270–82 and 18 (1902):49–63.

Sayad, A. 1982. "La naturalisation, ses conditions sociales et sa signification chez les immigrés Algeriens." Part 2, *Greco 13: Recherches sur les migrations internationales* 4–5:1–51.

———. 1984. "Etat, nation et immigration: L'ordre national à l'épreuve de l'immigration." *Peuples méditerranéens* 27–28:187–205.

Schieder, T. 1961. *Das deutsche Kaiserreich von 1871 als Nationalstaat.* Cologne: Westdeutscher Verlag.

———. 1985. "Typologie und Erscheinungsformen des Nationalstaats in Europa." In *Nationalismus,* ed. H. A. Winkler. Königstein/Ts: Athenäum.

Schmid, C. 1986. "Social Class, Race, and the Extension of Citizenship: The English Working Class and the Southern Civil Rights Movements." *Comparative Social Research* 9:27–46.

Schmitter, B. E. 1979. "Immigration and Citizenship in West Germany and Switzerland." Ph.D. thesis, University of Chicago.

Schnapper, D., and R. Leveau. 1987. "Religion et politique: Juifs et musulmans Maghrébins en France." Paper presented at the conference "Les musulmans dans la société française," organized by the Association Française de Science Politique (Paris, January 29–30, 1987).

Schuck, P. 1989. "Membership in the Liberal Polity: The Devaluation of American Citizenship." In Brubaker 1989a.

Schuck, P., and R. Smith. 1985. *Citizenship without Consent: Illegal Aliens in the American Polity.* New Haven, Conn.: Yale University Press.

Simmel, G. 1950. *The Sociology of Georg Simmel,* translated, edited, and with an introduction by K. H. Wolff. New York: Free Press.

Soboul, A. 1960. "De l'Ancien Régime à l'Empire: Problème national et réalités sociales." In *L'information historique.*

Szücs, J. 1981. *Nation und Geschichte.* Budapest: Corvina Kiadó.

Turner, B. 1986. *Citizenship and Capitalism: The Debate over Reformism.* London: Allen and Unwin.

von Thadden, R. 1987. "Umgang mit Minderheiten." Unpublished paper.

Walzer, M. 1970a. "The Obligation to Die for the State." In *Obligations: Essays on Disobedience, War, and Citizenship,* ed. Michael Walzer. Cambridge, Mass.: Harvard University Press.

———. 1970b. "The Problem of Citizenship." In *Obligations: Essays on Disobedience, War, and Citizenship,* ed. Michael Walzer. Cambridge, Mass.: Harvard University Press.

———. 1983. *Spheres of Justice.* New York: Basic Books.

Weber, E. 1976. *Peasants into Frenchmen.* Stanford, Calif.: Stanford University Press.

Wehler, H.-U. 1971. *Sozialdermokratie und Nationalstaat.* Göttingen: Vandenhoeck & Ruprecht.

Wenden, C. de, 1987. *Citoyenneté, nationalité et immigration.* Paris: Arcantière.

Wenden, C. de, ed. 1988. *La citoyenneté.* Paris: Edilig/Fondation Diderot.

Young, C. 1976. *The Politics of Cultural Pluralism.* Madison: University of Wisconsin Press.

Zolberg, A. 1981. "International Migrations in Political Perspective." In *Global Trends in Migration,* ed. M. Kritz et al. New York: Center for Migration Studies.

Zolberg, A. 1983. "Contemporary Transnational Migrations in Historical Perspective." In *U.S. Immigration and Refugee Policy,* ed. M. Kritz. Lexington, Mass.: Lexington Books.

# PART VI
## THE IMMIGRANT AND MULTICULTURALIST
## CRITIQUE

# 9
## *Multicultural Citizenship*
### WILL KYMLICKA

### 1. THE IMPORTANCE OF CITIZENSHIP

In a society that recognizes group-differentiated rights, the members of certain groups are incorporated into the political community not only as individuals, but also through the group, and their rights depend, in part, on their group membership. I have sometimes described these rights as forms of "differentiated citizenship." But can we still talk about "citizenship" in a society where rights are distributed on the basis of group membership?

Some liberals seem to regard this idea as a contradiction in terms. For them, citizenship is by definition a matter of treating people as individuals with equal rights under the law. This is what distinguishes democratic citizenship from feudal and other premodern views that determined people's political status by their religious, ethnic, or class membership. Hence John Porter insists that "the organization of society on the basis of rights or claims that derive from group membership is sharply opposed to the concept of society based on citizenship" (Porter 1987:128). We can find similar statements in the work of John Rawls and other recent liberal discussions of citizenship.[1]

The claim that differentiated citizenship is a contradiction in terms is overstated. If differentiated citizenship is defined as the adoption of group-specific polyethnic, representation, or self-government rights, then virtually every modern democracy recognizes some form of it. As Parekh notes, citizenship today "is a much more differentiated and far less homogeneous concept than has been presupposed by political theorists" (Parekh 1990:702).

However, critics of differentiated citizenship worry that, if groups are encouraged by the very terms of citizenship to turn inward and focus on their "difference," then, as Nathan Glazer put it in the American context, "the hope of a larger fraternity of all Americans will have to be abandoned" (Glazer 1983:227). Citizenship cannot perform its vital integrative function if it is group-differentiated—it ceases to be "a device to cultivate a sense of community and a common sense of purpose" (Heater 1990:295). Nothing will bind the various groups in society together, and prevent the spread of mutual mistrust or conflict. If citizenship is differentiated, it no longer provides a shared experience or common status. Citizenship would be yet another force for disunity, rather than a way of cultivating unity in the face of increasing social diversity. Citizenship should be a forum where people transcend their differences and think about the common good of all citizens (see, for example, Kukathas 1993:156; Kristeva 1993:7; Cairns 1993, 1995).

This is a serious concern and points to an important gap in much contemporary liberal theory. Recent political events and trends throughout the world—increasing voter apathy and long-term welfare dependency in the United States, the resurgence of nationalist movements in Eastern Europe, the stresses created by an increasingly multicultural and multiracial population in Western Europe, the backlash against the welfare state in Thatcher's England, the failure of environmental policies that rely on voluntary citizen cooperation, and so on—have made clear that the health and stability of a modern democracy depends not only on the justice of its basic institutions, but also on the qualities and attitudes of its citizens: for example, their sense of identity and how they view potentially competing forms of national, regional, ethnic, or religious identities; their ability to tolerate and work together with others who are different from themselves; their desire to participate in the political process in order to promote the public good and hold political authorities accountable; their willingness to show self-restraint and exercise personal responsibility in their economic demands, and in personal choices which affect their health and the environment; and their sense of justice and commitment to a fair distribution of resources. Without citizens who possess these qualities, "the ability of liberal societies to function successfully progressively diminishes" (Galston 1991:220).

Many classical liberals believed that a liberal democracy could be made secure, even in the absence of an especially virtuous citizenry, by creating checks and balances. Institutional and procedural devices such as the separation of powers, a bicameral legislature, and federalism would all serve to block would-be oppressors. Even if each person pursued her own self-interest, without regard for the common good, one set of private interests would check another set of private interests. In this way, Kant thought that the problem of good government "can be solved even for a race of devils." However, it has become clear that procedural-institutional mechanisms to balance self-interest are not enough, and that some level of civic virtue and public-spiritedness is required. Without this, democracies become difficult to govern, even unstable.[2]

Yet there is growing fear that the public-spiritedness of citizens of liberal democracies may be in serious decline.[3] Will the rise of group-based claims further erode the sense of shared civic purpose and solidarity? In answering this question, we need to keep in mind the distinction between the three forms of differentiated citizenship. In particular, we need to distinguish polyethnic and representation rights (in section 2), from self-government rights (in section 3).

## 2. POLYETHNICITY AND INCLUSION

Let's start with group representation rights. Generally speaking, the demand for representation rights by disadvantaged groups is a demand for *inclusion*. Groups that feel excluded want to be included in the larger society, and the recognition and accommodation of their "difference" is intended to facilitate this. Indeed, these representation rights can be seen as an extension of long-standing and widely accepted practices within liberal democracies. It has always been recognized that a majoritarian democracy can systematically ignore the voices of minorities. In cases where minorities are regionally concentrated, democratic systems have responded by intentionally drawing the boundaries of federal units, or of individual constituencies, so as to create seats where the minority is in a majority. Proponents of special representation simply extend this logic to nonterritorial groups who may equally be in need of representation (for example, ethnic minorities, women, the disabled). The familiar practice of defining geographic constituencies in such a way as to ensure representation of "communities of interest" is not seen as a threat to national unity — on the contrary, it is rightly seen as promoting civic participation and political legitimacy. Why then should guaranteed representation for nonterritorial communities of interest be seen as a threat to unity, rather than as evidence of a desire for integration? To be sure, there are enormous practical obstacles to such a proposal. However, the basic impulse underlying representation rights is integration, not separation.

Similarly, most polyethnic demands are evidence that members of minority groups want to participate within the mainstream of society. Consider the case of Sikhs who wanted to join the Royal Canadian Mounted Police but, because of their religious requirement to wear a turban, could not do so unless they were exempted from the usual requirements regarding ceremonial headgear. Or the case of Orthodox Jews who wanted to join the U.S. military but needed an exemption from the usual regulations so they could wear their yarmulkes. Such exemptions are opposed by many people, who view them as a sign of disrespect for "national symbols." But the fact that these men wanted to be a part of the national police force or the national military is ample evidence of their desire to participate in and contribute to the larger community. The special right they were requesting could only be seen as promoting, not discouraging, their integration.

Some demands for polyethnic rights take the form of withdrawal from the larger society, although this is more likely to be true of religious sects than of ethnic communities per se. The Amish and other Christian sects have been granted exemptions from the usual requirements regarding integration (for example, military service, compulsory education of children). But these are atypical, I believe. Moreover, it is important to note that these exemptions for religious groups have a very different origin and motivation from the current policy of "multiculturalism."

The decision to allow certain groups to withdraw from the larger society occurred many decades ago—often at the turn of the century—in response to the demands of white Christian and Jewish groups such as the Amish, Hutterites, Quakers, and Hasidim. "Multiculturalism" as an official government policy, by contrast, began in the late 1960s and 1970s, in the context of increasing immigration from nonwhite, non-Christian countries. And most of the group-differentiated policies that have arisen under the "multiculturalism" umbrella, and that are aimed at accommodating these new ethnic/religious groups, are not about withdrawing from the larger society. The case of the Sikhs in the Royal Canadian Mounted Police is a good example—the policy is intended not to allow Sikhs to withdraw from the larger society, but precisely to modify the institutions of mainstream society so that Sikhs can integrate into them as fully as possible.

Some recent immigrant groups make demands which are similar to the demands of older Christian sects. For example, some British Muslim groups have demanded the same sort of exemption from a liberal education granted to the Amish. But again these are atypical. Moreover, such demands have not been accepted in Canada, the United States, or Australia, since they are not the sort of demands that the new policy of polyethnicity was intended to meet. The philosophy underlying polyethnicity is an integrationist one, which is what most new immigrant groups want. It is a mistake, therefore, to describe polyethnic rights as promoting "ghettoization" or "balkanization."

Some people fear that polyethnic rights impede the integration of immigrants by creating a confusing halfway house between their old nation and citizenship in the new one, reminding immigrants "of their different origins rather than their shared symbols, society and future" (Citizen's Forum 1991:128). But these worries seem empirically unfounded. The experience to date suggests that first- and second-generation immigrants who remain proud of their heritage are also among the most patriotic citizens of their new countries (Whitaker 1992:255). Moreover, their strong affiliation with their new country seems to be based in large part on its willingness not just to tolerate, but to welcome, cultural difference.

Indeed, there is strikingly little evidence that immigrants pose any sort of threat to the unity or stability of a country. This fear was understandable 150 years ago, when the United States, Canada, and Australia began accepting waves of non-English immigrants. The idea of building a country through polyethnic immigration was quite unique in history, and many people thought it untenable. But that was 150 years ago, and there is no longer any reason for such fears to persist. It has become clear that the overwhelming majority of immigrants want to integrate, and have in fact integrated, even during the periods of large-scale influxes. Moreover, they care deeply about the unity of their new country (Harles 1993). To be sure, they want the mainstream institutions in their society to be reformed so as to accommodate their cultural differences and to recognize the value of their cultural heritage. But the desire for such polyethnic rights is a desire for inclusion which is consistent with participation in, and commitment to, the mainstream institutions that underlie social unity.

Indeed, those ethnic groups which seek polyethnic rights are often particularly concerned with clarifying the basis of national unity. As Tariq Modood notes:

> The greatest psychological and political need for clarity about a common framework and national symbols comes from the minorities. For clarity about what makes us willingly bound into a single country relieves the pressure on minorities, especially new minorities whose presence within the country is not fully accepted, to have to conform in all areas of social life, or in arbi-

trarily chosen areas, in order to rebut the charge of disloyalty.
(Modood 1994:64)

Why have so many commentators failed to see the integrative impulse of
polyethnic rights? In part it is prejudice against new immigrants, most of
whom are nonwhite and non-Christian. There seems to be a double standard
at work in many criticisms of polyethnic rights. While the special rights
granted to white Jewish and Christian groups to withdraw from the larger
society have at times been controversial, few people see these as serious
threats to social unity or stability, and they have been part of our political
culture for decades. But when accommodations were made for nonwhite,
non-Christian groups, people started complaining about the "tribalization"
of society and the loss of a common identity—even though these newer
polyethnic rights are in fact primarily intended to promote integration! It is
difficult to avoid the conclusion that much of the backlash against "multiculturalism" arises from a racist or xenophobic fear of these new immigrant
groups.

Moreover, it is likely that worries about the volatile relations between entrenched and long-standing national or racial groups get displaced
onto newer immigrants. For example, in the Canadian case, "the diversity
associated with multiculturalism is easier to 'blame' for disunity" than confronting the self-government demands of the Québécois or Aboriginals (Abu-
Laban and Stasiulus 1992:378). Similarly, I think that fears about the relations between whites and blacks in the United States are often displaced
onto the "ethnic revival." In each case, the modest demands of immigrants
provide an easier target than the demands of larger and more settled minorities, even though the former in fact pose little threat to the unity or stability of the country.

Finally, liberal assumptions about the relationship between citizenship and integration, particularly in the British context, have largely been
shaped by the experience of the working class. The working class provided
a relatively clear and successful example where common citizenship rights
helped integrate a previously excluded group into a common national culture. Many liberals (and socialists) have assumed that this model could
apply to other historically excluded groups, ignoring their very different
circumstances.

Consider the work of T. H. Marshall, one of the most influential
postwar theorists of citizenship. He believed that the working classes in
England were cut off from the "common culture" and were denied access
to a "common civilization" which should be seen as "a common possession

and heritage" (Marshall 1965:101–2). England was deeply divided along class lines, with little interaction between members of different classes, and that, combined with the lack of material resources, made it difficult for workers to take part in the broader cultural life of the country. They had their own subcultures, of course, which were often highly developed, but they were deprived of access to the national culture.

Marshall was deeply concerned with this cultural aspect of the exclusion of the working class. Indeed, he was more concerned with cultural exclusion than with material inequality per se. However, because the cultural exclusion of the working class derived from their socioeconomic standing, the most effective way to promote national integration was through the provision of material benefits, via the welfare state. Hence Marshall's focus was on expanding citizenship by the inclusion of universal "social rights" to education, health care, and social security programs. And there is ample evidence that these social rights have indeed served to promote the integration of the working class in various countries into the national culture.

Based on this example of the English working class, Marshall developed a theory about the integrative function of citizenship rights. He believed that the equal rights of citizenship would help promote national integration for previously excluded groups. These rights would generate "a direct sense of community membership based on loyalty to a civilization which is a common possession" (Marshall 1965:101–2).

However, it has become clear that the integration of the working class cannot be generalized in this way. There are many forms of cultural exclusion, and they interact with common citizenship in different ways (Barbalet 1988:93). In particular, Marshall's theory of integration does not necessarily work for culturally distinct immigrants, or for various other groups which have historically been excluded from full participation in the national culture — such as blacks, women, religious minorities, gays, and lesbians. Some members of these groups still feel excluded from the "common culture," despite possessing the common rights of citizenship.

In each of these cases, groups have been excluded from full participation not because of their socioeconomic status, but because of their sociocultural identity — their "difference." Of course, members of these groups are often materially deprived as well. But that is not the only cause of their cultural exclusion, and so providing material benefits will not necessarily ensure their integration into a common culture, or develop a sense of shared loyalty to a common civilization.

Like the working class (but unlike national minorities), these groups are demanding inclusion into the dominant national culture. But unlike the working class, [they need] group-differentiated rights... to feel accepted by the community and experience the "direct sense of community member-ship based on loyalty to a civilization which is a common possession" that Marshall saw as the basis of citizenship. The common rights of citizenship, originally defined by and for white, able-bodied, Christian men, cannot ac-commodate the special needs of these groups. Instead, a fully integrative citizenship must take these differences into account.

## 3. SELF-GOVERNMENT AND SEPARATISM

While polyethnic and representation rights can promote social integration and political unity, self-government rights pose a more serious challenge to the integrative function of citizenship. Both representation rights for disad-vantaged groups and polyethnic rights for immigrant groups take the larger political community for granted, and seek greater inclusion in it. Demands for self-government, however, reflect a desire to weaken the bonds with the larger political community, and indeed question its very authority and permanence.

It is worth exploring this point in some depth. When disadvantaged groups demand special representation, they generally take the authority of the larger political community for granted. They assume, as John Rawls puts it, that citizens are members of "one co-operative scheme in perpetu-ity," but that temporary special rights for oppressed groups are needed to achieve full membership in that cooperative scheme. Most polyethnic rights similarly take the authority of the larger polity for granted. They assume that immigrants will work within the economic and political institutions of the larger society, but that these institutions must be adapted to reflect the increasing cultural diversity of the population they serve.

In the case of self-government rights, the larger political commu-nity has a more conditional existence. National minorities claim that they are distinct "peoples," with inherent rights of self-government. While they are currently part of a larger country, this is not a renunciation of their origi-nal right of self-government. Rather it is a matter of transferring *some as-pects* of their powers of self-government to the larger polity, on the condi-tion that other powers remain in their own hands.

This condition is often spelled out in treaties or other terms of federation, for national minorities want their self-governing powers pro-tected securely and permanently. In this sense, the authority of the larger political community is derivative. In countries that are formed from the federation of two or more nations, the authority of the central government is limited to the powers which each constituent nation agreed to transfer to it. And these national groups see themselves as having the right to take back these powers, and withdraw from the federation, if they feel threatened by the larger community.

In other words, the basic claim underlying self-government rights is not simply that some groups are disadvantaged within the political community (representation rights), or that the political community is culturally diverse (polyethnic rights). Instead, the claim is that there is more than one political community, and that the authority of the larger state cannot be assumed to take precedence over the authority of the constituent national communities. If democracy is the rule of "the people," national minorities claim that there is more than one people, each with the right to rule itself.

Self-government rights, therefore, are the most complete case of differentiated citizenship, since they divide the people into separate "peoples," each with its own historic rights, territories, and powers of self-government; and each, therefore, with its own political community. They may view their own political community as primary, and the value and authority of the larger federation as derivative.

It seems unlikely that according self-government rights to a national minority can serve an integrative function.[4] If citizenship is membership in a political community, then, in creating overlapping political communities, self-government rights necessarily give rise to a sort of dual citizenship, and to potential conflicts about which community citizens identify with most deeply. Moreover, there seems to be no natural stopping point to the demands for increasing self-government. If limited autonomy is granted, this may simply fuel the ambitions of nationalist leaders who will be satisfied with nothing short of their own nation-state.

Democratic multination states which recognize self-government rights are, it appears, inherently unstable for this reason. At best they seem to be a modus vivendi between separate communities, with no intrinsic bond that would lead the members of one national group to make sacrifices for the other. Yet, liberal justice requires this sense of common purpose and mutual solidarity within the country.

It might seem tempting, therefore, to ignore the demands of national minorities, avoid any reference to such groups in the constitution, and insist that citizenship is a common identity shared by all individuals, without regard to group membership. This is often described as the American strategy for dealing with cultural pluralism.

But in fact the Americans have only applied this strategy in the context of integrating voluntary immigrants and involuntary slaves, who arrived in America as individuals or families. Generally speaking, a quite different strategy has been applied in the context of incorporating historically self-governing groups whose homeland has become part of the larger community, such as the American Indians, Alaskan Eskimos, Puerto Ricans, and native Hawaiians. Most of these national minorities are accorded some level of self-government within the American federation. And where the common citizenship strategy was applied to national minorities it has often been a spectacular failure. For example, the policy of pressuring American Indian tribes to relinquish their distinct political status, known as the "termination policy," had disastrous consequences, and was withdrawn in the 1950s.

Indeed, there are very few democratic multination states that follow the strict "common citizenship" strategy. This is not surprising, because refusing demands for self-government rights will simply aggravate alienation among national minorities, and increase the desire for secession. What is called "common citizenship" in a multination state in fact involves supporting the culture of the majority nation—for example, its language becomes the official language of the schools, courts, and legislatures; its holidays become public holidays. Moreover, a regime of common citizenship means that the minority has no way to limit its vulnerability to the economic and political decisions of the majority, since the boundaries and powers of internal political units are defined to suit the administrative convenience of the majority, not the self-government claims of the minority.

It is not surprising, then, that national minorities have resisted attempts to impose common citizenship on them. Rawls suggests that common citizenship promotes the political virtues of "reasonableness and a sense of fairness, a spirit of compromise and a readiness to meet others halfway" (Rawls 1987:21). But attempts to impose common citizenship in multination states may in fact threaten these virtues.

In the Ottoman Empire, for example, compromise between groups was traditionally ensured by the system of self-government for each "millet," thereby limiting mutual interference. In the mid-eighteenth century, however, the Ottomans stripped the millets of most of their self-governing power and tried to promote a common citizenship status that cut across religious and ethnic boundaries, so that everyone's political rights and identity were based on a common relationship to the Ottoman state, rather than membership in a particular millet. As Karpat notes, the result was disastrous, for once the self-governing status of the millets ended,

> the relative position of the religious and ethnic groups in the Ottoman Empire toward each other began to be decided on the basis of their numerical strength. Hence they were transformed

into minorities and majorities. It was obvious that sooner or later the views of the majority would prevail and its cultural characteristics and aspirations would become the features of the government itself. (Karpat 1982:163)

A similar process occurred when indigenous peoples in North America were accorded citizenship (often against their will), and so became a numerical minority within the larger body of citizens, rather than a separate, self-governing people. Rawls suggests that a strong sense of common citizenship is needed to deal with the danger that majorities will treat minorities unfairly. But common citizenship in a multination state helps create that danger in the first place, by transforming self-governing groups into numerical majorities and minorities.

Given this dynamic, imposing common citizenship on minorities which view themselves as distinct nations or peoples is likely to increase conflict in a multination state. Should the state then try to modify that national consciousness, so as to reduce or remove the minority's desire to form a distinct national society? This option is endorsed by David Miller, who says we should not "regard cultural identities as given, or at least as created externally to the political system," but rather should have "a stronger sense of the malleability of such identities, that is, the extent to which they can be created or modified consciously." Since "subcultures threaten to undermine the overarching sense of identity" needed for a generous welfare state, the state should promote "a common identity as citizens that is stronger than their separate identities as members of ethnic or other sectional groups" (Miller 1989:237, 279, 286–87).

But recent history suggests that *to some extent* national identities must be taken as givens. The character of a national identity can change dramatically, as the Quiet Revolution in Quebec shows. Equally dramatic changes have occurred recently amongst indigenous communities. But the identity itself — the sense of being a distinct national culture — is much more stable. Governments in Canada and the United States have, at times, used all the tools at their disposal to destroy the sense of separate identity amongst their national minorities, from residential schools for Indian children and the prohibition of tribal customs to the banning of French- or Spanish-language schools. But despite centuries of legal discrimination, social prejudice, or plain indifference, these national minorities have maintained their sense of having a national identity. Similarly, efforts by European governments to suppress the language and national identity of the Kurds, Basques, or other national minorities have had little or no success. And communist governments failed in their efforts to eradicate national loyalties. Despite a complete monopoly over education and the media, communist regimes were unable to get Croats, Slovaks, and Ukrainians to think of themselves primarily as "Yugoslavs," "Czechoslovaks," or "Soviets." Attempts to promote "pan-movements" that would supersede national identities—for example, attempts to create pan-Slavic or pan-Arabic states—have proven similarly futile (Fishman 1989:147).

It is no longer possible (if it ever was) to eliminate the sense of distinct identity which underlies these groups' desire to form their own national societies. If anything, attempts to subordinate these separate identities to a common identity have backfired, since they are perceived by minorities as threats to their very existence, and so have resulted in even greater indifference or resentment (Whitaker 1992:152–53; Taylor 1992a:64).

Much has been made in the recent literature of the social construction of national identity, and of the "invention of tradition" (Hobsbawm 1990). And of course much of the mythology accompanying national identities is just that—a myth. But it is important not to confuse the heroes, history, or present-day characteristics of a national identity with the underlying national identity itself. The former is much more malleable than the latter. Indeed, it seems that few if any national groups in the last hundred years have voluntarily assimilated, despite often significant economic incentives and legal pressures to do so. As Anthony Smith puts it, "whenever and however a national identity is forged, once established, it becomes immensely difficult, if not impossible (short of total genocide) to eradicate" (Smith 1993:131; cf. Connor 1972:350–51).

Since claims to self-government are here to stay, we have no choice but to try to accommodate them. Rejecting these demands in the name of common citizenship will simply promote alienation and secessionist movements. Indeed, recent surveys of ethnonationalist conflict around the world show clearly that self-government arrangements diminish the likelihood of violent conflict, while refusing or rescinding self-government rights is likely to escalate the level of conflict (Gurr 1993; Hannum 1990; Horowitz 1985).

Yet, as I noted earlier, accepting self-government demands is likely to lead to a desire for ever-increasing autonomy, even independence. Providing local autonomy reduces the likelihood of violent conflict, yet the resulting arrangements are rarely examples of harmonious cooperation between national groups. They often become "mere treaties of cooperation," in which quarrelsome groups "agree to cooperate only on a limited set of issues, if they can cooperate at all" (Ordeshook 1993:223). The sense of solidarity needed to promote the public good and to tackle urgent issues of justice is lacking. This seems increasingly true, for example, in Belgium and Canada.

We seem caught in a Gordian knot. Given this dynamic, some commentators conclude that the only solution to the problem of multination states is secession. According to Miller, where national identities have "already become so strong that what we have is really two separate nationalities living side by side," then "the best solution is ultimately likely to be the secession of one community" (Miller 1989:288). Similarly, Walzer argues that "if the community is so radically divided that a single citizenship is impossible, then its territory too must be divided" (Walzer 1983:62).

We are now back at John Stuart Mill's argument that a stable liberal democracy must be a nation-state, with a single national culture. If national minorities are unwilling to assimilate, they must secede and establish their own state.

Perhaps we should be more willing to consider secession. We tend to assume that secession is a moral and political catastrophe, but I suspect that few people today condemn the secession of Norway from Sweden in 1905. In the Norwegian case, the process of secession was (relatively) peaceful, and the result was two healthy liberal democracies where there used to be one. There is every reason to think that any future secession of Quebec from the rest of Canada would be similar. It is difficult to see why liberals should automatically oppose such peaceful, liberal secessions. After all, liberalism is fundamentally concerned not with the fate of states, but with the freedom and well-being of individuals, and secession need not harm individual rights.

However, secession is not always possible or desirable. Some national minorities, particularly indigenous peoples, would have trouble forming viable independent states. In other cases, competing claims over land and resources would make peaceful secession virtually impossible. In general, there are more nations in the world than possible states, and since we cannot simply wish national consciousness away, we need to find some way to keep multination states together.

## 4. THE BASIS OF SOCIAL UNITY
### IN A MULTINATION STATE

What then are the possible sources of unity in a multination state which affirms, rather than denies, its national differences? I do not have a clear answer to this question. Indeed, I doubt that there are any obvious or easy answers available.

There are important examples of stable multination states, such as Switzerland, which show that there is no necessary reason why the members of a national minority cannot have both a strong national consciousness and a strong sense of patriotism and commitment to the larger polity (Sigler 1983:188–92). This sense of patriotism is so strong that the Swiss are, in some ways, a single "people," as well as being a federation of peoples.

But there are all too many examples of countries where the institutionalization of national identities and rights has not prevented civil strife (for example, Lebanon and Yugoslavia). Moreover, some multination states whose long-term stability used to be taken for granted now seem rather more precarious (for example, Belgium).

What then are the conditions which help stabilize multination states? There are few discussions of this issue. To date, defenders of national self-government have been more concerned to argue that assimilation is not a viable source of unity than to explain what should take its place.

One suggestion is that social unity depends on "shared values." Obviously the citizens of any modern democracy do not share specific conceptions of the good life, but they may share certain political values. For example, one government commission in Canada developed a list of seven such values which Canadians shared: (1) a belief in equality and fairness; (2) a belief in consultation and dialogue; (3) the importance of accommodation and tolerance; (4) support for diversity; (5) compassion and generosity; (6) attachment to the natural environment; (7) a commitment to freedom, peace, and nonviolent change (Citizen's Forum 1991:34–44). The hope is that focusing on these shared values will provide grounds for social unity in Canada.

This idea is also found, in a more philosophical form, in many recent liberal theorists. Rawls, for example, claims that the source of unity in modern societies is a shared conception of justice. According to Rawls, "although a well-ordered society is divided and pluralistic ... public agreement on questions of political and social justice supports ties of civic friendship and secures the bonds of association" (Rawls 1980:540).

It is true that there often are shared political values within multination states, including a shared conception of liberal justice. However, it is not clear that these values, by themselves, provide a reason for two or more national groups to stay together in one country. For example, there may be (and probably is) a remarkable convergence of values between the citizens of Norway and Sweden, but is this any reason for them to reunite? I do not think so. The fact that they share the same values does not, by itself, explain whether it is better to have one state or two in that part of the world.

Similarly, there has been a pronounced convergence in values be-tween English- and French-speaking Canadians over the last thirty years (Taylor 1991:54). If the shared values approach were correct, we should have witnessed a decline in support for Quebec secession over this period, yet nationalist sentiment has in fact grown consistently. Here again, the fact that anglophones and francophones in Canada share the same principles of justice is not a strong reason to remain together, since the Québécois rightly assume that their own national state could respect the same principles. The same is true of the Flemish in Belgium.

Indeed, this reflects a very general trend. There has been a con-vergence of political values throughout the Western world, amongst both majority nations and national minorities. In terms of their political values, the Danes, Germans, French, and British have probably never been as similar as they are now. But this has not had any appreciable impact on the desire of these majority nations to retain their national independence. Why then should it diminish the desire of national minorities for self-government?

This suggests that shared values are not sufficient for social unity. The fact that two national groups share the same values or principles of justice does not necessarily give them any strong reason to join (or remain) together, rather than remaining (or splitting into) two separate countries. What more, or what else, is required for social unity? The missing ingredi-ent seems to be the idea of a *shared identity*. A shared conception of justice throughout a political community does not necessarily generate a shared identity, let alone a shared civic identity that will supersede rival national identities. People decide who they want to share a country with by asking who they identify with, who they feel solidarity with. What holds Americans together, despite their lack of common values, is the fact that they share an identity as Americans. Conversely, what keeps Swedes and Norwegians apart, despite the presence of shared values, is the lack of a shared identity.

Where does this shared identity come from? In nation-states, the answer is simple. Shared identity derives from commonality of history, lan-guage, and maybe religion. But these are precisely the things which are not shared in a multination state. If we look to strongly patriotic but culturally diverse countries like the United States or Switzerland, the basis for a shared identity often seems to be pride in certain historical achievements (for ex-ample, the founding of the American Republic). This shared pride is one of the bases of the strong sense of American political identity, constantly re-inforced in their citizenship literature and school curriculum.

But in many multination countries history is a source of resent-ment and division between national groups, not a source of shared pride.

The people and events which spark pride amongst the majority nation often generate a sense of betrayal amongst the national minority. Moreover, the reliance on history often requires a very selective, even manipulative, retelling of that history. Ernst Renan once claimed that national identity involves forgetting the past as much as remembering it. To build a sense of common identity in a multination state probably requires an even more selective memory of the past.

Shared values and an inspiring history no doubt help sustain solidarity in a multination state, but it is doubtful that either is sufficient by itself. How then can one construct a common identity in a country which contains two or more communities which view themselves as self-governing nations? The great variance in historical, cultural, and political situations in multination states suggests that any generalized answer to this question will probably be overstated.[5]

What is clear, I think, is that if there is a viable way to promote a sense of solidarity and common purpose in a multination state, it will involve accommodating, rather than subordinating, national identities. People from different national groups will only share an allegiance to the larger polity if they see it as the context within which their national identity is nurtured, rather than subordinated.[6]

This is difficult enough in a country which simply contains two nations (Belgium, for example). It gets much more complicated in countries which are not only multinational but also polyethnic, containing many national and indigenous groups, often of vastly unequal size, as well as immigrants from every part of the world. In this context, we need what Charles Taylor calls a theory of "deep diversity," since we must accommodate not only a diversity of cultural groups, but also a diversity of ways in which the members of these groups belong to the larger polity (Taylor 1991:74). For example, the member of an immigrant group in the United States may see her citizenship status as centered on the universal individual rights guaranteed by the constitution. Her ethnic identity, while important in various ways, may not affect her sense of citizenship, or what it is to be an American (or Canadian or Australian). The United States, for her, may be a country of equal citizens who are tolerant of each other's cultural differences.

But this model of belonging will not accommodate national minorities like the Puerto Ricans or Navaho. They belong to the United States through belonging to a national group that has federated itself to the larger country. According to a recent poll, 91 percent of the residents of Puerto Rico think of themselves as Puerto Ricans first, and Americans second (Rubinstein 1993:88). They do see themselves as Americans, but only because this does not require abandoning their prior identity as a distinct Spanish-speaking people with their own separate political community. The United States, for them, is a federation of peoples — English, Spanish, Indian — each with the right to govern itself.

Similarly, the immigrant model of belonging will not accommodate the francophones and indigenous peoples in Canada, for whom "the way of being a Canadian (for those who still want to be) is via their belonging to a constituent element of Canada," such as the Québécois or the Cree (Taylor 1991:75). For these groups, Canada is a federation of national groups which respect each other's right to be a distinct societal culture within Canada.

In countries that are both polyethnic and multinational, cultural groups are not only diverse, but they have diverse images of the country as a whole. People not only belong to separate political communities, but also belong in different ways. This means that the members of a polyethnic and multination state must not only respect diversity, but also respect a diversity of approaches to diversity. As Taylor puts it, an immigrant might see herself "as a bearer of individual rights in a multicultural mosaic," but she must nevertheless accept that a Puerto Rican, Navaho, or Québécois "might belong in a very different way... through being members of their national communities." And reciprocally, the Puerto Ricans, Navaho, and Québécois "would accept the perfect legitimacy of the 'mosaic' identity." This sort of "deep diversity" is "the only formula" on which a united polyethnic, multination state can be built (Taylor 1991:76).

What would hold such a multination state together? Taylor admits that this is an open question, but suggests that citizens might "find it exciting and an object of pride" to work together to build a society founded on deep diversity, and so be willing to make sacrifices to keep it together (Taylor 1991:76). This seems to beg the question. Why would citizens find this exciting rather than wearying, given the endless negotiations and complications it entails?

But Taylor is pointing in the right direction. A society founded on "deep diversity" is unlikely to stay together unless people value deep diversity itself, and want to live in a country with diverse forms of cultural and political membership. Even this is not always sufficient. For example, a sovereign Quebec would still be a very culturally diverse country, with immigrants from around the world, as well as a historically settled anglophone community, and various indigenous peoples, including the Cree, Mohawk, and Inuit. Secession rarely if ever creates homogeneous nation-states; it simply rearranges the pattern and size of groups. For citizens to want to keep a multination state together, therefore, they must value not just "deep diversity" in general, but also the particular ethnic groups and national cultures with whom they currently share the country.

The problem, of course, is that this sort of allegiance is the product of mutual solidarity, not a possible basis for it. If citizens already have a fairly strong sense of identity towards the other ethnic and national groups in the country, they will find the prospect of sustaining their deep diversity inspiring and exciting. But a vague commitment to the value of cultural diversity, by itself, may not generate a strong sense of identification with the existing country, or the particular groups that cohabit it.

As I noted earlier, some multination states do have this strong sense of mutual identification. This is obviously true of the Swiss. Canadians also have a reasonably strong sense of solidarity. For example, while over half of Quebecers attach priority, in their self-identify, to their status as Quebec citizens, compared with just under 30 percent who attach priority to Canadian citizenship, still 70 percent of Quebecers say they would be willing to make personal sacrifices that would benefit only Canadians outside Quebec (*L'actualité 1992*). This provides a level of goodwill that is not present in other multination states. And focusing on shared values, mythical history, or the excitement of deep diversity might help sustain that level of solidarity. But it is not clear how other multination states could try to create such a level of solidarity where it did not already exist. If two or more national groups simply do not want to live together, it may be impossible to create solidarity from scratch (Miller 1993:16 n. 14).

## 5. CONCLUSION

Some critics see the liberal commitment to common citizenship as evidence of an excessively legalistic understanding of citizenship which neglects the broader social and cultural aspects of membership. In fact, however, most liberal theorists have recognized that citizenship is not just a legal status, defined by a set of rights and responsibilities, but also an identity, an expression of one's membership in a political community. And it is precisely in the name of a strengthened civic identity that many liberals have clung to the principle of common citizenship.

That is, underlying much liberal opposition to the demands of ethnic and national minorities is a very practical concern for the stability of liberal states. Liberal democracies require citizens to have a fairly high level of self-restraint and mutual solidarity, and it is a fair question whether the politicization of ethnic and national differences is compatible with these requirements.

Yet I believe that fears in this area are often overstated. The demands of immigrants and disadvantaged groups for polyethnic rights and representation rights are primarily demands for inclusion, for full membership in the larger society. To view this as a threat to stability or solidarity is implausible, and often reflects an underlying ignorance or intolerance of these groups.

Self-government rights, however, do pose a threat to social unity. The sense of being a distinct nation within a larger country is potentially destabilizing. On the other hand, the denial of self-government rights is also destabilizing, since it encourages resentment and even secession. Concerns about social unity will arise however we respond to self-government claims.

A fundamental challenge facing liberal theorists, therefore, is to identify the sources of unity in a democratic multination state. The nineteenth-century English theorist A. V. Dicey once said that a stable multination federation requires "a very peculiar state of sentiment" among its citizens, since "they must desire union, and must not desire unity." Henri Bourassa made a similar point when he said that the "special development" of the French-Canadian nation "must come about in conjunction with the development of a more general patriotism that unifies us, without fusing us" (Cook 1969:149). Liberal theory has not yet succeeded in clarifying the nature of this "peculiar sentiment."

## NOTES

1. According to Rawls, a society in which rights and claims "depend on religious affiliation, social class, and so on . . . may not have a conception of citizenship at all; for this conception, as we are using it, goes with the conception of society as a fair system of cooperation for mutual advantage between free and equal persons" (Rawls 1989:241; cf. Heater 1990:285).

2. Galston 1991:215–17, 244; Macedo 1990:138–39. This may account for the recent interest in citizenship promotion amongst governments (see Britain's Commission on Citizenship, *Encouraging Citizenship* [1990]; Senate of Australia, *Active Citizenship Revisited* [1991]; Senate of Canada, *Canadian Citizenship: Sharing the Responsibility* [1993]). For further references and discussion, see Kymlicka and Norman 1994.

3. According to a recent survey, only 12 percent of American teenagers said voting was important to being a good citizen. Moreover, this apathy is not just a function of youth — comparisons with similar surveys from the previous fifty years suggest that "the current cohort knows less, cares less, votes less, and is less critical of its leaders and institutions than young people have been at any time over

the past five decades" (Glendon 1991:129; cf. Walzer, chapter 14 in this volume). The evidence from Great Britain is similar (Heater 1990:215).

4. This is true of most claims grounded in claims of self-government. But one particular aspect of self-government—guaranteed representation at the federal or intergovernmental level—clearly serves a unifying function. The existence of such group representation helps reduce the threat of self-government, by reconnecting the self-governing community to the larger federation. It is a form of connection which remains, and which can be drawn upon, when other connections are being weakened. This is true, I think, of Quebec's representation on the Supreme Court and of proposals for Aboriginal representation in the Senate.

5. European theorists are confronting these dilemmas as they seek to understand the nature of the European Community and the form of citizenship it requires. Habermas argues that European unity cannot be based on the shared traditions, cultures, and languages that characterized successful nation-states. Instead, European citizenship must be founded on a "postnational" constitutional patriotism based on shared principles of justice and democracy (Habermas 1992; Berten 1992; Ferry 1992). Others, however, argue that shared values are not a sufficient basis for unity, and that attention must also be paid to issues of identity (Taylor 1992b:61–65; Smith 1993).

6. As Taylor puts it in the Canadian case, to insist that Quebecers should put Canada first "makes no sense to Quebec federalists. . . . We belong to Canada by belonging to Quebec. If these allegiances get polarized to the point where one has to be put first, then our Canada has already been lost" (Taylor 1991).

## BIBLIOGRAPHY

AASA (American Association of School Administrators). 1987. *Citizenship: Goal of Education.* Arlington, Va.: AASA Publications.

Abu-Laban, Yasmeen, and Daiva Stasiulus. 1992. "Ethnic Pluralism under Siege: Popular and Partisan Opposition to Multiculturalism." *Canadian Public Policy* 18, no. 4:365–86.

Barbalet, J. M. 1988. *Citizenship: Rights, Struggle and Class Inequality.* Minneapolis: University of Minnesota Press.

Berten, André. 1992. "Identité européenne: Une ou multiple?" In Lenoble and Dewandre 1992.

Brilmayer, Lea. 1992. "Groups, Histories, and International Law." *Cornell International Law Journal* 25, no. 3:555–63.

Cairns, Alan. 1993. "The Fragmentation of Canadian Citizenship." In *Belonging: The Meaning and Future of Canadian Citizenship,* ed. William Kaplan. Montreal: McGill-Queen's Press.

———. 1995. "Aboriginal Canadians, Citizenship, and the Constitution." In *Reconfigurations: Canadian Citizenship and Constitutional Change.* Toronto: McClelland & Stewart.

Citizen's Forum on Canada's Future. 1991. *Report to the People and Government of Canada.* Ottawa: Supply and Services.

Connor, Walker. 1972. "Nation-Building or Nation-Destroying." *World Politics* 24:319–55.

Cook, Ramsey. 1969. *French-Canadian Nationalism: An Anthology.* Toronto: Macmillan.

Ferry, Jean-Marc. 1992. "Identité et citoyenneté européennes." In Lenoble and Dewandre 1992.

Fishman, Joshua. 1989. *Language and Ethnicity in Minority Sociolinguistic Perspective.* Clevendon: Multilingual Matters.

Galston, William. 1991. *Liberal Purposes: Goods, Virtues, and Duties in the Liberal State.* Cambridge: Cambridge University Press.

Glazer, Nathan. 1983. Ethnic Dilemmas: 1964–1982. Cambridge. Mass.: Harvard University Press.

Glendon, Mary Ann. 1991. *Rights Talk: The Impoverishment of Political Discourse.* New York: Free Press.

Gurr, Ted. 1993. *Minorities at Risk: A Global View of Ethnopolitical Conflict.* Washington, D.C.: Institute of Peace Press.

Habermas, Jürgen. 1992. "Citizenship and National Identity: Some Reflections on the Future of Europe." *Praxis International* 12, no. 1:1–19.

Hannum, Hurst. 1990. *Autonomy, Sovereignty, and Self-Determination: The Adjudication of Conflicting Rights.* Philadelphia: University of Pennsylvania Press.

Harles, John. 1993. *Politics in the Lifeboat: Immigrants and the American Democratic Order.* Boulder, Colo.: Westview.

Heater, Derek. 1990. *Citizenship: The Civic Ideal in World History, Politics and Education.* London: Longman.

Hobsbawm, E. J. 1990. *Nations and Nationalism since 1870: Programme, Myth and Reality.* Cambridge: Cambridge University Press.

Horowitz, D. L. 1985. *Ethnic Groups in Conflict.* Berkeley: University of California Press.

James, Susan. 1992. "The Good-Enough Citizen: Citizenship and Independence." In *Beyond Equality and Difference: Citizenship, Feminist Politics and Female Subjectivity,* ed. Gisela Bock and Susan James. London: Routledge.

Karpat, Kemal. 1982. "Millets and Nationality: The Roots of the Incongruity of Nation and State in the Post-Ottoman Era." In Benjamin Braude and Bernard Lewis, eds., *Christians and Jews in the Ottoman Empire: The Functioning of a Plural Society.* New York: Holmes & Meir.

Kristeva, Julia. 1993. *Nations without Nationalism,* trans. Leon S. Roudiez. New York: Columbia University Press.

Kukathas, Chandran. 1993. "The Idea of a Multicultural Society" and "Multiculturalism and the Idea of an Australian Identity." In *Multicultural Citizens: The Philosophy and Political Identity,* ed. Chandran Kukathas. St. Leonard's: Centre for Independent Studies.

Kymlicka, Will, and J. W. Norman. 1994. "Return of the Citizen." *Ethics* 104, no. 2:352–81.

Lenoble, Jacques. 1992. "Penser l'identité et la démocratie en Europe." In Lenoble and Dewandre 1992.

Lenoble, Jacques, and Nicole Dewandre, eds. 1992. *L'Europe au soir du siècle: Identité et démocratie.* Paris: Esprit.

Macedo, Stephen. 1990. *Liberal Virtues: Citizenship, Virtue and Community.* Oxford: Oxford University Press.

Marshall, T. H. 1965. *Class, Citizenship and Social Development.* New York: Anchor.

Miller, David. 1989. *Market, State and Community: The Foundations of Market Socialism.* Oxford: Oxford University Press.

———. 1993. "In Defense of Nationality." *Journal of Applied Philosophy* 10, no. 1:3–16.

Modood, Tariq. 1994. "Establishment, Multiculturalism, and British Citizenship." *Political Quarterly* 65, no. 1:53–73.

Norman, W. J. 1994. "Towards a Normative Theory of Federalism." In *Group Rights,* ed. Judith Baker. Toronto: University of Toronto Press.

Ordeshook, Peter. 1993. "Some Rules of Constitutional Design." *Social Philosophy and Policy* 10, no. 2:198–232.

Parekh, Bhikhu. 1990. "The Rushdie Affair: Research Agenda for Political Philosophy." *Political Studies* 38:695–709.

Parry, Geraint. 1991. "Paths to Citizenship." In *The Frontiers of Citizenship,* ed. Ursula Vogel and Michael Moran. New York: St. Martin's.

Pateman, Carole. 1988. "The Patriarchal Welfare State." In *Democracy and the Welfare State,* ed. Amy Gutmann. Princeton, N.J.: Princeton University Press.

Porter, John. 1987. *The Measure of Canadian Society.* Ottawa: Carleton University Press.

Rawls, John. 1980. "Kantian Constructivism in Moral Theory." *Journal of Philosophy* 77, no. 9.

———. 1987. "The Idea of an Overlapping Consensus." *Oxford Journal of Legal Studies* 7, no. 1.

———. 1989. "The Domain of Political and Overlapping Consensus." *New York University Law Review* 642:233–55.

Rubinstein, Alvin. 1993. "Is Statehood for Puerto Rico in the National Interest?" In *Depth: A Journal for Values and Public Policy* (Spring):87–99.

Sigler, Jay. 1983. *Minority Rights: A Comparative Analysis.* Westport, Conn.: Greenwood.

Smith, Anthony. 1993. "A Europe of Nations — or the Nation of Europe?" *Journal of Peace Research* 30, no. 2:129–35.

Taylor, Charles. 1991. "Shared and Divergent Values." In *Options for a New Canada,* ed. Ronald Watts and D. Brown. Toronto: University of Toronto Press.

———. 1992a. "The Politics of Recognition." In *Multiculturalism and the "Politics of Recognition,"* ed. Amy Gutmann. Princeton, N.J.: Princeton University Press.

———. 1992b. "Quel principe d'identité collective." In Lenoble and Dewandre 1992.

Walzer, Michael. 1983. *Spheres of Justice: A Defense of Pluralism and Equality.* Oxford: Blackwell.

Whitaker, Reg. 1992. *A Sovereign Idea: Essays on Canada as a Democratic Community.* Montreal: McGill-Queen's University Press.

# 10

## Toward a Postnational Model of Membership
### YASEMIN NUHOĞLU SOYSAL

. . . Guestworkers in Western nation-states . . . even without formal citizenship status . . . are incorporated into various legal and organizational structures of the host society. . . . Reflecting upon guestworker membership, I analyze the changing structure and meaning of citizenship in the contemporary world. I introduce a new model of membership, the main thrust of which is that individual rights, historically defined on the basis of nationality, are increasingly codified into a different scheme that emphasizes universal personhood. I formalize the model by comparing it with the national model of citizenship and specifying its distinctive elements. The articulation of this model sets the stage for the further elaboration of dualities in the rules of the postwar global system, which, while insisting on the nation-state and its sovereignty, at the same time legitimate a new form of membership that transcends the boundaries of the nation-state.

### GUESTWORKERS AND CITIZENSHIP: OLD CONCEPTS, NEW FORMATIONS

The postwar era is characterized by a reconfiguration of citizenship from a more particularistic one based on nationhood to a more universalistic one based on personhood. Historically, citizenship and its rights and privileges have expanded in waves, with changes in how the national public is defined in relation to class, gender, and age (Marshall 1964; Ramirez 1989; Turner 1986a, 1986b). Each wave has represented the entry of a new segment of population into the national polity; workers, women, and children were eventually included in the definition of citizenship.[1] This universalizing movement has made exclusions based on any criteria of ascribed status incompatible with the institution of citizenship (Turner 1986a:92–100). The expansion, however, was limited from within: the rights of men, women, and children, as individuals, were defined with respect to their membership in a particular nation-state. In that sense, the expansion of rights protracted and reinforced particularities ordained by national attributes. In contrast, in the postwar era, an intensified discourse of personhood and human rights has rent the bounded universality of national citizenship, generating contiguities beyond the limits of national citizenry. Accordingly, contemporary membership formations have superseded the dichotomy that opposes the national citizen and the alien, by including populations that were previously defined as outside the national polity. Rights that used to belong solely to nationals are now extended to foreign populations, thereby undermining the very basis of national citizenship. This transformation requires a new understanding of citizenship and its foundation.

Recent studies recognize the disparity between the national citizenship model and the membership of postwar migrants in European host countries. Tomas Hammar (1986, 1990), for instance, argues that foreigners who are long-term residents of European states, and who possess substantial rights and privileges, should be given a new classification, and suggests the term *denizen*. In the same vein, Brubaker (1989a, 1989b) maintains that the membership forms generated by postwar immigration deviate from the norms of classical nation-state membership, which he views as "egalitarian, sacred, national, democratic, unique, and socially consequential." In acknowledging these deviations, he offers a model of "dual membership" organized as concentric circles: an inner circle of citizenship, based on nationality, and an outer circle of denizenship, based on residency. Both Hammar and Brubaker contend that, in regard to rights of immigrants, the crucial determinant is residence, not citizenship. Similar versions of the denizen model have been discussed in Heisler and Heisler 1990, Layton-Henry 1990a, Fullinwider 1988, and d'Oliveira 1984.

Heisler and Heisler (1990) attribute the emergence of the denizenship status to the existence of a "mature" welfare state. They suggest that the elaborate redistribution machinery and the "ethos of equality" of the welfare state have led to the widening of the scope of citizenship in European societies. States of Europe have indeed expanded their comprehensive welfare apparatuses to guestworkers and their families. However, there is nothing inherent about the logic of the welfare state that would dictate the incorporation of foreigners into its system of privileges. Welfare states are also conceived as "compelled by their logic to be closed systems that seek to insulate themselves from external pressures and that restrict rights and benefits to members" (Freeman 1986:51; see also Leibfried 1990). Not that this logic of closure is empirically realized in the world of welfare states. Many of the most advanced welfare states, especially those that are small in size and trade-dependent, have open economies that operate as part of an increasingly integrated global economy (Katzenstein 1985; Cameron 1978).[2] Nevertheless, welfare states are expected to operate with the assumption of closure: the effective distribution of welfare among citizens and maintenance of high standards of benefits and services require the exclusion of noncitizens (see Schuck and Smith 1985; Walzer 1983). As such, the welfare state is universal only within national boundaries.

The denizenship model depicts changes in citizenship as an expansion of scope on a *territorial* basis: the principle of domicile augments the principle of nationality. Denizens acquire certain membership rights by virtue of living and working in host countries. Within this framework, denizenship becomes for the nation-state and its citizenry an irregularity that should be corrected in the long run (see Heisler and Heisler 1990, and the articles in Brubaker 1989c and Layton-Henry 1990b).

In construing changes in citizenship as territorial, these studies remain within the confines of the nation-state model. They do not recognize the changing basis and legitimacy of membership or the recent, fundamental changes in the relationship between the individual, the nation-state, and the world order. As I see it, the incorporation of guestworkers is no mere expansion of the scope of national citizenship, nor is it an irregularity. Rather, it reveals a profound transformation in the institution of citizenship, both in its institutional logic and in the way it is legitimated. To locate the changes, we need to go beyond the nation-state.

## A Model for Postnational Membership

This section introduces a model of membership that delineates the contemporary restructuring and reconfiguration of citizenship. The summary in the table compares this model, which I call *postnational,* with the classical model of national citizenship as conceptualized in political sociology. The two models differ in various dimensions. A comparative discussion, in terms of each dimension, follows.

## TIME PERIOD

The modern history of citizenship begins with the French Revolution. Although the idea of national citizenship emerged at the time of the Revolution, the realization of this particular form of membership occurred much later. Only quite recently has national citizenship become a powerful construct. The classical instruments for creating a national citizenry, the first compulsory education laws and universal (male) suffrage acts, were not enacted before the mid-nineteenth century (Ramirez and Soysal 1989; Soysal and Strang 1989). Moreover, construction of the dichotomy between national citizens and aliens, through the first immigration and alien acts, and made visible in the introduction of passports, identity cards, and visas, did not take place until as late as the First World War.[3]

TABLE 1. COMPARISON OF NATIONAL AND POSTNATIONAL MODELS OF MEMBERSHIP

| DIMENSION | MODEL I: NATIONAL CITIZENSHIP | MODEL II: POSTNATIONAL MEMBERSHIP |
|---|---|---|
| TIME PERIOD | 19th to mid-20th centuries | Postwar |
| TERRITORIAL | Nation-state bounded | Fluid boundaries |
| CONGRUENCE BETWEEN MEMBERSHIP AND TERRITORY | Identical | Distinct |
| RIGHTS/PRIVILEGES | Single status | Multiple status |
| BASIS OF MEMBERSHIP | Shared nationhood (national rights) | Universal personhood (human rights) |
| SOURCE OF LEGITIMACY | Nation-state | Transnational community |
| ORGANIZATION OF MEMBERSHIP | Nation-state | Nation-state |

The reconfiguration of citizenship is mainly a postwar phenomenon. Even as the nation-state and its membership became authorized and taken-for-granted, its classificatory premises were beginning to be contested.

By the 1960s, the classical model of nation-state membership was loosening its grip on the Western world, while consolidation of national polity and citizenship was an impassioned item on the agenda of many countries in Africa and Asia. The increasing flow of goods and persons and the large magnitude of labor migrations after World War II have facilitated this process.

## TERRITORIAL DIMENSION

The classical model is nation-state bounded. Citizenship entails a territorial relationship between the individual and the state (Bendix 1977; Weber 1978). It postulates well-defined, exclusionary boundaries and state jurisdiction over the national population within those boundaries. The model thus implies a congruence between membership and territory: only French nationals are entitled to the rights and privileges the French state affords—nobody else.

In the postnational model, the boundaries of membership are fluid; a Turkish guestworker can become a member of the French polity without French citizenship. By holding citizenship in one state while living and enjoying rights and privileges in a different state, guestworkers violate the presumed congruence between membership and territory. The growing number of dual nationality acquisitions further formalizes the fluidity of membership.[4]

The fluid boundaries of membership do not necessarily mean that the boundaries of the nation-state are fluid. Neither does it imply that the nation-state is less predominant than before.[5] Indeed, the nation-states, still acting upon the national model—since their existence is predicated on this model—constantly try to keep out foreigners by issuing new aliens laws and adopting restrictive immigration policies. However, these continued attempts testify that European states have not succeeded in controlling the influx of foreigners. In particular, such measures have failed to prevent migratory flows justified on humanitarian grounds—political asylum and family unification, two major sources of persisting immigration to European countries.

## RIGHTS AND PRIVILEGES

The classic order of nation-states expresses formal equality in the sense of uniform citizenship rights. Citizenship assumes a single status; all citizens are entitled to the same rights and privileges. The postnational model, on the other hand, implies multiplicity of memberships—principal organizational form for empires and city states. As we have seen in the case of guestworkers, the distribution of rights among various groups and citizens is not even. In the emerging European system, certain groups of migrants are more privileged than others: legal permanent residents, political refugees, dual citizens, and nationals of common market countries.[6]

In earlier polities, multiplicity of membership was also a given, but inequality was considered a "natural" characteristic of social order. Differential membership status, such as that of slaves, was thus constructed as part of the formal definition of the polity. Modern polities, however, claim a uniform and universal status for individuals. As Turner (1986a:133) comments, in the modern polity "the particularistic criteria which define the person become increasingly irrelevant in the public sphere." What makes the case of the guestworker controversial is that it violates this claim for unitary status.[7] Rendering differential status unjustifiable within the framework of universalistic personhood, the modern polity encourages a climate for diverse claims to and further expansion of rights.

## BASIS AND LEGITIMATION OF MEMBERSHIP

In the classical model, shared nationality is the main source of equal treatment among members. Citizenship invests individuals with equal rights and obligations on the grounds of shared nationhood. In that sense, the basis of legitimacy for individual rights is located within the nation-state.

However, guestworker experience shows that membership and the rights it entails are not necessarily based on the criterion of nationality. In the postnational model, universal personhood replaces nationhood; and universal human rights replace national rights. The justification for the state's obligations to foreign populations goes beyond the nation-state itself. The rights and claims of individuals are legitimated by ideologies grounded in a transnational community, through international codes, conventions, and laws on human rights, independent of their citizenship in a nation-state. Hence, the individual transcends the citizen. This is the most elemental way that the postnational model differs from the national model.

Universal personhood as the basis of membership comes across most clearly in the case of political refugees, whose status in host polities rests exclusively on an appeal to human rights. Refugees are in essence stateless (some carry a United Nations passport) but are nonetheless still protected and granted rights as individuals.[8] Similarly, the most universalized aspects of citizenship are those immediately related to the person — civil and social rights — which are often the subject of international conventions and discourse. These rights are more commonly secured in international codes and laws, and they permeate national boundaries more easily than universal political rights that still imply a referential proximity to national citizenship.

## ORGANIZATION OF MEMBERSHIP

While the basis and legitimation of membership rights have shifted to a transnational level, membership itself is not really organized in a new scheme. In both models, the responsibility of providing and implementing individual rights lies with national states. In other words, one still has to go through, for instance, the German, British, or French welfare system. The state is the immediate guarantor and provider, though now for "every person" living within its borders, noncitizen as well as citizen. Actually, the very transnational normative system that legitimizes universal personhood as the basis of membership also designates the nation-state as the primary unit for dispensing rights and privileges (Meyer 1980).

This is critical to explaining why residency in a state is consequential in securing various rights. The world is still largely organized on the basis of spatially configured political units; and topographic matrixes still inform the models and praxis of national and international actors. Hence the nation-state remains the central structure regulating access to social distribution. The material realization of individual rights and privileges is primarily organized by the nation-state, although the legitimacy for these rights now lies in a transnational order.

## TRANSNATIONAL SOURCES OF MEMBERSHIP

How can we account for the manifest changes in national citizenship, that celebrated and stubborn construction of the modern era? As it stands, postnational membership derives its force and legitimacy from changes in the transnational order that defines the rules and organization of the nation-state system. I regard two interrelated lines of development as crucial in explaining the reconfiguration of citizenship.

The first one concerns a transformation in the organization of the international state system: an increasing interdependence and connectedness, intensified world-level interaction and organizing, and the emergence of transnational political structures, which altogether confound and complicate nation-state sovereignty and jurisdiction (Abu-Lughod 1989a, 1989b; Boli 1993; Meyer 1980; Robertson 1992). I refer not only to growth in the volume of transactions and interactions, which, in relative terms, has not changed significantly over the last century (Thomson and Krasner 1989). More important are qualitative changes in the intensity of these interactions, and their perception by the parties involved.

In the postwar era, many aspects of the public domain that used to be the exclusive preserve of the nation-state have become legitimate concerns of international discourse and action. The case of guestworkers clearly demonstrates this shift. The host states no longer have sole control over migrant populations. The governments of the sending countries and extranational organizations of various kinds also hold claims vis-à-vis these populations, in regard to their lives, education, welfare, family relations, and political activities.[9] A dense set of interactions facilitated by inter- and transnational market and security arrangements (NATO, the EC [European Community, now the European Union], and the UN system) constrain the host states from dispensing with their migrant populations at will. In fact, this system not only delegitimizes host state actions that attempt to dispense with foreigners; it obliges the state to protect them.

This is a different picture from that of nineteenth-century conceptions of the international system, which assume a world of discrete nation-states with exclusive sovereignty over territory and population. In the postwar period, the nation-state as a formal organizational structure is increasingly decoupled from the locus of legitimacy, which has shifted to the global level, transcending territorialized identities and structures. In this new order of sovereignty, the larger system assumes the role of defining rules and principles, charging nation-states with the responsibility to uphold them (Meyer 1980, 1994). Nation-states remain the primary agents of public functions, but the nature and parameters of these functions are increasingly determined at the global level.

The intensification and connectedness of the global system do not necessarily signal that nation-states are organizationally weaker or that their formal sovereignty is questioned. Rather, it refers to the explicitness of global rules and structures, and the increasing invocation of these rules. In that sense, nation-states, as authorized actors, function concurrently with inter- and transnational normative structures, ordering and organizing individuals' lives.

The second major development is the emergence of universalistic rules and conceptions regarding the rights of the individual, which are formalized and legitimated by a multitude of international codes and laws. International conventions and charters ascribe universal rights to persons regardless of their membership status in a nation-state. They oblige nation-states *not* to make distinctions on the grounds of nationality in granting civil, social, and political rights. The Universal Declaration of Human Rights (1948) unequivocally asserts that "all beings are born free and equal in dignity and rights, independent of their race, color, national or ethnic origin." The International Covenant on Civil and Political Rights (1966) further imposes a responsibility on the state to respect and ensure the rights of "all individuals within its territory and subject to its jurisdiction" (Goodwin-Gill, Jenny, and Perruchoud 1985:558). The European Convention on Human Rights (1950) expounds almost identical provisions, with further protection against the collective expulsion of aliens. Both the Universal Declaration of Human Rights and the European Convention have been incorporated into the constitutions and laws of many countries.[10]

In addition to these principal codes of human rights, many aspects of international migration, including the status of migrant workers and their particular rights, have been elaborated and regularized through a complex of international treaties, conventions, charters, and recommendations. Some of these instruments originated in the early 1950s, at the onset of large-scale labor migration. Over time, their span has expanded to include entry and residence, the rights to choice and security of employment, working conditions, vocational training and guidance, trade-union and collective bargaining rights, social security, family reunification, education of migrant children, and associative and participatory rights, as well as individual and collective freedoms. These conventions differ in scope. Some have universal application; others are country-specific. Nonetheless, they all aim to set standards for the "equitable" treatment of migrants and the elimination of disparities between nationals and migrants of different categories.

The conventions concluded under the aegis of the International Labor Office (ILO) and the Council of Europe are especially noteworthy.[11] According to the ILO Convention of 1949, the contracting states agree to treat migrant workers "without discrimination in respect of nationality, race, religion, or sex" regarding employment, conditions of work, trade union membership, collective bargaining, and accommodation (ILO n.d.:2). The 1975 convention goes further, promoting the social and cultural rights of migrant workers and their families, in addition to provisions strictly concerned with labor. It explicitly states that the participating countries will take all steps to assist migrant workers and their families "to maintain their own culture" and to provide for their children "to learn their own mother tongue" (ILO 1986:7).

In a similar vein, the 1955 Convention of the European Council on Establishment requires the contracting parties "to treat the nationals of the other contracting states on a basis of equality and to secure for them the enjoyment of civil rights . . . [and] the same economic rights as are possessed by nationals of the state in which the alien is established" (Plender 1985:3). Later conventions of the Council (1961, 1977) introduce provisions regarding freedom of association and information, residence and work permits, social security, social and medical assistance, and family reunification. More recently, the Council has given priority to extending the lists of individuals' rights, specifically to include further rights in the cultural and political spheres. The Council organizes meetings and conferences to promote cultural rights and make national and local authorities aware of "specificities" of minorities, both native and foreign.

More generally, the United Nations has produced a series of instruments with implications for international migration and migrants. The UNESCO Declaration on Race and Racial Prejudice (1978) extends provisions for the cultural rights of migrants—the right to be different, to have one's cultural values respected, and to receive instruction in one's mother tongue. The United Nations Convention on the Protection of the Rights of All Migrant Workers and Their Families, adopted in 1990, aims to establish universal standards that transcend national definitions of foreigners' status. The convention guarantees minimum rights to every migrant, including women and undocumented aliens and their families (see *International Migration Review* 1991). In doing so, it constructs the category of "migrant worker," including such subcategories as "seasonal worker" and "frontier worker," as a universal status with legitimate rights. The ILO and the European Council also have provisions dealing specifically with illegal aliens and their protection (Niessen 1989).

Lastly, political refugees are protected by a set of international legal instruments designed to ensure their rights. According to the Geneva Convention on the Legal Status of Refugees (1951), persons shall not be forced to return to their country of origin if they have a "well-founded fear of persecution" for reasons of race, religion, nationality, membership of a particular social group or political opinion. The Convention further guarantees treatment in the country of asylum equal with that of nationals in regard to religious freedom, acquisition of property, rights of association, and access to courts and public education (Plender 1985).

The multitude and scope of these instruments are impressive. The rights defined and codified assure not just the economic, civil, and social rights of individual migrants—membership rights, in Marshall's terms— but also the cultural rights of migrant groups as collectivities. Within this context, the collective rights of foreigners—the right to an ethnic identity, culture, and use of one's native tongue—emerge as a locus of international legal action.[12] . . .

The most comprehensive legal enactment of a transnational status for migrants is encoded in European Communities law. Citizenship in one EC member state confers rights in all of the others, thereby breaking the link between the status attached to citizenship and national territory. The provisions specify a migrant regime under which European Community citizens are entitled to equal status and treatment with the nationals of the host country. The basic tenets of this regime are as follows:

- Citizens of member states have the right to free movement, gainful employment, and residence within the boundaries of the Community.
- Community law prohibits discrimination based on nationality among workers of the member states with regard to employment, social security, trade union rights, living and working conditions, and education and vocational training.
- Community law obliges host states to facilitate teaching of the language and culture of the countries of origin within the framework of normal education and in collaboration with those countries.
- The Commission of the European Community recommends full political rights in the long run for Community citizens living in other member states. Under current arrangements, they have the right to vote and stand as candidates in local and European elections.[13]

These rights are protected by a growing body of directives, regulations, and laws that locates them within a human rights context (Commission of the European Communities 1989). Moreover, the 1991 Maastricht treaty has created the status of citizen of the Community, to "strengthen the protection of the rights and interests of the nationals of its member states." The treaty foresees a multilevel citizenship structure that guarantees rights independently of membership in a particular state. Thus, the Community as a supranational organization establishes a direct relationship with individuals in the member nation-states. As such, "European citizenship" clearly embodies postnational membership in its most elaborate legal form. It is a citizenship whose legal and normative bases are located in the wider community, and whose actual implementation is assigned to the member states.

At present, the new Community citizenship and the free-movement provision do not apply to nationals of non-EC countries, who constitute the majority of the migrant populations in Europe. For non-EC migrants, the Community has issued guidelines toward the equalization of their status with that of nationals of EC countries. In 1989, for example, the Community adopted the Charter of the Fundamental Rights of Workers, which requires the member states to guarantee workers and their families from nonmember countries living and working conditions comparable to those of EC nationals. More directly, with its authority to engage in international treaties, the Community has made agreements with several non-EC sending countries. These bilateral agreements incorporate the rights of non-EC foreign workers into the legal framework of the Community with provisions in regard to social security, working conditions, and wages, under which workers and their families from signing countries can claim benefits on equal terms with community citizens (Callovi 1992).[14]

My intention in citing all of these instruments and regimes is to draw attention to the proliferation of transnational arrangements, grounded in human rights discourse, that address the rights and interests of migrants and refugees. These instruments and regimes provide guidelines as to the management of migrant affairs for national legislation, by standardizing and rationalizing the category and status of the international migrant. Like other transnational instruments, the charters and conventions regarding guest-workers do not for the most part entail formal obligations or enforceable rules. This does not mean that they do not effect binding dispositions. By setting norms, framing discourses, and engineering legal categories and legitimate models, they enjoin obligations on nation-states to take action. They define goals and levels of competence, and compel nation-states to achieve specific standards. They form a basis for the claims of migrants shaping the platforms of migrant organizations as well as other public interests. They generate transnational activity and stir up publicity regarding migrant issues.

One of the ways international instruments affect nation-state action on migrants is through the construction of migrants as a legal category. Statutes on aliens, migrant workers, and refugees, which entitle migrants to claim legal protection on the basis of human rights, are now established branches of international law (Perruchoud 1986). In the case of the European Community and the European Council, extragovernmental bodies have been established, to interpret and give meaning to international codes and laws, thereby both constraining and enabling nation-state jurisdiction in many ways. One such example is the European Court of Human Rights. According to the European Convention of Human Rights, individual citizens of the European Council countries, as well as nongovernmental organizations or groups, can appeal directly to the European Court, whose decisions are binding on member states. In the last two decades, the caseload of the European Court has increased drastically, with some 5,500 complaints filed each year (Lester 1993). The Court has given a significant number of rulings on individual rights in recent years, including decisions on immigration and family unification.

Corresponding to this growth in the activity of the European Court, national courts increasingly invoke the European Human Rights Convention. The resulting panoply of human rights arrangements generates interesting cases. For example, in 1992, a Sudanese political refugee in Germany fled to Britain for asylum, fearing racial persecution in Germany. The British government decided to send him back to Germany, his first port of entry; however, a British high-court judge ordered the government to halt the deportation in accord with the European Convention on Human Rights, acknowledging that in Germany he might be in danger of attack by neo-Nazis (*Economist,* 15 February 1992). In an earlier case, some East-African Asians, by appealing to the European Convention of Human Rights, were able to contest their exclusion from the United Kingdom under the 1968 Commonwealth Immigrants Act, which subjected the populations from the New Commonwealth to immigration controls (Plender 1986). Thereby, an international human rights instrument superseded the decision of the British Parliament.

The Court of Justice of the European Community, another supranational legal arrangement, oversees individual or state-level complaints that fall within Community Law. The Court has the task of harmonizing national laws with those of the Community. Fourteen percent of the cases brought before the European Court of Justice between 1953 and 1986 were related to the free movement of workers and their dependents, the right of abode and work, and other social issues (Commission of the European Communities 1987). The European Convention on Human Rights has been cited frequently by the Court of Justice in elaborating the general principles of Community law and making decisions (Brown and McBride 1981).

In addition to their effect in the realm of legal rights, transnational laws, rules, conventions, and recommendations also directly influence nation-state policy and action. Let me cite some examples to illustrate this point. The inspiration for foreigners' assemblies and advisory councils came from a directive of the fifth session of the European Conference on Local Powers in 1964 (Sica 1977). Acting upon this directive, European host governments established several such assemblies and councils between 1968 and 1978 (Miller 1981). In creating specialized social service centers for migrants, the EC Commission's recommendation of 1962 constituted the basis upon which many national governments acted (Dumon 1977). In the early 1970s, the participation rights for foreigners in the workplace were mainly introduced by the expansion of the European Community law and practice. Similarly, the European Community General Directive on Education of Migrant Workers (1977) afforded a backdrop for national provisions for teaching migrant children their own language and culture. In collaboration with sending countries, many European host states have established arrangements for such instruction.

Existing national policies are also sometimes revised in response to transnational instruments. In Sweden, limitations on the political activity of aliens were rescinded in 1954 as an effect of the European Convention on Human Rights and Fundamental Freedoms (Hammar 1985b). Similarly, in 1985 the Austrian Supreme Court ruled the Foreigners Police Law unconstitutional, "since it did not accord with Article 8 of the European Convention on Human Rights, . . . interfering with private and family life" of migrants (Bauböck and Wimmer 1988:664). This decision resulted in an amendment of the law, requiring the foreigners police to take into account an individual's family situation and length of residence before making a decision about deportation.

All of these examples substantiate the impact of transnational instruments in the rationalization of the status of international migrant. Migrants' rights increasingly expand within the domain of human rights, supported by a growing number of transnational networks and institutions. The crucial point is that this intensified transnational modus operandi very much determines the discourse of membership and rights on the national level. The universalistic conceptions of rights and personhood become formally institutionalized norms through the agency of an array of collectivities — international governmental and nongovernmental organizations, legal institutions, networks of experts, and scientific communities. These collectivities, by advising national governments, enforcing legal categories, crafting models and standards, and producing reports and recommendations, promote and diffuse ideas and norms about universal human rights that in turn engender a commanding discourse on membership.[15] The same discourse is adopted by states, organizations, and individuals in granting and claiming rights and privileges, thereby reenacting the transnational discourse.

Human rights discourse is widely evoked in national policy language and government rhetoric pertaining to the rights of international migrants. As Catherine de Wenden remarks, since 1981, French immigration policies have been transformed from "a mere body of laws dealing with labor" to legislation and governmental guidelines that prescribe "equal treatment of foreigners and nationals, and human rights." Over the years, the basic rights of migrants, including "the fundamental right to a family life" and the "expression and representation of migrants in a multicultural France," have become part of policy discourse (de Wenden 1987). After the electoral victory of conservative and centrist parties in 1993, the French parliament passed a series of restrictive laws concerning the nationality code, family unification, and illegal immigration. The restrictions were criticized not only by civil rights groups and opposition parties, but also by prominent cabinet members, expressing concerns about human rights (*New York Times,* 23 June 1993).[16] The French Constitutional Council ruled against the legislation concerning family unification on the grounds that it would violate the rights of migrants as individuals. The Council reasoned that "foreigners are not French, but they are human beings" (*Le Monde,* 16 August 1993).

Germany's policy language and official rhetoric have also changed over time. In 1981, Richard von Weizsaecker, then the mayor of West Berlin, insisted that foreigners must decide between repatriation and becoming Germans (Castles 1985). In the 1990s, however, Berlin offers its foreign residents a "multicultural society" and "no forced integration," as was noted in the official address of the secretary of the Berlin City State at a conference at the Free University in June 1990. The term *multicultural society* is invoked in public debates and has gained currency among experts on foreigners' issues and government officials responsible for implementing policies of integration.

As attacks on migrants and asylum seekers have risen, the debate about easing Germany's restrictive nationality law and allowing dual citizenship has intensified. The argument of the Social Democratic Party for extending dual citizenship was that "it would send a signal to our foreign residents that we fully recognize them as human beings" (Reuter news agency, 4 June 1993).[17] The major rally organized by the government to protest the killings of three Turkish migrants by neo-Nazis convened under a banner proclaiming that "Human Dignity Is Inviolable" (*Boston Globe,* 8 November 1992). In addressing another such protest, Richard von Weizsaecker, the president of Germany, reasserted the theme of human dignity: "The first article of our constitution does not say 'the dignity of Germans is inviolable' but 'the dignity of man is inviolable'" (United Press International, 3 June 1993).

In much official debate, arguments for furthering the rights of migrants are typically presented in terms of the inalienable right of personhood. For example, the Belgian delegation to the 1981 Conference of European Ministers, in making a case for multicultural policies, reasoned that "any attempt to deprive a people of its history, culture, and language produces human beings who are incomplete and incapable both of forming plans for the future and of participating in community life and politics. It is to prevent alienation of this kind that any initiative permitting multilingual and multicultural education and a well-developed community life must be encouraged" (Council of Europe 1981:205). Claims for the political rights of migrants are framed within the same discourse: "The migrant's integration — apart from economic, social, and cultural aspects — involves the question of political participation, since the migrant has a political dimension, as does any other human being; his status in the receiving country cannot be divorced from this fundamental dimension" (*International Migration* 1977:78, citing the conclusions of the seminar on Adaptation and Integration of Permanent Immigrants of the Intergovernmental Committee for Migration [ICM]). Such an understanding of political rights clearly contradicts the construction of the individual's political existence as a national citizen.

Migrants themselves repeatedly urge the universalistic concept of personhood as the grounding principle for membership rights. Claims for membership become publicly coded as human rights, as is clearly discernible from the platforms and action programs of foreigners. In its sixth congress in Stockholm, the European Trade Union Confederation called for a more "humanitarian European unity," referring to the rights of migrant workers, especially those from the non-EC countries (*Ikibin'e Dogru,* 29 January 1989). Debates about local voting rights invariably center on the universal/humanistic versus national/particularistic controversy. The most notable argument put forth is that "the right to take part in the political process of one's country of residence is an essential aspect of human life" (Rath 1990:140). In their manifesto for local voting rights, the foreigners' organizations in Switzerland explicitly referred to humans' "natural right" of self-determination. The motto of the 1990 voting rights campaign of migrants in Austria was "Voting Rights Are Human Rights" (*Milliyet,* 10 October 1990). All these claims portray suffrage not only as a participatory right, but as an essential aspect of human personhood.

Human rights discourse dominates calls for cultural rights, as well. Multiculturalism, the right to be different and to foster one's own culture, is elementally asserted as the natural and inalienable right of all individuals. What is ironic is that the preservation of particularistic group characteristics — such as language, a customary marker of national identity — is justified by appealing to universalistic ideas of personhood. The Turkish Parents Association in Berlin demands mother-tongue instruction in schools on the grounds that "as a human being, one has certain natural rights. To learn and enrich one's own language and culture are the most crucial ones" (from the 1990 pamphlet of the association). In the same vein, the Initiative of Turkish Parents and Teachers in Stuttgart publicized its cause with the slogan "Mother Tongue Is Human Right" (*Milliyet,* 4 October 1990).

Urging Islamic instruction in public schools, migrant associations also assert the natural right of individuals to their own cultures. During the 1987 national elections, Islamic associations in Britain justified their demands for the observance of Islamic rules in public schools and the recognition of Muslim family law by invoking the Declaration of Human Rights and the Declaration on the Elimination of All Forms of Intolerance Based on Religion or Belief (Centre for the Study of Islam and Christian-Muslim Relations 1987). In May 1990, when the local authorities refused to permit the opening of another Islamic primary school, the Islamic Foundation in London decided to take the issue to the European Court of Human Rights. As part of the debate over the *foulard* affair in France, the head of the Great Mosque of Paris declared the rules preventing the wearing of scarves in school to be discriminatory. He emphasized personal rights, rather than religious duties: "If a girl asks to have her hair covered, I believe it is her most basic right" (*Washington Post,* 23 October 1989). Accordingly, the closing statement of the fourth European Muslims Conference made an appeal for the rights of Muslims as "human beings" and "equal members" of European societies (*Kirpi,* July 1990:15).

In all of these examples, the prevalence of transnational discourse is evident. Membership rights are recast as human rights; governments, organizations, and individuals recurrently appeal to this "higher-order" principle. The changes I have delineated indicate not only the empirical extension of rights, but the existence of legitimate grounds upon which new and more extensive demands can be made. The dominance of human rights discourse, and the definition of individuals and their rights as abstract universal categories, license even foreign populations to push for further elaboration of their rights. The fact that rights, and claims to rights, are no longer confined to national parameters supports the premise of a postnational model of membership.

One caveat: although my discussion draws on cases from Western Europe, the arguments I develop are not exclusive to Europe. As the transnational norms and discourse of human rights permeate the boundaries of nation-states, the postnational model is activated and approximated worldwide. However, in countries where the nation-building efforts are still under way, or are contested by alternative groups or ideologies, national citizenship constitutes a significant category and has important organizational consequences. In such cases, the boundaries between citizens and noncitizens are sharply constructed, without much space for ambiguity. The expulsion of hundreds of thousands of Ghanaian laborers from Nigeria in 1983 is an example (Plender 1985). Similarly, during the 1990 Gulf war, when the Yemeni government sided with Iraq, Saudi Arabia deported about a half-million Yemeni workers, some of whom were longtime residents (Esman 1992). In most of these countries, definitions and categories of foreign labor and their rights are not as elaborately codified and institutionalized as they are in the West. In several of the Gulf countries, for example, there are few labor codes, and international labor conventions have not been ratified (Nakhleh 1977).[18] Foreign workers in these systems are generally excluded from most forms of participatory rights and entitlements. Obvious examples are Turks in Libya, Indians and Pakistanis in Saudi Arabia, and Filipinos and Sinhalese in other Gulf states—but, note also the Palestinians in Israel and Iranians and Koreans in Japan.

## The Dialectics of Postnational Membership and the Nation-State

Unfolding episodes of world politics in the 1990s may seem to contradict my assertions about postnational membership and the declining significance of national citizenship. Consider the reinventions and reassertions of national(ist) narratives throughout the world: fierce struggles for ethnic or national closure, in former Yugoslavia, Somalia, India, and Ireland; the violent vocalization of antiforeigner groups throughout Europe, accompanied by demands for restrictive refugee and immigration policies.

How can we account for these seemingly contradictory propensities? In order to untangle such trends from the perspective of this essay, let me return to the dialectical dualities of the global system with which I began.

The apparent paradoxes reflected in postwar international migration emanate from the institutionalized duality between the two principles of the global system: national sovereignty and universal human rights. The same global-level processes and institutional frameworks that foster postnational membership also reify the nation-state and its sovereignty.

The principle of human rights ascribes a universal status to individuals and their rights, undermining the boundaries of the nation-state. The principle of sovereignty, on the other hand, reinforces national boundaries and invents new ones. This paradox manifests itself as a deterritorialized expansion of rights despite the territorialized closure of polities. The postwar period has witnessed a vast proliferation in the scope and categories of universalistic rights. Human rights have expanded beyond a conventional list of civil rights to include such social and economic rights as employment, education, health care, nourishment, and housing. The collective rights of nations and peoples to culture, language, and development have also been recodified as inalienable human rights. Women's rights have become "women's human rights" of freedom from gender violence and "certain traditional or customary practices, cultural prejudices and religious extremism" (from the draft document of the 1993 World Conference on Human Rights, cited in the *New York Times,* 16 June 1993).[19]

Incongruously, inasmuch as the ascription and codification of rights move beyond national frames of reference, postnational rights remain organized at the national level. The nation-state is still the repository of educational, welfare, and public health functions and the regulator of social distribution. Simply put, the exercise of universalistic rights is tied to specific states and their institutions. Even though its mode and scope of action are increasingly defined and constrained by the wider global system, the sovereign nation-state retains the formally and organizationally legitimate form venerated by the ideologies and conventions of transnational reference groups such as the UN, UNESCO, and the like.

Expressions of this duality between universalistic rights and the territorially confined nation-state abound. Faced with a growing flux of asylum seekers in the 1990s, Western states have defensively reconsidered their immigration policies. Regulation of immigration is often articulated as indispensable to national sovereignty, and several host countries have initiated restrictions.[20] On the other hand, the category of refugee has broadened to encompass new definitions of persecution. For example, Canada's Immigration and Refugee Board has begun to grant asylum to women persecuted because of their gender; cases involving rape, domestic violence, and states' restrictions on women's activities qualify for asylum (*New York Times,* 27 September 1993). France recognized "genital mutilation" as a form of persecution in granting asylum to a West African woman (*New York Times Magazine,* 19 September 1993). In the United States, an immigration judge in San Francisco granted asylum to a gay Brazilian man, as a member of a "persecuted social group" in his home country (*New York Times,* 12 August 1993). So, even as Western states attempt to maintain their boundaries through quantitative restrictions, the introduction of expanding categories and definitions of rights of personhood sets the stage for new patterns of asylum, making national boundaries more penetrable.

A parallel dynamic is also manifest in the German government's attempts to control the flow of refugees. At the end of 1990, a significant number of Gypsies from Yugoslavia was denied asylum, but nonetheless allowed to stay after much public debate concerning human rights (*Süddeutsche Zeitung,* 23 November 1990). In 1992, the German government again decided to repatriate Gypsies, "who do not qualify for asylum," to Romania. This time, to "compensate" for human rights, Germany pledged financial aid to assist the Gypsies "reintegrate" into Romanian society (*Boston Globe,* 1 November 1992).[21] Thus, while acting in its "national interest" by denying entry to potential refugees, the German state simultaneously extends its responsibilities beyond its national borders by "providing for the welfare" of deportees.

The European Community, as an emerging political entity, is not immune to the dualities of the global system either. The doctrine of human rights is frequently invoked in European Community texts and provisions. For instance, the Maastricht treaty and other EC conventions declare that immigration policies will comply with "international commitments" to human rights and the "humanitarian traditions" of EC states. Concurrently, the Community is engaged in boundary-maintaining activities through arrangements such as "European citizenship" and the Schengen agreement. While the latter aims at drawing the borders of a supranational entity through common visa and immigration procedures, the former reconstitutes an exclusionary membership scheme at a supranational level. However, constrained by its own discourse, conventions, and laws, the Community establishes, and compels its member states to provide, an expanding range of rights and privileges to migrants from both EC and non-EC countries.

These seemingly paradoxical affinities articulate an underlying dialectic of the postwar global system: while nation-states and their boundaries are reified through assertions of border controls and appeals to nationhood, a new mode of membership, anchored in the universalistic rights of personhood, transgresses the national order of things.

The duality embedded in the principles of the global system is further reflected in the incongruence between the two elements of modern citizenship: identity and rights. In the postwar era, these two elements of citizenship are decoupled. Rights increasingly assume universality, legal uniformity, and abstractness, and are defined at the global level. Identities, in contrast, still express particularity, and are conceived of as being territorially bounded. As an identity, national citizenship—as it is promoted, reinvented, and reified by states and other societal actors—still prevails. But in terms of its translation into rights and privileges, it is no longer a significant construction. Thus, the universalistic status of personhood and postnational membership coexist with assertive national identities and intense ethnic struggles.

Indeed, the explosion of nationalism can be construed as an exponent of the underlying dialectic of the postwar global system. More and more collectivities are asserting their "national identities" and alleging statehood on the basis of their acclaimed "nationness." These claims are fed and legitimated by the highly institutionalized principle of political sovereignty and self-determination, which promises each people an autonomous state of its own. As political practice, national sovereignty may be contested (as in the case of Kuwait and Iraq during the Gulf war), but as a mode of organization, it is yet to have an alternative. Sovereignty provides a protected status in the international realm, authenticated by membership in the United Nations. Thus, even when previous nation-states are dissolving (for example, the Soviet Union and Yugoslavia), the emerging units aspire to become territorial states with self-determination, and the world political community grants them this right. The new (or would-be) states immediately appropriate the language of nationhood, produce anthems and flags, and, of course, pledge allegiance to human rights.

The principle of self-determination further reinforces expressions of nationalism, since, for sovereign statehood, a nationally bounded and unified population is imperative. Therefore, collectivities that have been previously defined simply as ethnicities, religious minorities, or language groups reinvent their "nationness," accentuate the uniqueness of their cultures and histories, and cultivate particularisms to construct their "others" (see Hobsbawm 1990).[22]

At another level, the collective right to self-determination and to political and cultural existence is itself increasingly codified as a universal human right.[23] Claims to particularistic identities, cultural distinctiveness, and self-determination are legitimated by reference to the essential, indisputable rights of persons, and, thus, are recast as world-level, postnational rights. This recodification is, in fact, what Roland Robertson (1992:100) calls "the universalization of particularism and the particularization of universalism." What are considered particularistic characteristics of collectivities — culture, language, and standard ethnic traits — become variants of the universal core of humanness. In turn, as universal attributes and human rights, they are exercised in individual and collective actors' narratives and strategies.

Framing political self-determination and collective cultural rights as universalistic prerogatives occasions ever-increasing claims and mobilizations around particularistic identities. An intensifying world-level discourse of "plurality" that encourages "distinct cultures" within and across national borders contributes to this new dynamism. An identity politics, energized by narrations of collective pasts and accentuated cultural differences, becomes the basis for participation, and affords the means for mobilizing resources in the national and world polities. If one aspect of this dynamism is relegitimization and reification of nationness, the other is its fragmentation, displacement of its meaning, and hence its delegitimization.

A growing tendency toward regionalisms (sometimes separatisms) and their recognition by the central states fragments existing nations and nationalities into infinitely distinct ethnicities and cultural subunits. In Europe more and more groups seek economic and linguistic autonomy on the basis of their regional identities — Bretons, Corsicans, Basques, and Occitans in France; Scots and Welsh in Britain; Lombards and Sardinians in Italy. And European states, even those that have long resisted linguistic and cultural diversity, increasingly accommodate autonomous entities (as in Spain) and provide for regional languages (as in France and Italy).[24] The multiplication of particularisms and subsequent fragmentation disrupt the presumed contiguities of nationness and undermine the territorial sanctity of nation-states.

Furthermore, as particularistic identities are transformed into expressive modes of a core humanness, thus acquiring universal currency, the "nation" loses its charisma and becomes normalized. The idea of nation becomes a trope of convenience for claims to collective rights and identity. Even groups that may not fit the classic definitions of a nation refer to themselves as such: gays and lesbians claim a "Queer Nation"; the Deaf define themselves as a national subgroup with its own cultural peculiarities and language; and indigenous peoples request to be called, not tribes, but nations, and seek a vote in the United Nations. In this universalizing flux, "the ways of 'doing' identity" (Robertson 1992:99) become standardized exercises, with common themes and modes of presentation. At the center of this activity lies the construction of official taxonomies, with reference to routine markers and attributes of culture; that is, the placid images of cuisines, crafts, life-styles, religious symbols, folklores, and customs.

In the context of this normalizing trend, national identities that celebrate discriminatory uniqueness and naturalistic canonizations of nationhood become more and more discredited. It is, for instance, increasingly difficult to protect and practice a code of nationality that inscribes "blood" or "lineage" as its primary principle. Note the widespread reaction to Germany's blood-based citizenship and naturalization laws, and the German government's decision to overhaul these "outdated" laws (Reuter news agency, 12 June 1993). Similarly, national canons that valorize ancestral warmaking and symbols of patriarchy are increasingly less enticing as vehicles for doing identity. It has been truly amazing to observe the remaking of the "Vikings," from warrior forefathers to spirited long-distance traders.[25]

All of these recontextualizations of "nationness" within the universalistic discourse of human rights blur the meanings and boundaries attached to the nation and the nation-state. The idea of the nation persists as an intense metaphor, at times an idiom of war. However, in a world within which rights, and identities as rights, derive their legitimacy from discourses of universalistic personhood, the limits of nationness, or of national citizenship, for that matter, become inventively irrelevant.

## Notes

1. The first international acknowledgment of children's rights was the Declaration of the Rights of the Child, adopted in Geneva in 1923 (Underhill 1979). In 1990, the Convention on the Rights of the Child became international human rights law, affirming the rights of children to survival, protection, development, and education (*International Herald Tribune,* 1 October 1990). See also Boli and Meyer 1987 and Ramirez 1989 for the incorporation of children's rights into national constitutions and agendas.

2. Katzenstein (1985) argues that economic openness and vulnerability to fluctuations in the global economy facilitate welfare and corporatist arrangements in the small states of Europe. Similarly, Cameron (1978) shows that trade dependence has a positive effect on social spending in European countries. Freeman (1986) acknowledges the increasing openness of national economies but considers it a source of tension for the "viability" of the welfare state.

3. Laws had been enacted sporadically to control certain population flows, but systematic immigration regulation and control of aliens were established only after World War I in most European countries (Hammar 1986). The "work permit" is also a relatively new innovation; from the early nineteenth century until the 1920s, one did not need such a permit to enter a country as a fully empowered economic actor.

4. In Sweden, there were 100,000 people with dual citizenship in 1985. Each year, about 10,000 new cases are added (Hammar 1985a). France has over one million Franco-Algerian dual nationals (de Rham 1990). In 1985, the total number of people holding dual citizenship in Western Europe was estimated to be between 3 million and 4 million (Perotti, Costes, and Llaumett 1989).

5. All of the common indicators of state strength show an increase throughout the century (Boli 1987, 1993). At the same time, nation-states are becoming much more vulnerable to outside influences.

6. The 1981 British Nationality Act even formalizes this "multiple status" through legal categories. According to the act, British citizenship is a three-tier system, composed of British citizens, British overseas citizens, and citizens of dependent territories, each with a differential set of rights (Handsworth Law Centre 1985).

7. Contemporary polities like South Africa and Israel that ventured to institutionalize such unequal statuses have been strongly condemned and have failed to maintain their status quo.

8. The very existence of the category "refugee," referring to persons whose most basic rights are denied in their own countries by their own states, demonstrates the fragility of the ideals of personhood and citizenship. Ironically,

refugee status does not apply to people under the sovereignty of their own government, whatever the violation of their basic human rights.

9. See Heisler 1986 for the involvement of sending countries in matters related to the lives of migrants. Most states, for example, recruit and send their own teachers and clergy to perform educational and religious functions for their citizens abroad.

10. Other regional human rights conventions include the American Declaration of the Rights and Duties of Man (1948), the American Convention on Human Rights (1969) accompanied by the Inter-American Court of Human Rights (1979), and the African Charter on Human and People's Rights (1981). Though not in effect, the Arab Charter of Human Rights (1971) and the Draft Arab Covenant on Human Rights (1979) also exist (Donnelly 1986).

11. See Böhning 1988 for a review of ILO activities and labor standards regarding the protection of migrant workers. The Council of Europe, an institution entirely separate from the European Community, principally engages in promoting treaties and agreements between member countries concerning a broad range of human rights and social and economic affairs.

12. Certain collective rights are already included in national legislation. For example, Sweden, the Netherlands, and Belgium recognize the right to use the mother tongue and have arrangements to provide for it. Also, all European Community countries have legislation allowing religious rituals that involve slaughtering animals (Poulter 1986).

13. The provision for local and European voting rights awaits the enactment of the Maastricht treaty, which was ratified by all EC member states in 1993.

14. In 1990, the European Community had agreements with five immigrant-sending countries: Turkey, Algeria, Morocco, Tunisia, and Yugoslavia.

15. These collectivities are referred to as "transnational moral entrepreneurs" (Nadelmann 1990), "epistemic communities" (Ruggie 1975), and "rationalized others" (Meyer 1994).

16. Justice Minister Pierre Méhaignerie and Social Affairs Minister Simone Veil opposed the proposed legislation on identity checks for foreigners, arguing that it may lead to racial discrimination.

17. The call for dual citizenship has also received support from the liberal Free Democrats (FDP), a partner in the ruling coalition, and such prominent members of the Christian Democrats (CDU), the major partner in the coalition, as the president of parliament, Rita Süssmuth, and the mayor of Berlin, Eberhard Diepgen. In addressing a workshop at the Center for European Studies at Harvard University in January 1992, Barbara John, head of the Office of Foreigners' Affairs in Berlin, likened Germany's existing citizenship codes to "tribal membership," and advocated changes toward "club membership."

18. There are regional protocols and charters that aim at regulating migration for employment, including the Protocol on Free Movement of Persons of the Economic Community of West African States and the Charter of the

Organization of African Unity, but they do not contain provisions as comprehensive as the ones I have discussed.

19. The 1993 World Conference on Human Rights was a forum for expanding and redefining human rights beyond their conventional scope. The Conference recognized for the first time the rights of "poor nations" to economic development and the right of women to protection on the basis of gender as inviolable human rights (*New York Times*, 21 June 1993).

20. An urgency about "control over borders" summarizes official rhetoric. In defending Austria's new restrictive asylum law, the director of immigration reasoned that "in international migration, there is a point at which it becomes chaotic and there is no longer a means to control it" (*New York Times*, 10 August 1993).

21. Germany has concluded similar financial aid agreements with other refugee-sending countries such as the former Yugoslavia, Poland, the Czech Republic, and Russia. In 1991, an agreement with the former Yugoslavia for the "reintegration" of Macedonian Gypsies promised a program that included financing of kindergartens and job-training facilities (*Business Week*, 9 September 1991). The practice is not limited to Germany. When Albanian asylum seekers were sent back in 1991, the Italian government allocated "an emergency economic and financial aid package" for Albania (SOPEMI 1992:30).

22. After the political transformations in Eastern Europe, the Baltic states of Latvia and Estonia and the Czech Republic launched exclusive national citizenship schemes creating large noncitizen minorities from populations that had citizenship previously.

23. The right to self-determination is recognized by two major instruments of human rights: the International Covenant on Civil and Political Rights, and the International Covenant on Economic, Social, and Cultural Rights. The first article of both covenants proclaims that "all peoples have the right of self-determination. By virtue of that right, they freely determine their political status and freely pursue their economic, social, and cultural development" (quoted in Dinstein 1976:106).

24. Spain comprises 17 regions with varying degrees of autonomy, some with separate languages. In 1991, Italy recognized 11 minority languages, giving regional authorities substantial discretion to implement bilingualism in schools (*Financial Times*, 22 November 1991). In 1993, the French government asked local authorities to develop bilingual education programs in regions with such indigenous languages as Breton, Flemish, Occitan, Basque, and Catalan (*New York Times*, 3 May 1993).

25. My thanks to John Meyer for reminding me of this point. In 1992 a Viking exhibition, the first of its kind, toured Europe with the usual fare — food tents, on-the-spot craft production, dances and singing, and face painting. The image presented was a tame, domestic one, supplanting the "barbaric" swords, shields, and carnage customarily associated with the Vikings. Similarly, in 1988,

the exhibit "Süleyman, the Magnificent" toured the world and recast the "warlike" reign of that Ottoman sultan as a history of arts, architecture, and legal and administrative reforms.

## BIBLIOGRAPHY

Abu-Lughod, Janet L. 1989a. *Before European Hegemony: The World System, a.d. 1250–1350.* London: Oxford University Press.

———. 1989b. "Restructuring the Premodern World System." Paper presented at the annual meeting of the American Sociological Association, San Francisco.

Bauböck, Rainer, and Hannes Wimmer. 1988. "Social Partnership and 'Foreigners Policy': On Special Features of Austria's Guest-Worker System." *European Journal of Political Research* 16:659–82.

Bendix, Reinhard. 1977. *Nation-Building and Citizenship: Studies of Our Changing Social Order.* Berkeley and Los Angeles: University of California Press.

Böhning, W. R. 1988. "The Protection of Migrant Workers and International Labour Standards." *International Migration* 26:133–45.

Boli, John. 1987. "World Polity Sources of Expanding State Authority and Organization, 1870–1970." In *Institutional Structure: Constituting State, Society, and the Individual,* ed. George M. Thomas et al. Newbury Park, Calif.: Sage.

———. 1993. "Sovereignty from a World Polity Perspective." Paper presented at the annual meeting of the American Sociological Association, Miami.

Boli, John, and John W. Meyer. 1987. "The Ideology of Childhood and the State: Rules Distinguishing Children in National Constitutions, 1870–1970." In *Institutional Structure: Constituting State, Society, and the Individual,* ed. George M. Thomas et al. Newbury Park, Calif.: Sage.

Brown, L. Neville, and Jeremy McBride. 1981. Observation on the Proposed Accession by the European Community to the European Convention on Human Rights. *American Journal of Comparative Law* 29:691–705.

Brubaker, William Rogers. 1989a. Introduction to Brubaker 1989c.

———. 1989b. "Membership without Citizenship: The Economic and Social Rights of Noncitizens." In Brubaker 1989c.

Brubaker, William Rogers, ed. 1989c. *Immigration and Politics of Citizenship in Europe and North America.* Lanham, Md.: University Press of America.

Callovi, Giuseppe. 1992. "Regulation of Immigration in 1993: Pieces of the European Community Jig-Saw Puzzle." *International Migration Review* 26:353–72.

Cameron, David R. 1978. "The Expansion of the Public Economy: A Comparative Analysis." *American Political Science Review* 72:1243–61.

Castles, Stephen. 1985. "The Guests Who Stayed—The Debate on 'Foreigners Policy' in the German Federal Republic." *International Migration Review* 19:517–34.

Centre for the Study of Islam and Christian-Muslim Relations (Birmingham). 1987. "Muslim Demands of the British Political Parties." *News of Muslims in Europe,* no. 40:6–7.

Commission of the European Communities. 1987. "New Rights for the Citizens of Europe." European File, no. 11/87. Luxembourg: Office for Official Publications of the European Communities.

———. 1989. "The European Community and Human Rights." European File, no. 5/89. Luxembourg: Office for Official Publications of the European Communities.

Council of Europe. 1977. *European Convention on the Legal Status of Migrant Workers.* Strasbourg.

———. 1981. "European Migration in the 1980s: Trends and Policies." Conference of European Ministers Responsible for Migration Affairs, Strasbourg, 6–8 May 1980, Records. Strasbourg.

de Rham, Gérard. 1990. "Naturalisation: The Politics of Citizenship Acquisition." In Layton-Henry 1990b.

de Wenden, Catherine Wihtol. 1987. "France's Policy on Migration from May 1981 till March 1986: Its Symbolic Dimension, Its Restrictive Aspects and Its Unintended Effects." *International Migration* 25:211–20.

Dinstein, Yoram. 1976. "Collective Human Rights of Peoples and Minorities." *International and Comparative Law Quarterly* 25:102–20.

d'Oliveira, H. U. Jessurun. 1984. "Electoral Rights for Non-Nationals." *Netherlands International Law Review* 31:59–72.

Donnelly, Jack. 1986. "International Human Rights: A Regime Analysis." *International Organization* 40:559–642.

Dumon, W. A. 1977. "The Activity of Voluntary Agencies and National Associations in Helping Immigrants to Overcome Initial Problems." *International Migration* 15: 113–26.

Esman, Milton J. 1992. "The Political Fallout of International Migration." *Diaspora* 2: 3–41.

Freeman, Gary P. 1986. "Migration and the Political Economy of the Welfare State." *Annals of the American Academy of Political and Social Science* 485:51–63.

Fullinwider, Robert K. 1988. "Citizenship and Welfare." In *Democracy and the Welfare State,* ed. A. Gutmann. Princeton, N.J.: Princeton University Press.

Goodwin-Gill, Guy S. 1989. "International Law and Human Rights: Trends Concerning International Migrants and Refugees." *International Migration Review* 23:526–46.

Goodwin-Gill, Guy S., R. K. Jenny, and Richard Perruchoud. 1985. "Basic Humanitarian Principles Applicable to Non-Nationals." *International Migration Review* 19:556–69.

Hammar, Tomas. 1985a. "Election Year '85: Immigrant Voting Rights and Electoral Turnout." *Current Sweden,* no. 336. Stockholm: Swedish Institute.

———. 1985b. "On Immigrant Status and Civic Rights in Sweden." Paper presented to the research group, European Consortium for Political Research, Paris.

———. 1986. "Citizenship: Membership of a Nation and of a State." *International Migration* 24:735–47.

———. 1990. *International Migration, Citizenship, and Democracy.* Aldershot: Gower.

Handsworth Law Centre. 1985. *Immigration Law Handbook: A Comprehensive Guide to Immigration Law and Practice.* 3d ed. Birmingham.

Heisler, Barbara Schmitter. 1986. "Immigrant Settlement and the Structure of Emergent Immigrant Communities in Western Europe." *Annals of the American Academy of Political and Social Science* 485:76–86.

Heisler, Martin O., and Barbara Schmitter Heisler. 1990. "Citizenship — Old, New, and Changing: Inclusion, Exclusion, and Limbo for Ethnic Groups and Migrants in the Modern Democratic State." In *Dominant National Cultures and Ethnic Identities,* ed. J. Fijalkowski, H. Merkens, and F. Schmidt. Berlin: Free University.

Hobsbawm, Eric. 1990. *Nations and Nationalism since 1780: Programme, Myth, Reality.* Cambridge: Cambridge University Press.

ILO (International Labor Office). 1986. *The Rights of Migrant Workers: A Guide to ILO Standards for the Use of Migrant Workers and Their Organizations.* Geneva: ILO Publications.

———. N.d. *Provisions of the ILO Conventions and Recommendations Concerning Migrant Workers.* Geneva: ILO Publications.

*International Migration.* 1977. Third Seminar on Adaptation and Integration of Permanent Immigrants: Conclusions and Recommendations 15:17–83.

*International Migration Review.* 1991. U.N. International Convention on the Protection of the Rights of All Migrant Workers and Members of Their Families. Special Issue 25(4).

Katzenstein, Peter J. 1985. *Small States in World Markets: Industrial Policy in Europe.* Ithaca, N.Y.: Cornell University Press.

Layton-Henry, Zig. 1990a. "Citizenship or Denizenship for Migrant Workers?" In Layton-Henry 1990b.

Layton-Henry, Zig, ed. 1990b. *The Political Rights of Migrant Workers in Western Europe.* London: Sage.

Leibfried, Stephan. 1990. "Sozialstaat Europa? Integrationsperspektiven europäischer Armutsregimes." Nachrichtendienst des Deutschen Vereins für öffentliche und private Fürsorge (NDV) 70:296–305.

Lester, Anthony. 1993. "Britain Wrong on Human Rights." *Financial Times,* 26 May.

Marshall, T. H. 1964. *Class, Citizenship and Social Development.* Garden City, N.Y.: Doubleday.

Meyer, John W. 1980. "The World Polity and the Authority of the Nation-State." In *Studies of the Modern World System,* ed. A. Bergesen. New York: Academic Press.

———. 1994. "Rationalized Environments." In *Institutional Environments and Organizations,* ed. W. R. Scott and J. W. Meyer. Newbury Park, Calif.: Sage.

Miller, Mark J. 1981. *Foreign Workers in Western Europe: An Emerging Political Force.* New York: Praeger.

Nadelmann, Ethan A. 1990. "Global Prohibition Regimes: The Evolution of Norms in International Society." *International Organization* 44:479–526.

Nakhleh, Emile A. 1977. "Labor Markets and Citizenship in Bahrayn and Qatar." *Middle East Journal* 31:143–56.

Niessen, Jan. 1989. "Migration and (Self-) Employment, Residence, and Work Permit Arrangements in Seventeen European Countries." Maastricht: European Center for Work and Labor. Manuscript.

Perotti, Antonio, André Costes, and Maria Llaumett. 1989. "L'Europe et l'immigration." Part 1: "Les constats." *Migrations société* 1:23–46. Paris: CIEMI.

Perruchoud, R. 1986. "The Law of Migrants." *International Migration* 24:699–716.

Plender, Richard. 1985. "Migrant Workers in Western Europe." *Contemporary Affairs Briefing* 2, no. 14.

———. 1986. "Rights of Passage." In *Towards a Just Immigration Policy,* ed. A. Dummett. London: Cobden Trust.

———. 1988. *International Migration Law.* 2d ed., rev. Dordrecht: Martinus Nijhoff.

Poulter, Sebastian M. 1986. *English Law and Ethnic Minority Customs.* London: Butterworths.

Ramirez, Francisco O. 1989. "Reconstituting Children: Extension of Personhood and Citizenship." In *Age Structuring in Comparative Perspective,* ed. D. Kertzer and K. W. Schaie. Hillsdale, N.J.: Lawrence Erlbaum Associates.

Ramirez, Francisco O., and Yasemin Nuhoğlu Soysal. 1989. "Women's Acquisition of the Franchise: An Event History Analysis." Paper presented at the annual meeting of the American Sociological Association, San Francisco.

Rath, Jan. 1990. "Voting Rights." In Layton-Henry 1990b.

Robertson, Roland. 1992. *Globalization: Social Theory and Global Culture*. London: Sage.

Ruggie, John Gerard. 1975. "International Responses to Technology: Concepts and Trends." *International Organization* 29:557–83.

Schuck, Peter H., and Rogers M. Smith. 1985. *Citizenship without Consent: Illegal Aliens in the American Polity*. New Haven, Conn.: Yale University Press.

Sica, Mario. 1977. "Involvement of the Migrant Worker in Local Political Life in the Host Country." *International Migration* 15:143–52.

SOPEMI-Netherlands. 1992. *Migration, Minorities and Policy in the Netherlands*. Report for the Continuous Reporting System on Migration of the OECD.

Soysal, Yasemin Nuhoğlu, and David Strang. 1989. "Construction of the First Mass Education Systems in Nineteenth-Century Europe." *Sociology of Education* 62:277–88.

Thomson, Janice E., and Stephen D. Krasner. 1989. "Global Transactions and the Consolidation of Sovereignty." In *Global Changes and Theoretical Challenges: Approaches to World Politics for the 1990s*, ed. E. O. Czempiel and J. N. Rosenau. Lexington, Mass.: Lexington Books.

Turner, Bryan S. 1986a. *Citizenship and Capitalism: The Debate over Reformism*. London: Allen and Unwin.

———. 1986b. "Personhood and Citizenship." *Theory, Culture, and Society* 3:1–16.

Underhill, E. 1979. "The Situation of Migrant and Refugee Children in Relation to the United Nations Declaration of the Rights of the Child." *International Migration* 17:122–38.

Walzer, Michael. 1983. *Spheres of Justice: A Defense of Pluralism and Equality*. New York: Basic Books.

Weber, Max. 1978. *Economy and Society: An Outline of Interpretive Sociology*, vol. 1, ed. G. Roth and C. Wittich. Berkeley and Los Angeles: University of California Press.

# PART VII
## THE FEMINIST CRITIQUE

# 11
## *Citizenship in a Woman-Friendly Polity*
### Kathleen B. Jones

Some feminists have argued that women are, at best, second-class citizens in most Western democracies. Not only do women lack the full complement of "rights" included in citizenship, but also the conceptualization of citizenship in these systems — the characteristics, qualities, attributes, behavior, and identity of those who are regarded as full members of the political community — is derived from a set of values, experiences, modes of discourse, rituals, and practices that both explicitly and implicitly privileges men and the "masculine" and excludes women and the "female." As feminists, we have contended that in Western political discourse, citizenship remains defined as an activity practiced in an androcentric field of action and represented through the codes of a phallocentric discourse.[1]

Consequently, some of us have claimed that even if women achieve juridical/legal equality, gain more adequate political representation in lawmaking and administrative bodies, and possess the economic means and personal motivation to practice their rights, and even if women's duties to the state are broadened to include military service, women's membership in the political community still will be less full than men's. Women cannot be seen in public space as women citizens who act politically on their own ground, with their full being-female, because the discourse of citizenship is itself gendered. The dominant conceptualization of citizenship displaces "women, their work, and the values associated with that work from the culturally normative definitions of objectivity, morality, citizenship, and even, of human nature."[2] Within the perspective of the dominant view, it is not women who enter public space but persons who happen to be female.[3] Women's becoming entitled to claim the rights and duties of citizenship remains, in this view, unremarkable except that the numbers of those who make such claims increases.

Such critiques imply that unless we directly challenge the dominant gendered political discourse, women's experiences and self-understandings will be fit into existing paradigms that privilege elite men's behavior and norms, and the relationship between gender and citizenship will be reduced to the "presence or absence of actual women" among the ranks of citizens, ignoring the problem of how the identity of the citizen is described and resisting the idea that women's political practices may subvert the meaning of citizenship itself.[4] In the realm of political theory, feminist formulations constitute just such a subversion. What is behind the detailed investigations of women's experiences of the political is the impulse to articulate the "historically evolv[ing] content of [a] social movement"—the women's movement—which suggests a transformed theory and practice of citizenship.[5] When we claim that we can neither describe nor explain women's political behavior fully within the contours of existing paradigms, we are really questioning the relationship between theory and practice, between concepts and action, or between language and experience. Our project is neither to impose abstract categories onto a presumptively passive social reality nor to assume that social experiences produce concepts in an unmediated, automatic way. Among feminist theorists, some claim that language constructs experience, while others claim that language reflects, or at least only partly shapes, experiences. All of these theorists, nevertheless, are challenging the lions that guard the canonical literature on citizenship.[6]

As feminist theorists, we have foregrounded in our work the sexist bias that sets the terms of membership in Western liberal democracies. In these polities, a citizen is one whose membership is contingent upon the ultimate subordination of the specific bonds of gender, race, and class—indeed, all particularized identities—in favor, most often, of a national identity and loyalty to the state. To become a citizen is to trade one's particular identity for an abstract, public self. But the identification of citizens and the definition of citizenship is derived from the representation of the behavior of a group with particular race, gender, and class characteristics (white, male elites) as the model of citizenship for all individuals. The discursive power of this group includes the ability to define normatively the practice of citizenship. In other words, citizenship is delimited conceptually by falsely universalizing one particular group's practice of it. "Woman qua woman — as symbol of attachment to individual bodies, private interests and natural feeling — represents all that war and citizenship are supposed to contain and transcend," writes Genevieve Lloyd.[7]

We have contended that the values, experiences, modes of discourse, rituals, and practices of those "other" groups excluded categorically from the definition of citizenship might found citizenship in a different way, at least in a way that permits a more diversified and pluralistic model.[8] Just as feminist studies of women's activities and daily life provided the basis for an alternative conceptualization of work, so feminist studies of women's political participation — both implicitly and explicitly feminist practices — provide the basis for an alternative discourse on citizenship.[9] Whether the concept of citizenship can withstand the pressure of these "others," or whether some new concept of political action and political membership is required remains to be seen.

We have just begun to undertake the difficult task of providing new definitions for concepts like citizenship and political action. Much of what feminist theory has contributed exists in fragmentary form, yet to be synthesized and developed into a coherent alternative perspective. Yet this project has critical normative and methodological significance for political science as a field and for the construction of a polity consistent with feminist principles. Whom we recognize as citizens depends upon what qualifies as the behavior of citizens. This, in turn, affects how we study the behavior of citizens and how we claim that behavior might differ in a feminist, woman-friendly community. Revisioning women's experiences, without assuming that those experiences contain, in any literal sense of the word, implicit meanings, has prompted us to rethink the basic categories of political analysis.

The notion of citizenship in a woman-friendly polity is not sufficiently represented by traditional liberal language and discourse about the characteristics and activities of citizenship, which express citizenship primarily in juridico-legal terms as the individual practice of rights. Nor does the orthodox socialist conceptualization of the "citizenship" of associated producers articulate richly enough the textures of feminist citizenship. Moreover, we feminists also have not formulated or articulated a coherent theory of feminist citizenship.

Several themes emerge in feminist political discourse that are particularly relevant to the development of a new theory of citizenship. The focus of some feminist theorists on issues of sexuality, reproduction, and the physical self suggests a renewed attention to the "body" in the "body politic." From this perspective, citizenship is defined as a practice of embodied subjects whose sex/gendered identity affects fundamentally their membership and participation in public life. Within any discourse that defines citizenship as the armed struggle to defend one's way of life, women's bodies are problematic. Since this discourse defines women as weak and as needing (men's) protection, women cannot become active in their own defense without either calling into question their identity as women or threatening the sexual iconography upon which the discourse is based.[10] Some feminists have noted that specific representations of female embodiment and sexuality have "served the purposes both of sexual and [of] racial domination." In this account sexual harassment is a political strategy designed to structure public space in ways that endanger women, hampering or precluding their mobility and regulating the extent to which they can be present in public.[11] When women have acted publicly in ways that challenge the status quo, the official representation of their behavior often has questioned their identity as women or has caricatured such women as sexually wanton and licentious. The conceptual shift suggested in certain feminist studies of women's political action away from armed defense to empowerment as the model for defining women's participation in the activities of citizenship unsettles the connection between male bodies and citizenship.

The feminist politicization of the body and of everyday, private/personal reality increases the range, intensity, and modes of political action. If the scope of politics is broadened by the aphorism "the personal is political," then the arenas for political action (the architecture of public space), the depth of personal commitment and connection to political activity, and the forms of political participation are transformed. Correspondingly, new duties and responsibilities are added to the obligations of members of the political community, and new demands are placed on the state or other organized, political decision-making bodies. Also, new rights are described, for instance, the right to be free from sexual harassment.

Feminist discourse often is permeated by a language that speaks in familial and intimate tones. In our descriptions of the (ideal) social relations among citizens, we tend to replace the disembodied, impersonal descriptors of citizenship that we inherited from classical liberalism with kinship metaphors. Both classical liberals and Enlightenment philosophers employed, to some extent, the family as a metaphor for society. Yet they also distinguished the ways that relations among citizens were different from familial, intimate relations. It was not simply that relations among citizens occurred in public space. The bonds constituted by citizenship subordinated all personal loyalties and allegiances to loyalty to a more abstract entity, the polity. Citizens were shorn of "the particular and ascribed characteristics which distinguish[ed] them in the private sphere, and [thus they] appear[ed] as unrelated equals."[12] With the possible exception of the language of liberal feminism, we feminists have returned to descriptions of political action in familial or personal terms: sisters, mothers, lovers, friends are the citizens of a feminist political community. Nevertheless, we are increasingly aware that applying the logic of intimate relations to the organization of political life is fraught with contradictions, since the shared principles of equality, mutuality of respect, and consensual decision making in face-to-face contexts are called upon to serve the apparently divided purposes of maintaining community and protecting individual interests from erasure.[13]

Our general emphasis on relationships as definitive of personality and selfhood implies a renewed critique of the concept of autonomy embedded in Western political philosophy. Like Marx, many feminists see the individual as the ensemble of social relationships. Yet we include among the central, determinant relationships modes of sexual, personal, and productive activity. Our concern has been to explore the ways that socially connected selves engage in political action as citizens.

Certain feminists have strongly reacted to women's exclusion from, or segregation within, different political forums. They have objected to women's relative lack of access to conventional arenas of political decision making, as well as to women's unequal representation in leadership positions in radical organizations for political change. Feminist ideas about political institutions stress participation almost to the point of obsession. Thus, we have emphasized democratic forms of organization that complement notions of egalitarian citizenship. Connected to this is a return to the Hobbesian stress on homologous authority relations. If democracy is to be sustained, then it must be the mode of organizing society at all levels: in the family, the workplace, the community, and the state.

Related to this rejection of partial democracy is the search for new forms of organization that both are humane and reflect more open and ambiguous organizational structures and behavioral codes. Critical of the way that modern bureaucracies substitute norms of efficiency and depersonalized decision-making rules for flexible administrative methods, some feminist theorists have begun to explore the hidden structures of power that construct the citizen of the modern state as client-beneficiary and, hence, as a regulated subject. This theory recognizes that the neoprotectionism of welfare state systems has a different effect on women's and men's experiences of citizenship, especially poor women for whom client activities are the dominant form of political participation. Their "citizenship" is reduced to making what the state defines as legitimate economic claims.

Our stress on cross-cultural differences among women, often not highlighted enough in feminist theory, has led us to emphasize the importance of building an international feminist community. This shifts the boundaries of political action away from citizenship as a relationship between the state and its subjects toward a model of politics and public space more consistent with anarchist and communitarian principles. Interestingly, feminist political theory provides another kind of critique of the nation-state as an outmoded political form: a way for us to begin to tackle the theories of international politics based on balance-of-power theses long dominant in political science. The implications of this insight have not yet been explored fully.

Finally, besides redesigning the shape of politics, feminist theory suggests a new grammar and ethos of political action. If gender is made one of the central categories of political analysis, then all political knowledge is influenced by it. Because the meaning of being a political actor is affected significantly by the characteristics of gender-defined practices, as well as by the convictions and beliefs structuring what modern theorists mean by "private" life, the political action of women might differ from that of men. Whether this is something to be regretted or applauded is a source of division among feminists, with some of us advocating "maternal thinking," others of us stressing the possibilities of a "woman-centered" science, and still others of us alarmed at the implications of any celebration of "woman's culture."[14] Nevertheless, concepts such as "maternal thinking" carry epistemic weight to the extent that they retrieve traditional female activities from the heap of politically irrelevant experiences. For instance, if nurturing is considered to reflect identifiable, historically specific moral codes and forms of knowledge, these alter the way that we define the characteristics of the citizen and study the practice of citizenship. At least, such a definition of nurturing provides a critique of the limits "of a rights-based conception of the individual and a view of social justice as equal access."[15]

The articulation of a new feminist theory of citizenship that encompasses these themes is the combined result of a critical reassessment of women's practices and women's values, and the search for the ways to construct a political community responsive to women's complex social locations. It represents the effort to read these practices, values, and locations in ways that rupture the text of Western political discourse.

## THE BODY POLITIC

From the origins of political philosophy, the question of the body, especially the female body, has plagued the architects of states. Plato subscribed to the view that the wants of the flesh disrupted the business of politics.

Nature should be subordinated to reason, and the human body should be subjected to rigorous discipline to prevent any alienation of loyalty to the community. Although women could become philosophers, they could achieve this only insofar as their femaleness was circumscribed by the dictates of the state. For Aristotle, not only were women excluded from participating in politics, but also their contributions to the ends of the state were limited to the production of the mere necessities of existence and to reproduction, literally, of those who might become citizens.[16]

Plato's and Aristotle's fears of sexuality and the body permeate the works of early Christian theorists as well. The apostle Paul wrote of unification through the body of Christ, but it is a transcendence of the body and all of the temptations of the flesh that he and later the church fathers had in mind. Still later, Augustine promised equality through an escape from the body into the city of God.[17]

For sixteenth- and seventeenth-century theorists, as well as their eighteenth-century successors, the term *passions* had political import. It was a term not to be conflated with "the body" nor expressly gender defined, although it was often represented metaphorically as a feminized drive. As Joan Scott has noted, the terms of modern discourse during this time were not "explicitly about gender, but they relied on references to it, the gendered 'coding' of certain terms, to establish their meanings."[18]

For Machiavelli, the passions were the stuff of politics. The play of fortune and the passions were accepted, but they required a cunning prince to outwit the chicanery of these female forces that could undo states: "Fortune is a woman and, if you wish to keep her down, you must beat her and pound her."[19] For Rousseau, the female body becomes the symbol of all that is dangerous to political order if not properly contained. Paradoxically, Rousseau makes domesticated female sexuality the cement of the social order. The only way to ensure political order was to segregate the sexes and educate them to their appropriate aims, taking care that the passionate aims of women were not allowed to hold sway in public space. "But let mothers deign to nurse their children, morals will reform themselves, nature's sentiments will be awakened in every heart, the state will be repeopled."[20]

Feminist theorists have considered how these conceptualizations of the body and the passions limit the political status of women. What is it about women's bodies, as metaphor and reality, that makes them unfit for citizenship? Early liberal feminists seem to have glossed over the problematics of the body. John Stuart Mill and Mary Wollstonecraft advocated the integration of women into the political arena by "extending the liberal principles of freedom, equality, and rationality to women through a process of education."[21] These opportunities for integration, however, were assumed to be irrelevant for the majority of women, who continued to be constrained within the home by child-rearing responsibilities. . . . Both Mill and Wollstonecraft maintained that the sense of justice and duty developed within the "private" sphere of the home was incompatible with justice in the civil, public sense. The situation could be improved insofar as women became rational mothers, practitioners of what Wollstonecraft called "enlightened rational affection."[22] Still, as Carole Pateman argues, this programmatic approach accepted implicitly the bifurcation of the body (and particularized concerns) and rational discourse, without fully exploring the structural factors and representational practices that make this bifurcation sex specific. Women, as "familial" creatures, and love, as particularized passion, were set opposed irrevocably to political virtue and public duty. The implications of the liberal understanding of citizenship was that, if women were to become full citizens, then women would have to become like men.

The political language of liberalism proved incapable of expressing the broadened scope of citizenship that would include full-bodied participation. Rousseau's solution had entailed a rigid segregation of roles that excluded women from citizenship, even though he acknowledged the critical functions that women performed as mothers of citizens, and even though he embraced, as civic virtues, the values of sentiment and tradition that had been associated historically with a feminized sensibility.[23] The dilemma confronting modern political theory from the eighteenth century on was how to recognize the political relevance of sexual differences, and how to include these differences within definitions of political action and civic virtue without constructing sexually segregated norms of citizenship. In short, the task was to construct a theory of political equality and citizenship that granted the individual personhood of women without denying that women had differing needs and interests from men.[24]

In their efforts to rejuvenate feminist theory in the late 1960s, feminists began developing an implicit critique of disembodied citizenship in their analyses of the structure and ideology of patriarchy. Inveighing against the centuries-old exclusion of women from public life dictated by the presumed limitations of the female body — particularly its reproductive functions — feminists constructed different theories of how to "transform women into public persons with a public identity."[25]

In much of this early work, the emphasis on transforming women reflects a characterization of women's lives as straitjacketed and apolitical. As Gerda Lerner has noted, the predominance of the "oppressed group model" tends to present a one-dimensional view of women's experiences that denies categorically that there is anything positive or politically valuable about them.[26] Ironically, this view incorporates the devaluation of women's experiences and accepts the patriarchal reading of the significance of women's lives that it claims to be criticizing. One particularly extreme formulation is Shulamith Firestone's call for the remaking of women so that they can be freed from the oppression of their bodies. If artificial reproduction, tabooless sexuality, contract-bound living groups, and a fully age- and sex-integrated workforce were established, Firestone argues, women would no longer be treated as second-class citizens. Although this view clearly refutes the notion that the family, sexuality, and the mode of production are realms beyond the scope of politics, the complete permeation of the private by public imperatives does erase the dialectic that preserves a vital tension between individual and communal dimensions of human experience.

A much less extreme formulation of political integration explains the ways that women's roles, especially in the family and in subordinate positions in the workforce, "restrict the resources women need to be integrated into politics as full citizens . . . [and] teach them to be something other than full citizens."[27] In addition to emphasizing the need to redistribute familial responsibilities, this approach stresses the importance of eradicating the psychological barriers to women's full inclusion in public life. It promises that the integration of the private and the public worlds will accomplish this and have a transformative effect on the values of both. Yet even this formulation begs the question of the nature of the public roles for which women will be liberated, and the conflicts with public duty that men's fuller integration into the private realm will create for men.

In another direction, "difference feminism" emphasizes the political significance of female culture and finds in the pluralism of rituals, practices, myths, and stories evidence of the best and the worst of the lives of women. If a woman's body limits her citizenship, the problem is rooted in the ways that the activities of citizenship are represented to exclude a body that does not easily fit military-corporate uniforms. Citizenship has to be redefined to accommodate women's bodies in their concrete, historically changing forms. This requires a model of citizenship that allows for differences in age, color, and physical strength, that accepts the sexuality/sensuality of political actors, that accommodates pregnancy, parturition, and menstrual cycles, and that encourages the articulation of interests and the pronouncement of authority in voices of many registers.[28]

If this latter school of theory embraces the values of the "concrete, the particular, and the bodily" identified with the social world of women,[29] its proponents have not always been careful to disentangle these values from the context of domination that threatens to transform every alternative voice into a new song of self-sacrifice.[30] In other words, they have not always clarified the way that the values of "women's culture" can be used to transform the public arena and contribute to the articulation of specifically political norms. Nor have they acknowledged fully that this emphasis on difference sometimes renews the demand, à la Rousseau, for maintaining the sexual segregation of activities and modes of consciousness in order to preserve the presumed purity of women's civic virtue.

There is a need to "embrace the cherished ideals and precious human values that flow from the social world of women"; at the same time it is imperative "to sever those ideals and values from patterns of male domination and female subordination." The ways that this balance can be accomplished in theory and practice need to be developed further. Yet, as Jean Bethke Elshtain suggests, implicit in this rethinking of women's relationship to public power is a rich vision of the social. Elshtain writes about the feminist reappropriation of Antigone: "To reaffirm the standpoint of Antigone for our own time is to portray woman as one who resists the imperious demands and overweening claims of state power when these run roughshod over deeply rooted and particular values and identities. Women must learn to defend without defensiveness." It is possible to develop a "transformed vision of the human community against the arid plane of bureaucratic statism."[31]

Regardless of the side one takes in this debate, a major impact of feminist theory has been to reintroduce the problem of the body into political discourse. Feminist theory has made it impossible to ignore the fact that citizens act as embodied subjects whose interests reflect their biological and psychosocial reality. Once we fully acknowledge the problem of the body, then we must also challenge the adequacy of the "rights" formulation of citizenship.[32]

In two areas, pornography and reproductive rights, thinking about the political significance of women's bodies has been extraordinarily vital. One of the claims that feminists have made about pornography is that it prevents women from achieving equal rights and equal respect. Until women can be free from harassment by sexually explicit imagery that represents them as bodies to be exploited, their citizenship will be denied one of the rights that belong to all individuals: the right to control one's body. Similarly, feminists claim the right to reproductive freedom for all women on the grounds that women's bodies belong to them.[33]

Both of these issues reveal the political complexity of women's bodies. Although proprietary claims have merit, they do not exhaust the debates surrounding the questions of pornography and reproduction. If women's bodies belong to them, then the decision to participate in pornographic films should belong to the individual alone. Yet some feminists appeal to other values to limit the absoluteness of this right. If women recognize the ways that representations of female sexuality construct images of women as passive objects of male desire, then, these feminists imply, women have an obligation to other women not to participate in the fabrication or circulation of these images, regardless of what they might be free to do as individuals who own their own bodies. Similarly, the question of whether women alone possess their wombs finds its mirror image in the debate about surrogate mothering. If a woman's body belongs solely to her, there is, strictly speaking, no more reason to prohibit womb leasing than there is to forbid prostitution. Yet some feminists have argued against surrogacy and prostitution, recognizing that the body is not merely a natural object or an individual possession; it is a historical object, affected by economic and political structures that mediate its expressiveness. It is also an intrinsic feature of human subjectivity. The body is not a mere container of the self.[34]

Acknowledging the body makes the concept of strict equality more difficult to apply. In a democratic polity, citizens are meant to enjoy equal individual rights. Still, biological, social, and discursively defined differences make the granting of the same rights to different persons more likely to sustain a hierarchy of rights than a uniformity of status. Some philosophers argue that sexual differences should be made no more relevant to the allocation of political rights and responsibilities than eye color is.[35] Yet difference feminists argue that the history of gender reveals it to be connected fundamentally to personal and political identity. Even if we object to a particular set of gender arrangements, they claim, this does not permit us to discard the concept of gender altogether in the design of more just social worlds. In this sense, gender is a different sort of category than class since gender necessitates only relations of difference, whereas class by definition requires relations of inequality.

## CHANGING POLITICAL SPACE

Despite the fact that feminists have been reciting the phrase "the personal is political" for years, traditional political science continues to conduct its research in a business-as-usual fashion. The major concepts of contemporary Western political thought are built on an acceptance of the nineteenth-century idea that the public is fundamentally distinct from the private and the personal. This distinction informs the discipline and shapes the methodology of traditional political science. As Elshtain has noted, the consequence is that all of "those aspects of social reality that go into making a person what he or she is fall outside the frame of formal, abstract analysis."[36] The dominant idea of citizenship could not be more abstracted from lived experience.

Many feminist studies have contributed to exposing the exclusion of women from political science research. A significant body of scholarship has been produced, largely by women in the profession, that challenges the assumption that women participate in politics significantly less than men and attempts to explain persistent differences in patterns of nonparticipation in nonsexist ways. A number of works also have explored the behavior of women political elites and have considered the public policy process surrounding women's issues.[37]

Despite the proliferation of important work by and about women, the epistemological and methodological framework of most of this research remains wedded to traditional definitions of politics and political behavior.[38] It represents the amassing of considerable evidence concerning women's contributions to politics. However, paraphrasing Gerda Lerner's analysis of similar approaches in women's history, these researchers apply questions from traditional political science to women and try to fit women's behavior into the empty spaces of political science scholarship. The obvious limitation of this work is that it leaves unchallenged the adequacy of the traditional categories of political analysis to describe and explain women's political attitudes, behavior, and "interests." Instead, the pervasive assumption of this research is that "those stereotyped characteristics held up as the masculine ideal (for example, aggressiveness, competitiveness, and pragmatism, and so on) are the norms of political behavior as well."[39]

This kind of research has been extremely important in documenting women's political lives, but it does not do justice to the insight that women's experiences in the so-called private sphere also are political. This insight emerged particularly forcefully in the context of women's participation in the civil rights and antiwar movements of the sixties. Women in these movements came to feel that they were relegated to traditionally "female" roles in the organizations. Not only were they denied equal access to leadership positions, but also their participation in the intellectual aspects of movement work was derided by the men whenever the women raised questions about the politics of the sexual division of labor. The most explosive issues, however—ones that challenged the narrowness of traditional understandings of politics and of the dynamics of solidarity—were those at the intersection of racial and sexual politics. As Sara Evans notes, the presence of white women in the civil rights movement contributed at the same time to the incipience of feminism among white women, to the development of deep rifts between white women and black women, and to tensions between black men and black women.

White women gained self-confidence and a growing sense of political efficacy as they engaged in political organizing. Strong black women in southern communities who had a long history of participation were their inspiring models. Yet black women felt that white women were protected by the privilege of their race from the more dangerous tasks and the more dehumanizing consequences of challenging racism in the South. Black women were subject to more police brutality and to more frequent jailings than were white women. At the same time, political tensions were created by sexual liaisons between white women and black men. If white women refused black men's sexual advances, they were accused by black men of being racists. If they accepted, black women felt their womanhood was being called into question and that they were being betrayed by their sisters. "The rising anger of black women would soon become a powerful force within the Student Non-Violent Coordinating Committee, creating a barrier that shared womanhood could not transcend," Evans writes. Ironically, the ideology of black separatist politics suggested the need for a separatist women's movement as well. Given the historical context of the civil rights struggles, this heightened black women's already keen sense of divided loyalties. When white women began to feel themselves the targets of derision from all sides, and especially from "white men in a white movement" (the leaders of the northern New Left), the women's movement's emerging discourse of "sexual exploitation" and "objectification" seemed to describe these women's experiences most closely and thus appealed to them.[40]

It is fruitful to apply the lessons of this history to the ways that we characteristically define citizenship. The definition of political action has been used in the history of political theory to describe the ontology of the citizen, but what counts as political action has been limited largely to formal interactions between citizens and the state. If citizens are not abstractions but concrete, socially located individuals who share certain identities with others like them, and who interact publicly and privately with each other and with the state and other institutions, then we need a new political science to consider the ways that the multifaceted dimensions of these interactions structure the space of politics and pattern alliances within and between certain groups. Moreover, women's experiences in the private sphere are political in the double sense of constructing an identifiable set of interests, virtues, and values that can be expressed in public, or politically relevant, terms and in the sense of creating, at least potentially, a group that shares those interests, virtues, and values. Yet, the experiences of any women are the experiences of particular women—women of a specifiable nationality, race, class, age, sexual preference, and religious background. Consequently, the political alliances that potentially can be grounded in women's experiences are not inherent in those experiences in any unmediated way. Specifiable differences that at least arguably distinguish women, as individuals and as groups, from each other serve to locate women in a social world of multiple, sometimes competing, identities and loyalties. We need a methodology that explores the political dimensions of the private sphere and the complexity of the politics of identity, instead of a litany of studies that replicate the dichotomy between the public and the private, a dichotomy borrowed from nineteenth-century constructions of politics.

Beginning with Gabriel Almond and Sidney Verba's *The Civic Culture,* the political significance of familial behavior has been investigated widely. The field of political socialization has since produced a considerable body of research that explores the ways in which certain structures of familial experience—like patterns of authority, language and conceptual development, and participatory opportunities—construct different expectations and capacities for different family members.[41] Feminist scholars, such as Virginia Sapiro, have drawn on this earlier work to consider what "the substantive connections between private gender roles and political roles might be." Sapiro's work is significant because it explores how different gender roles contribute to the construction of different understandings of citizenship. For instance, she finds that more "privatized" women—women whose lives are dominated by private roles, concerns, and values even when they are involved in public life—are the group most likely to see citizenship as a passive, political support role and the least likely to see citizenship as a matter of activism.[42]

Research that describes more accurately the significance of women's participation, that explores the direction and outcome as well as factors affecting the rate of traditional forms of participation (such as voting and campaign activities) is important because we need a fuller understanding of the motivations, self-understandings, and potentially transformative effects of women's political participation. This of course requires detailed case studies as well as quantitative research. It also requires the careful examination of other topics directly connected to policy—such as welfare politics, the operation of the criminal justice system, and both state and non-state regulation of sexuality and reproduction, employment and economic development, and immigration laws. The experience of citizenship is strongly determined by the development of public policy in these arenas, as well as by the activities of lobbying and voting.

Nevertheless, our investigation of citizenship should not be limited only to forms of participation that have been defined traditionally as political, or to those that can be measured easily through standard quantitative analyses. The implications of the "personal is political" in studies of political involvement can be understood by considering the difference between characterizing women's traditional roles, as housewives and mothers, for example, as politically isolated and generally politically ignorant ones, and representing those roles as a significant political mechanism both for continuing the segregation of dominant public institutions along sexual lines, as well as, potentially, for undermining dominant hierarchies.

In her study of the political life of Indian women, Tonia Devon argues that women are politically ignorant because they are less informed about "the ruling party, political slogans, the national anthem, Mahatma Gandhi, and Indian Independence Day" than are men. Perhaps it is more accurate to say that there are differences in the kinds of political knowledge available to, and considered appropriate for, men and women, with men having more global, and women more parochial knowledge. Devon finds that women in India, regardless of whether they are employed outside the home, are relatively uninformed about traditional topics of politics compared with men. This, she speculates, is because of the widely internalized view that "politics is not a subject for women."[43] Yet this view *is* political knowledge: it is knowledge of the proper place for women and the values that place represents.

The beginning of a new definition of political participation is suggested in Sidney Verba's reassessment of the classical distinction between political participation and a more "parochial relation" to the polity. In an essay that extends his earlier work, Verba notes that "particularized contacting" of the government by citizens to resolve "some problem whose relevance is limited to the individual or the family" also is political participation. Because so many problems that were once resolved by families or nongovernmental associations are now being taken over by the state, it is time to acknowledge that the distinction "among the parochial, the subject and the citizen require[s] some revision," Verba writes.[44] Although the political significance of families as training grounds for citizenship had been well documented, feminists have seized the insight that turning to the state for the redress of apparently private grievances constitutes political participation.

Yet this redefinition requires refinement. None of Verba's evidence points to the significance of gender variables in mobilizing individuals or groups to petition the government for aid. Nation-state differences are reported, but whether these vary by sex is unknown. Moreover, the spatial dimensions of citizenship remain institutional. Interests count as political insofar as they are translated into petitions to or claims against the government. This neglects other factors that might weigh into the definition of political participation, such as processes that politicize issues previously defined as personal problems and the personally transformative effects of group identification (consciousness-raising).[45] These variables discursively reconstruct public space as they express problems in public terms, even if the government is not directly and immediately implicated. For instance, women's experiences of threat and danger have focused attention on certain features of the political geography of sexuality and personal freedom. "Take-Back-the-Night" marches against sexual harassment, rape, and pornography on college campuses are examples of a definition of participation that is focused not on government action but on the reclamation of public space itself.

An extraordinary historical example of the distinctiveness and significance of women's reclamation of public space is to be found in the impressive, though largely undocumented, participation of women in the revolutionary actions of the Paris Commune of 1871. When the Paris Commune declared its autonomy from the Versailles government on March 18, 1871, thousands of women found themselves in politics: literally positioning their bodies between the Versailles troops, who had been sent to quell the revolt, and the Paris National Guard, who were defending the Commune on the hills of Montmartre; driving ambulances; sewing uniforms; writing for the Commune press; educating the children of Communards and Communardes in newly reclaimed public schools; and defending the city of Paris on gunboats along the Seine. The actions and in some cases deaths of women represented their new claim on public space as "citoyennes"—women citizens—and the creation of the Commune as a new social form. The Commune represented to its supporters a place wherein the republican ideology that had consigned women to silence in the domestic sphere would give way to men and women workers who would rule themselves. To the enemies of the Commune, women's presence in this reconfigured public space represented a transgression and defamation of the sexual geography of public order that supported the French republic itself. These opponents presented women's actions in the conflict as those of whores, thieves, sexually licentious creatures, and even she-men, since these women had the audacity to carry guns and wear pants.

The architecture of public space and its relevance for the potential political mobilization of women is explored in the work of contemporary feminist urban geographers who have investigated how the literal design of cities and suburban residential areas has segregated the concerns of women.[46] The ways that urban policies reinforce this segregation, what I call the sexual geography of political action, has yet to be appreciated fully in feminist theories of citizenship. Evans reports that the experiences of women in the civil rights movement in the South, and the later experiences of northern women working in the organizational drives of the New Left, led to the recognition of important black women leaders in isolated communities who were often unnoticed when the power centers and lines of power were assumed to be male controlled. Some of the most important organizational successes of these movements came as the result of these women-to-women networks operating outside the dominant boundaries of political geography. In Detroit, for instance, women's mobilization of ghettoes around the concerns of sanitation, housing, and recreation centers created an effective network where men's efforts to mobilize around the issue of employment had failed.[47]

## CHANGING POLITICAL BEHAVIOR

Few studies of women and citizenship have employed anything but traditional definitions and measures of political participation, despite the facts that women generally are located in markedly different contexts and socialized to different skills than are men. Usually, participation is defined as voting, campaign involvement, influencing the vote of another, following political (electoral) events in the media, and other formal political actions. Feminist theory's innovation about politics has been to recognize that standard definitions of politics tend to be male biased, that is, based on norms derived from activities in arenas traditionally dominated by men and their interests.

Barbara Nelson's studies of the impact of economic marginality on women's political activity is representative of this approach. Nelson shows how structural factors effected the construction of a two-tiered system of citizenship: relatively powerless, predominantly female client-citizens and more powerful, disproportionately male electoral-citizens. As the ranks of electoral-citizens swelled with more women participants, the class dimensions of these forms of citizenship became highlighted. Nelson's claim is that ordinary definitions of citizenship that focus exclusively on particular activities in which all individuals may, in the abstract, engage fail to consider the political significance of real economic marginality affecting a particular sector of these individuals.

Nelson's work suggests a notion presented more explicitly in the writings of Scandinavian feminists, that welfare state liberalism creates a different sort of citizenship derived from social policy entitlements that construct "segmented and fragmented citizenship patterns"[48] varying by class and nation. Moreover, Nelson argues that some women's status as clients who represent the claims of groups of people categorized by need contradicts the liberal state's emphasis on individualized claims for social benefits. Consequently, the experience of citizenship by poor women underscores "the inherent tension in liberalism between women's commitment to (and responsibility for) families and their full exercise of citizenship" in all its dimensions.[49] Poor women's primary relationship to the state as mothers demonstrates graphically the limits of liberalism. In the face of very real economic and ideological factors limiting the participation of many, it is difficult for liberalism to achieve its goal of equal and independent civic standing as the basis of citizenship.

Similarly, Helga Hernes argues that, despite highly developed social service programs in Scandinavian countries, women's status as citizens still is marked by inequality, underrepresentation, discrimination, and subordination. Women have been incorporated into the state as client-citizens, or as low-level service worker–citizens — as recipients and deliverers of benefits under programs designed for them largely by a male-dominated establishment. Yet they, and their interests, generally are absent from the corporatist system that establishes the priorities of the public sector. Women are not the ones who define the state's priorities. Hernes describes the Scandinavian state as a "tutelary state," where the nature of women's citizenship is marked primarily by their transition from private to public dependency.[50] Since women are more likely to be the immediate beneficiaries of a stable public sector, Hernes hypothesizes that women are more likely to be the supporters of public growth and regulation. The irony is that women are supporting the growth and development of an institution that incorporates women without necessarily incorporating greater representation for them in the arenas and institutions that shape their lives.

Yet Hernes has concluded in a later essay that any adequate account of contemporary citizenship in Scandinavia must include the entitlements and claims aspect, as well as the participatory aspect of citizenship "in order to grasp the interplay between material rights, multilevel participation and political identities." This hypothesis furthers her earlier arguments by suggesting that it is possible that new forms of political identity formation and group consciousness especially connected to women's multifaceted experiences of citizenship in modern welfare state systems might be evolving. In

Scandinavian countries, there is an increasing possibility of "political identity formation within the legal administrative system." Certain legal and political reforms, such as incorporation of client recommendations for policy implementation, have added participatory dimensions to the task of the client, enabling women to "become more active in negotiating the content and forms of delivery of their entitlements."[51]

Birthe Siim has extended this analysis of the nature of women's citizenship by emphasizing the importance of paying attention to national differences between welfare systems. The state's increasing role in providing services has not transformed women into dependent client-citizens universally. Rather, Siim argues, in the Scandinavian countries women's role as consumers of state-provided services has made them less dependent on the state as clients than in systems like the United States and Britain, where weaker welfare systems have increased women's reliance on the state as clients. She also has contributed to the redefinition of political activity by criticizing Hernes's earlier bias toward conceptualizing political influence as participation in formal "power from above" types of politics, as opposed to women's activities in social movements, or "power from below."[52] Men and their interests may continue to dominate in the formal arenas of power, but women's ability to construct alternative arenas of influence is not lacking altogether, and it may augur forms of participation that are less bureaucratic, more democratic, and more personalized.

## Politics among Friends

Finally, consider the significance of rhetorical strategies that represent the feminist political community as a familial group (sisters) or a friendship group. Like other radical protest movements that emerged in the late 1960s, the women's movement has stressed the need to transform the organization of political life to make it more consonant with principles of equality and face-to-face relationships. In place of the more distant and alienated interactions of citizens of bureaucratic systems, leaders of the women's movement have proposed intimate forms of interaction and have based models of political life on idealized models of the family and on friendship groups. In this analysis affective ties replace functional ones as the cement of a social order, the creative development of personality substitutes for the pursuit of instrumental goals, and a shared sense of community takes the place of the competitive norms of capitalist culture. Similarly, trust supplants suspicion as the motivating political impulse.

These normative criteria did not originate in the sixties. Many socialist-inspired movements, such as the Israeli kibbutzim, have claimed to be founding a new politics. We feminists have employed a language laced with kinship and friendship metaphors to express our commitment to the search for alternative forms of social living derived from female experience, forms of living that would stress the emotional as well as the cognitive dimensions of human action within a political context that would be more free and equal. The seventies phrase "sisterhood is powerful" carries these meanings, as well as the connotation that relationships heretofore regarded as private and personal had political implications.

Defining the citizen in the feminist polity as a sister or a friend transforms the characteristics of citizenship in at least two ways. First, belonging to the polity as one belongs to a family intensifies the experience of membership. Families tend to be institutions that demand total commitment from their members. Since we have complained that political life is characterized by fragmented, depersonalized relationships that are necessary evils rather than positive goods, it is appropriate for us to choose a language that distinguishes our vision of politics from bureaucratized, utilitarian modes of sociality. In families, individuals are nurtured and cared for as persons as opposed to being regarded as functions.

Second, family and friends develop a solidarity that is stronger and deeper than the formal connections among mere citizens. Whereas loyalty to the modern state is often a tenuous and fragile relationship, loyalty in the family and among friends is postulated as more continuous and less capricious. Thus, familial and friendship relations can involve all dimensions of the person, not simply certain aspects of the individual. The kinds of psychological bonds that tie the individual to the family and to friends are arguably more complex than the connections between the individual and the state. Body, heart, and will are involved intimately in family life and among friends.

As feminists, we tend to stress the positive dimensions of these aspects of membership in the feminist polity. Yet, as a number of authors have noted, there are negative sides to this transformed vision of citizenship.[53] The kind of commitment that is expected from a sister exacts a toll that is not always consistent with the feminist stress on autonomy and self-development. If personal conflicts develop among family members or feminist citizens, the expectation of loyalty may be transformed from a sense of security into a sense of restriction, or an even more self-destructive sense of obligation. The feminist stress on commitment, and the demand for a total involvement of the person may gloss over the extent to which this entails an excessively disciplinary strategy. The phrase "politically correct" behavior captures the tension and contradiction that some feminists feel as various forms of sibling rivalry emerge within the feminist polity. The intimate connection binding feminist citizens as members of a community with shared identifiable goals and promising nurturance and support has proven to be founded, at least in part, on guilt and the threatened punishment of disownership for those sisters who do not conform.

The obligations that followed from this new theory of citizenship often are burdensome beyond many people's capacity. Ironically, the feminist citizen model may validate the idealized image of an all-nurturing, all-loving woman even as it rejects the patriarchal system that created that image. Of course, the expectation is that these caretaking relations will be reciprocal and no longer identified as necessarily women's or certain women's responsibilities. Still, the methods for guaranteeing this often are unspecified. Moreover, the ability to dissent from the feminist "general will" is more limited when the political community is modeled on a familial relationship than when it is based on a friendship group. The obligation to defend one's family seems stronger, less subject to the judgments of rationality and will that the idea of political obligation entails, and it conflicts with the stress on voluntarism that some feminist theorists have considered to be the foundation of all social relationships. In fact, as Martha Ackelsberg notes, we feminists often used a "charged language of kin relationships to describe a relationship that is distinctly not one of kin."[54]

Since all dimensions of a person's life are implicated in familial relationships, and, to a lesser extent, in friendships, the potential for loss of any preserve of privacy is great. The closer the group is knit together, the greater the subtle, but coercive, threats to any idea of individual autonomy. In 1975, discussing the potential conflict between personal autonomy and the search for community reflected in radical political movements for social change, including the women's movement, Jane Mansbridge noted that "even in the absence of conscious state or corporate direction, if every member of a society were expected to participate politically through . . . a group, individuals might no longer be free to use participation for their own ends. They might easily be drawn into groups whose ends they did not share and find themselves manipulated in ways they did not intend."[55] These dilemmas continue to be experienced by some participants in the women's movement, and yet the limits of transforming citizenship into friendship are often only implicit in feminist theory.

Nevertheless, there is a sense in which the positive stress on stronger and more intimate connections to community and, by implication, the more deeply felt sense of political obligation is consistent with another aspect of feminist political theory that argues for alternative conceptualizations of selfhood and practices of political judgment. Instead of conceptualizing society as one founded contractually, in which obedience to authorities is exchanged for protection, some feminists prefer the concept of a society founded through promises. This is in part because the exchange of obedience for protection describes the traditional form of the relationship between the sexes and thus extends the hierarchical and dependent aspects of that relationship into the political realm. Instead of an exchange between unequals, the self-assumed obligation "of promising . . . creat[es] . . . a relationship . . . based on trust, keeping faith and responsibility." Such a relationship expresses better than a contract the sorts of political relations between citizens that feminists have been endorsing: "horizontal and multifaceted ties of self-assumed political obligation."[56]

Other dilemmas emerge when the bonds between members of the feminist polity are based on certain aspects of maternalism. The virtues of commitment to relationships, love, and caring for others are held up as ideal bonds between citizens that are meant to temper the individualist, rights-based, contractual model of citizenship that views the public realm as one of competition rather than community building.[57] This view alerts us to the limits of the traditional concept of citizenship, which requires that we accept the disciplinary terms that it imposes. The traditional concept of citizenship assumes the necessity of annihilating all other particular loyalties to locality, family, sex, class, and race in order for citizenship to become a relationship among equals. The extremity of this annihilation is reflected quite profoundly in the image of what Elshtain calls "Spartan motherhood": the mother who responds to the calls of civic duty by offering her sons to the exigencies of armed civic virtue.[58] The rights and obligations of citizenship appear to depend on the suspension of the primacy of these other dimensions of human identity and to place the citizen's loyalty at odds, at least theoretically, with these other allegiances.

Yet the ways that women have made these other bonds central to their experiences have been documented in feminist analyses.[59] One possible implication of such research is that women experience more acutely than men the alienation from these bonds that citizenship as currently defined and practiced requires. A different implication is that the traditional concept of citizenship depends on the assumption of a combative, oppositional perspective on political action that has been associated, symbolically, with a masculinist process. The attempt to suffuse a notion of citizenship with the intimacy and particularity of these other bonds, like the maternal one, finds its limit in the traditional concept of citizenship itself.

## CONCLUSION

Can we feminists construct a theory of citizenship that is at once intimate and political? Is the concept of citizenship adequate to express the behavior of those in the redefined polity that our theories have elaborated? The question, for the present, is an open one. It can be said, however, that a polity that is friendly to women and the multiplicity of their interests must root its democracy in the experiences of women and transform the practice and concept of citizenship to fit these varied experiences, rather than simply transform women to accommodate the practice of citizenship as it traditionally has been defined.

Bettina Aptheker writes about considering the advantage of the position at the crossroads of multiple worlds that many women have occupied: "We traipse back and forth every day, sometimes several times a day between the cultures of our existence: the women's cultures, the men's cultures, the children's cultures, the work cultures, the class cultures, the lesbian cultures, the 'straight' cultures, the racial cultures, the ethnic cultures, the church cultures." Rooting a "politics of our own," she argues, requires not the effort to "find the least common denominator around which to unite" but, instead, "abandon[ing] oppositional ways of thinking."[60]

If we abandon oppositional ways of thinking, worlds open up to us. Borders become permeable; different women become visible as the different sorts of women they are, but with the potential to act in solidarity through their differences. Since, as feminists have been contending, the concept and practice of citizenship now rests on excluding women and representations of the female by definition, women's visibility threatens to disrupt the system of international (dis)order founded on the assumption of competition, and occasional cooperation, among nation-states. Women's political presence as gendered beings, marking the presence of those who have actually and symbolically been excluded from full citizenship, signals the possibility of shifting the boundaries of citizenship away from nationalism toward multicultural community. If women represent everything that citizenship opposes, what happens to citizenship, as concept and practice, when women's experiences and symbolism become incorporated?

Neither citizenship nor the experiences of women should be seen as static and fixed by nature, however. Rather, they are part of an ongoing historical process of the transformation of modern society and modern political communities — a process that continually renegotiates the boundaries of public space and redefines the characteristics of those who occupy it as full members — as citizens.

## NOTES

1. Recent feminist political theory has contributed to the debate about the scope and meaning of citizenship and the nature of political action in the modern age. See, for example, Susan Okin, *Women in Western Political Thought* (Princeton, N.J.: Princeton University Press, 1979), p. 233; Genevieve Lloyd, "Selfhood, War and Masculinity," in *Feminist Challenges: Social and Political Theory*, ed. Carole Pateman and Elizabeth Gross (Boston: Northeastern University Press, 1986), p. 63–76; Jean Bethke Elshtain, *Women and War* (New York: Basic Books, 1987); and Joan Landes, *Women and the Public Sphere in the Age of the French Revolution* (Ithaca, N.Y.: Cornell University Press, 1988).

2. Evelyn Fox Keller, "Feminist Perspectives on Science Studies," *Barnard Occasional Papers on Women's Issues* 3 (Spring 1988):10–36, esp. 13.

3. Virginia Sapiro made the important distinction between the representation of "citizens who happen to be women" and representing women "*because* they are women" in her "When Are Interests Interesting? The Problem of Political Representation of Women," *American Political Science Review* 75 (Sept. 1981):701–16. See also Anna G. Jonasdottir, "On the Concept of Interest, Women's Interests, and the Limitations of Interest Theory," in *The Political Interests of Gender*, ed. Kathleen B. Jones and Anna G. Jonasdottir (London: Sage, 1988), pp. 33–65.

4. Keller, "Feminist Perspectives," p. 15.

5. Andrew Feenberg, "The Question of Organization in the Early Marxist Work of Lukács: Technique or Practice?" in *Lukács Today*, ed. T. Rockmore (New York: Reidel, 1988), pp. 126–56, esp. 130.

6. Among feminists who stress that language constructs experience, see, for example, Kathy Ferguson, "Subject-Centeredness in Feminist Discourse," in Jones & Jonasdottir, *Political Interests of Gender*, pp. 66–78.

7. Lloyd, "Selfhood, War and Masculinity," p. 76.

8. See, for example, Mary Dietz, "Context Is All: Feminism and Theories of Citizenship," *Daedalus* 116, no. 4 (Fall 1987):1–24, esp. 12–13.

9. Compare Bettina Aptheker, *Tapestries of Life: Women's Work, Women's Consciousness, and the Meaning of Daily Experience* (Amherst: University of Massachusetts Press, 1989), esp. pp. 167–230.

10. See Zillah Eisenstein, *The Female Body and the Law* (Berkeley and Los Angeles: University of California Press, 1988).

11. Adrienne Rich, "Disloyal to Civilization: Feminism, Racism and Gynephobia," in *Lies, Secrets and Silence*, ed. Adrienne Rich (New York: Norton, 1979), pp. 275–310, esp. 291; Catharine MacKinnon, *Feminism Unmodified:*

*Discourses on Life and Law* (Cambridge, Mass.: Harvard University Press, 1987), esp. pp. 46–62.

12. Carole Pateman, " 'The Disorder of Women': Women, Love, and the Sense of Justice," *Ethics* 91 (Oct. 1980):24.

13. Bonnie Zimmerman, *The Safe Sea of Women* (Boston: Beacon, 1990).

14. Karen Offen, "Defining Feminism: A Comparative Historical Approach," *Signs* 14, no. 1 (Autumn 1988):119–57. See also Offen's exchanges with Ellen DuBois and Nancy Cott, "Comment and Reply," *Signs* 15, no. 1 (Autumn 1989):195–209.

15. Dietz, "Context Is All," p. 12. See also Elshtain, *Women and War.*

16. Plato, *The Republic,* trans. Allan Bloom (New York: Basic Books, 1968), esp. bks. 4–6; Aristotle, *The Politics,* trans. Ernest Barker (Oxford: Oxford University Press, 1946).

17. John Phillips, *Eve: The History of an Idea* (New York: Harper, 1984), esp. pp. 119–47.

18. Joan Scott, "Gender: A Useful Category of Historical Analysis," *American Historical Review* 91, no. 5 (1986):1053–75, esp. 1073.

19. Niccolo Machiavelli, *The Prince and Other Works,* trans. Allan Gilbert (New York: Hendricks House, 1964), p. 176.

20. Jean-Jacques Rousseau, *Emile,* trans. Allan Bloom (New York: Basic Books, 1979), p. 46.

21. Pateman, " 'The Disorder of Women,' " p. 31.

22. Mary Wollstonecraft, *A Vindication of the Rights of Woman* (Middlesex: Penguin, 1975), pp. 264–65.

23. Jean Bethke Elshtain, *Meditations on Modern Political Thought: Masculine/Feminine Themes from Luther to Arendt* (New York: Praeger, 1986).

24. Sheila Rowbotham, "What Do Women Want: Woman Centered Values and the World As It Is," *Dalhousie Review* 64, no. 4 (Winter 1984–85):649–65.

25. Jean Bethke Elshtain, "Antigone's Daughters," in *Families, Politics, and Public Policy,* ed. Irene Diamond (New York: Longman, 1983), pp. 300–311, esp. 302.

26. Gerda Lerner, "Placing Women in History," in *The Majority Finds Its Past,* ed. Gerda Lerner (New York: Oxford University Press, 1979), esp. pp. 145–47.

27. Virginia Sapiro, *The Political Integration of Women: Roles, Socialization and Politics* (Urbana: University of Illinois Press, 1983), p. 172.

28. See Elshtain, "Antigone's Daughters"; Kathleen Jones, "Dividing the Ranks: Women and the Draft," *Women and Politics* 4, no. 4 (1984):75–87; Rowbotham, "What Do Women Want" and Ruth L. Smith and Deborah M. Valenze, "Mutuality and Marginality: Liberal Moral Theory and Working-Class Women in Nineteenth-Century England," *Signs* 13, no. 2 (Winter 1986): 277–98.

29. Dorothy E. Smith, "A Sociology for Women," in *The Prism of Sex: Essays in the Sociology of Knowledge,* ed. Julia A. Sherman and Evelyn Torton Beck (Madison: University of Wisconsin Press, 1979), pp. 135–88.

30. See Kathy Ferguson's discussion of this in *The Feminist Case against Bureaucracy* (Philadelphia: Temple University Press, 1984).

31. Elshtain, "Antigone's Daughters," pp. 304, 307, 308.

32. Rosalind Petchesky, *Abortion and Women's Choice* (New York: Longman, 1983).

33. On pornography, see the relevant essays in MacKinnon, *Feminism Unmodified.*

34. See Robin West, "Jurisprudence and Gender," *University of Chicago Law Review* 55, no. 1 (Winter 1988):1–72.

35. Richard Wasserstrom, "Racism and Sexism," in *Philosophy and Social Issues,* ed. Richard Wasserstrom (Notre Dame, Ind.: University of Notre Dame Press, 1980).

36. Elshtain, "Antigone's Daughters," p. 307.

37. R. Darcy, Susan Welch, and Janet Clark, *Women, Elections and Representation* (New York: Longman, 1987).

38. Kathleen B. Jones, "Towards the Revision of Politics," in Jones and Jonasdottir, *Political Interests of Gender,* pp. 11–32.

39. Susan Bourque and Jean Grossholz, "Politics as Unnatural Practice," *Politics and Society* 4, no. 2 (1974):225–66, esp. 229.

40. Sara Evans, *Personal Politics: The Roots of Women's Liberation in the Civil Rights Movement and the New Left* (New York: Vintage, 1980), pp. 60, 82.

41. Gabriel Almond and Sidney Verba, *The Civic Culture: Political Attitudes and Democracy in Five Nations* (Princeton, N.J.: Princeton University Press, 1963). For a current review of the arguments and biases of *The Civic Culture,* see Gabriel Almond and Sidney Verba, eds., *The Civic Culture Revisited* (Boston: Little, Brown, 1980).

42. Sapiro, *Political Integration of Women,* pp. 53, 107.

43. Tonia Devon, "Up from the Harem: The Effects of Class and Sex on Political Life in Northern India," in *Perspectives on Third World Women: Race, Class and Gender,* ed. Beverly Lindsay (New York: Praeger, 1980), pp. 123–42, esp. 134.

44. Sidney Verba, "The Parochial and the Polity," in *The Citizen and Politics: A Comparative Perspective,* ed. Sidney Verba and Lucien Pye (New York: Greylock, 1978), pp. 4–5.

45. Arthur Miller, Anne Hildreth, and Grace L. Simmons, "Political Mobilization and Gender Consciousness," in Jones and Jonasdottir, *Political Interests of Gender,* pp. 106–34.

46. Dolores Hayden, *The Grand Domestic Revolution* (Cambridge, Mass.: MIT Press, 1981).

47. Evans, *Personal Politics,* pp. 51–53, 140–45.

48. Helga Hernes, "The Welfare State Citizenship of Scandinavian Women," in Jones and Jonasdottir, *Political Interests of Gender,* pp. 187–213, esp. 191.

49. Barbara Nelson, "Women's Poverty and Women's Citizenship: Some Political Consequences of Economic Marginality," *Signs* 10, no. 2 (Winter 1984):209–31.

50. Helga Hernes, "Women and the Welfare State: The Transition from Private to Public Dependence," in *Patriarchy in a Welfare Society,* ed. Harriet Holter (Oslo: Universitetsforlaget, 1984), pp. 26–45.

51. Hernes, "Welfare State Citizenship of Scandinavian Women," pp. 189, 207.

52. Birthe Siim, "Toward a Feminist Rethinking of the Welfare State," in Jones and Jonasdottir, *Political Interests of Gender,* pp. 160–86.

53. For a positive view, see Janice Raymond, *A Passion for Friends* (Amherst: University of Massachusetts Press, 1986).

54. Martha Ackelsberg, " 'Sisters' or 'Comrades'? The Politics of Families and Friends," in Diamond, ed., *Families, Politics, and Public Policy,* p. 346.

55. Jane Mansbridge, "The Limits of Friendship," in *Participation in Politics,* ed. J. R. Pennock and J. Chapman (New York: New York University Press, 1975), p. 264.

56. Carole Pateman, *The Problem of Political Obligation: A Critical Analysis of Liberal Theory* (New York: Wiley, 1979), pp. 170, 174.

57. Dietz, "Context Is All," pp. 10–11.

58. Elshtain, *Women and War.*

59. Mary Belenky, Blythe Clinchy, Nancy Goldberger, and Jill Tarule, *Women's Ways of Knowing* (New York: Basic Books, 1986).

60. Aptheker, *Tapestries of Life,* pp. 251, 253.

# PART VIII
## MULTIPLE CITIZENSHIPS

# 12

## The Dynamics of Citizenship in Israel and the Israeli-Palestinian Peace Process

### GERSHON SHAFIR AND YOAV PELED

The Declaration of Principles signed by Israel and the Palestine Liberation Organization (PLO) in September 1993 marked a dramatic about-face in Israel's traditional policy towards the PLO and the Palestinian issue in general. This turn of events came as a surprise not only to journalists and commentators following day-to-day political events but also to scholars engaged in the academic study of Israeli society.

Our purpose in this essay is not to provide a comprehensive explanation for the Oslo agreement and the subsequent development of Israeli-Palestinian relations. Such an endeavor would require a detailed analysis of both structural and conjectural factors that have converged at a particular time to achieve this political and diplomatic breakthrough. Our aim is to construct a theoretical framework out of various conceptualizations of citizenship that can account for the moderation in Israeli policy and, more broadly, for social change. While the liberal conception of citizenship, being the most universal, is commonly the one put forth for legitimational purposes in most societies, the actual citizenship discourse in each particular society may consist of alternative conceptions of citizenship, superimposed on one another. By "citizenship," in other words, we must understand not only a bundle of formal rights, but the entire mode of incorporation of individuals and groups into the society. Changing citizenship rights and patterns of participation in society frequently express and legitimate other kinds of social change.

The field of our analysis will be the five major politically constructed ethnic and religious groups—ashkenazim, mizrachim (respectively, Jews hailing from Europe and the West and from the Middle East and North Africa), citizen Palestinians, noncitizen Palestinians, and Orthodox Jews—that comprise the basic skeleton of Israel's citizenship structure. These groups are stratified into a set of roughly concentric circles, from core to periphery, that constitute a hierarchical and fragmented citizenship structure.

A fruitful way of examining Israeli society is by analyzing the interaction between those exclusionary and universalist practices that resulted from two imperatives that have coexisted uneasily and have vied for dominance within it: a colonial, frontier imperative and a democratic, civic imperative. Our thesis is that in the last two decades Israeli society has been moving steadily away from its frontier origins, and corresponding republican citizenship ideals, and assuming more and more the character of civil society and its attendant liberal citizenship practices. It is this dynamic, we argue, that has propelled Israeli governments to undertake multiple domestic reforms and take advantage of the opportunities presented by international developments and adopt a policy of accommodation. It is these changes, we argue, that will continue to nurture the peace process, in spite of the uncertainties that accompany it. At the same time, arrayed against the liberal citizenship is an ethnonationalist citizenship discourse that mobilizes and justifies the opposition to the peace process.

## COLONIALISM AND DEMOCRACY

A frontier society is "a territory or zone of interpenetration between two previously distinct societies" in ongoing conflict. According to Lamar and Thompson, "probably the nearest contemporary approach to the kind of frontier...where rival societies compete for control of the land is to be found in Israel" (Lamar and Thompson 1981:7, 312). Conventional analyses of Israeli history have highlighted those characteristics of the Zionist settlement project that seem to demarcate it from other colonial encounters. However, Shafir's study of the formative period of Zionist settlement in Palestine—1882 to 1914—showed that the Israeli case does resemble that of some of the other European overseas colonial societies, such as Australia, the northern United States, South Africa, and Algeria. All of those experiences were shaped by the exclusionary practices of colonization and the resultant frontier struggles with already existing societies (Shafir 1996).

The political institutions and political culture of the *Yishuv* (Jewish community in pre-1948 Palestine), which later served as foundations for the Israeli state, were shaped by the Jewish-Palestinian frontier struggle. The settlement project was predicated on the construction of an economic sector based on cooperative principles, with Labor Zionism's most famous social innovation, the *kibbutz,* at its center. This economic sector, employing only Jews and under the control of the Labor Zionist movement, was formed and supported by two pillars: the World Zionist Organization's Jewish National Fund and the agricultural workers' Histadrut (trade union). The aims of the JNF and the Histadrut were the removal of land and labor, respectively, from the market, thus closing them off to Palestinian Arabs. The economy they built gradually developed into an economic empire encompassing, at its height, agricultural, industrial, construction, marketing, transportation, and financial concerns, as well as a whole network of social service organizations. At the same time, this economic infrastructure played a crucial role in maintaining the political and cultural hegemony of the Labor Zionist movement, thus ensuring the privileged position of a large segment of *ashkenazi* Jews.

The cooperative colonies of Labor Zionism, where the conflict with the Palestinian Arab population was at its most intense, emphasized the civic virtue of *chalutziyut* (pioneering): the redemptive activity of the pioneers, consisting of physical labor, agricultural settlement, and military defense. The *kibbutzim* and the Labor movement, consequently, were seen as a republican community of virtuous and dedicated individuals, committed to a common moral purpose — the fulfillment of Zionism. The Labor movement's elite position was justified, ideologically, by interpreting the notion of "pioneering" in a sweeping fashion, as characterizing all individuals associated with the Labor Zionist movement, even those who had long abandoned the settlements, and agricultural work in general, in favor of administrative or political functions (Shapiro 1976). Israel's *ashkenazi,* state-building elite has utilized the *republican conception of citizenship* in order to legitimize the privileges it derived from the colonial project through its control of the state and other public institutions.

Thus the foundation was laid for distinguishing between the civic virtue (or "desert") not only of Jews and Arabs, but also between the *ashkenazi* and the *mizrachi* groups within the Jewish community, based on their presumed contributions to the project of Zionist redemption (Peled 1992). The different historical trajectories of the two communities reflected the superior organizational ability of the *ashkenazi* workers, which placed them in a better position to procure resources from the World Zionist Organization. The *ashkenazi* settler-workers legitimated their demands, however, by drawing a distinction between themselves as "idealistic" and the *mizrachi*, for example, Yemenite Jews, as "natural" workers. "Idealistic workers" were the stuff pioneers were made of, blazing the trail and setting moral standards for the community. "Natural workers," on the other hand, were to be foot soldiers in the Zionist campaign, adding "quantity" to the pioneers' "qualitative" efforts (Shafir 1996). This distinction between "quality" and "quantity" was meant to bridge the gap between the pioneers' claim to be a dedicated, exclusive vanguard, deserving of special privileges, and the continuing desire to draw the Jewish masses to Palestine. This proved to be of crucial importance in the 1950s and 1960s, when the pioneers, now occupying all dominant positions in society, had to deal with a massive influx of *mizrachi* immigrants.

But the *Yishuv* was also a *democratic* community, where individual rights and the procedural rules of democracy were respected. This was mandated by its semivoluntary nature and the need to keep all Jewish social sectors within its bounds, for demographic and legitimational purposes. Both the *ashkenazi* and the *mizrachi* ethnic groups were part of the Jewish ethnonation and as such shared the same *völkisch, or ethnonational, citizenship* granted in Israel to all Jewish immigrants upon arrival. As Jews immigrating under the Law of Return, *mizrachi* immigrants were granted all civil and political rights. At the same time, however, they were socially marginalized: sent to settle in border areas and in towns deserted by Palestinians in 1948, to beef up the military, and to provide unskilled labor for the country's industrialization drive (Smooha 1978; Bernstein and Swirski 1982). The resultant "ethnic gap" between *ashkenazim* and *mizrachim* has persisted, and in some respects even widened, to this day (Kraus and Hodge 1990:66, 68).

In a circle peripheral to the Jewish core are the Palestinian Arab citizens of the State of Israel. Though they are Israeli citizens, until 1966 they were ruled through a military administration that clearly violated their citizenship rights. Since the abolition of the military administration, Palestinian citizens have enjoyed political rights on an individual basis. Israel's Palestinian citizens, now about 20 percent of its population, share with Jews a *liberal citizenship*. As to social rights, these have been tied in Israel, in truly republican manner, to the performance of military service. Since most Palestinian citizens are not called up (by administrative practice, rather than by law), this exemption has been used to justify the abridgement of their social rights (Kretzmer 1990:98–107). They have also been excluded from political citizenship in the republican sense, that is, from participating in attending to the common good of society.

This exclusion was formalized in 1985, in an amendment to the law governing elections to the Knesset, which stated that a list of candidates shall not participate in elections to the Knesset if its goals, explicitly or implicitly, or its actions seek to "negate the existence of the State of Israel as the state of the Jewish people." Another clause annuls lists that seek to "negate the democratic character of the State." Israel's Palestinian citizens then possess individual liberal rights but are forbidden to advance a collective vision of the common good of society that would be incompatible with the Zionist vision (Peled 1992). In fact, one of the major arguments heard against the legitimacy of the peace process, and of the Rabin-Peres government that pursued it, is that they both depended on the support of Palestinian political parties.

The outer circle of the Israeli citizenship hierarchy comprises the Palestinian Arab population in the occupied West Bank and Gaza Strip that was effectively, but not legally, incorporated into Israel in 1967. These Palestinians lived for twenty-seven years under military occupation and possessed no effective civil, political, or social rights. By virtue of being occupied, Palestinian residents of the occupied territories were *neither citizens nor members of Israeli society.* They functioned merely as Israel's metics: a cheap and flexible labor supply, and captive consumers and taxpayers (Semyonov and Lewin-Epstein 1987).

Though integrated into Israel in many respects, all the occupied territories were effectively ruled until 1994–95 by a military government whose commanders were authorized to replace previous civilian laws with military decrees. The legal system, moreover, was openly split. While Palestinian residents of the occupied territories were subject to military law, Israeli settlers in these territories continued to be subject to Israeli civil law even for violations committed in the occupied territories. In short, the particularistic aspect of the Israeli legal system — applying two sets of laws to two different populations residing in the same territory and ruled by the same government — reached its high (or low) point in the West Bank and Gaza (Benvenisti 1990).

In sharp contrast to the restrictions imposed on the two groups of Palestinians, citizens and noncitizens, Orthodox Jews, though they are divided between a majority of opponents and a minority of supporters of Zionism, are the recipients of a variety of privileges. In large part this is due to the reliance of the Zionist movement on the religious tradition for legitimation and mobilizational purposes. A central manifestation of the status of

Jewish religion is the cultural autonomy granted to Orthodox Jews. The Israeli legal system, however, allows Orthodox Jews not only to lead their own autonomous life but also to control key aspects of the life of all Jews in the country. Israel granted rabbinical courts exclusive jurisdiction over marriage and divorce of all Jews in Israel. (Similar laws were enacted with respect to the religious courts of non-Jewish communities.) The most important practical consequence of this law is that, by and large, civil marriage and the possibility of interreligious marriage is not available to Israeli citizens (Zucker 1983:100–121). Cultural autonomy is most pronounced in the existence of two autonomous, but state-financed, religious educational systems and in the deferment or exemption of yeshiva (religious academy) students and religious women from military service. Though military service is one of the pioneering Zionist activities, from which Israel's Arab citizens are also barred or exempt, Orthodox Jews suffer no disability for their lack of service. Orthodox Jews resemble a corporate entity, which carries not only rights but also privileges.

## HIERARCHY OF CITIZENSHIPS

The tension between the exclusionary impetus of frontier society and the inclusionary impetus of civil society in both the *Yishuv* and the State of Israel has expressed itself in a hierarchical and fragmented citizenship structure. In other words, the state and the Histadrut have been mobilizing societal resources and dispensing rights, duties, and privileges, in accordance with a multilayered and complex index of memberships. This citizenship structure has been mediated and made ideologically coherent by the simultaneous use of three conceptions of citizenship—liberal, republican, and ethnonationalist—each with its own definition of the array of social groups comprising the society.

The differential allocation of entitlements, obligations, and domination by the mobilizational Israeli state has proceeded in a number of stages. First, the liberal idea of citizenship has functioned to separate citizen Jews and Palestinians from the noncitizen Palestinians in the occupied territories and abroad, whether these Palestinians were conceptualized as refugees or as stateless, rightless subjects of Israel's military occupation. Then the ethnonationalist discourse of inclusion and exclusion has been invoked to discriminate between Jewish and Palestinian citizens within the sovereign State of Israel. Finally, the republican discourse has been used to legitimize the different positions occupied by the major Jewish ethnic groups: *ashkenazim* versus *mizrachim*.

This framework was little altered until the 1980s. When the State of Israel was founded in 1948, the discourse of *mamlachtiyut* (statehood) was invoked to legitimate the transition to independence. This ethos emphasized the shift from sectoral interests to the general interest, from semivoluntarism to binding obligation, from foreign rule to political sovereignty. Equal application of the law was of paramount importance if the state was to assert its authority over the various Jewish social sectors, which had enjoyed a large degree of autonomy in the *Yishuv* (Peled 1992). As understood in the context of *mamlachtiyut,* the uniform rule of law did not entail, however, a neutral, liberal state or a universal, liberal citizenship structure. The state was to continue to be committed to the values of *chalutziyut* and to demand such commitment from its citizens. *Mamlachtiyut,* then, was not meant to displace the pioneering mobilizing ethos or abandon the settlement project; quite the contrary, it was meant to endow them with the organizational and political resources of a sovereign state. Thus, under the legitimational guise of universal liberal citizenship, individuals and social groups continued to be treated by the state in accordance with their presumed contributions to the common good as defined by the Zionist project (Kimmerling 1985:272).

## THE POLITICS OF LIBERALIZATION AND DECOLONIZATION

As our survey of citizenship conceptions and practices demonstrates, the fragmented Israeli citizenship structure resulted from, facilitated, and depended upon a highly intrusive but formally democratic state, engaged in intensive mobilization and control of societal resources. Starting in the 1980s, the Israeli state, like other states, began to lose its paramount place vis-à-vis society and the citizenship hierarchy gradually began to unravel. It was undermined from the bottom and the top, that is, by those who had nothing to lose and those who had everything to gain by changing it, rather than by the groups placed in the middle of it — *mizrachi* Jews and citizen Palestinians. The *mizrachim,* who helped the Likud Party to victory in 1977, had not been able to demand real improvement in their socioeconomic conditions following this victory, and citizen Palestinians had not launched their own *intifada* or joined that of their noncitizen relatives. We suggest that it is precisely the intermediate location of these two groups, that is, the fact that both of them had a lot to lose by rocking the boat, that prevented them from challenging the established order on their own. Over the years, however, and especially since the 1980s, the hierarchical citizenship began to unravel from the bottom and the top simultaneously.

At the bottom, the least privileged group, noncitizen Palestinians, rose up in the *intifada,* their first effective act of resistance since 1967. The *intifada,* which broke out in December 1987, revealed a break in Israel's citizenship structure, precisely at the point where the gap between its universalist liberal pretensions and its exclusionary practices was widest. Morally, the brutally oppressive methods used by Israel's security forces to suppress the *intifada* forced the Israeli public to face, in a way it never had to do before, the discrepancy between the two systems of law prevailing on both sides of the Green Line. The *intifada* alone could not defeat Israel militarily nor cripple its economy. However, coming as it did at a time when economic and political liberalization strained the resources of the state, both morally and materially, it added considerable force to the argument that the traditional, colonial citizenship discourse should be discarded in favor of a new, civil discourse.

At the top, members of the veteran *ashkenazi* elite have gradually come to realize that the colonial citizenship discourse with its corresponding social institutions, which was crucial for Israel's state- and nation-building and provided the Labor movement with much of its identity, glory, and privileges, was no longer necessary and even may have become a hindrance to their economic interests. Over the years, Israel's economic development, funded to a very large extent by externally generated resources, has weakened the state's and Histadrut's control of the economy in favor of private business interests (Shalev 1992). This sectoral shift has manifested itself in policy changes that began as early as the late 1960s and have gradually intensified over the last two decades. Among these changes were "substantial privatization, the institution of a stable exchange rate, reduced capital subsidies and increasing governmental resistance to 'bailouts,' and cuts in the defense budget and budget deficit" (Shalev 1993). Similar changes, allowing market forces to play a greater role in the labor market and providing foreign goods and investments easier access to the Israeli market, have also been effected (Razin and Sadka 1993).

The *ashkenazi* elite has outgrown the confines of its colonial phase of development and now seeks to venture out into the world. Since members of these new elites feel confident enough to compete in the open market, both domestically and internationally, their concern is no longer to be protected within this market, but rather to expand it as much as possible. As long as the Israeli-Arab conflict destabilized the region, however, Israel was ignored by multinational companies and remained outside the international investment circuit. Not surprisingly, prominent Israeli business leaders, as well as academic economists, were among the most vocal catalysts and supporters of the breakthrough in Israeli-Palestinian relations. The "selling" of the peace accords by Israeli political leaders was done not only by promising an end to the *intifada* and security for the Israeli public, but even more emphatically by presenting peace as a key to unprecedented prosperity (cf. *Globes,* November 1993).

Electorally, the new elites have expressed themselves primarily through Chug Mashov (Feedback Circle), the important neoliberal, pro-peace wing of the Labor Party, and the liberal Meretz Party, which have become the main champions of privatization and economic liberalization, as well as of the peace process. In the Histadrut general elections of May 1994, this peace and privatization block, headed by former Labor Minister of Public Health Hayim Ramon, won 46 percent of the vote. Thus the Histadrut, the umbrella organization of the Labor movement's cooperative economic institutions, was captured by its bitterest enemies and has since shed all of its productive assets as well as its all-important health care system. This process is also likely to bring about a major realignment of the Israeli party system through the crystallization of two political blocks: a neoliberal, peace and privatization block, and a traditional Zionist block, advocating the retention of both the welfare state and much of the occupied territories.

The *ashkenazi* elite, correspondingly, lost much of its interest in maintaining the primacy of republican citizenship with its emphasis on a strong state and on communal public-spiritedness. It was this colonial citizenship discourse, however, that had justified the delegitimation of the Palestinians' national rights. The gradual decline of this discourse and its replacement by a civil, more liberal discourse had the effect, when combined with the *intifada*'s impact, of moving the Rabin-Peres government to moderate its opposition to Palestinian nationalism and begin to shed the occupied Palestinian territories.

The declining of the republican citizenship, however, was only in part replaced with a liberal citizenship discourse; simultaneously it was challenged by the ethnonationalist citizenship discourse that gained in importance after the 1967 war. This *völkisch* citizenship discourse itself was strengthened by absorbing into itself and being transformed by Orthodox Judaism and its doctrines of the religious significance of the Promised Land and of its Jewish domination as a precondition for messianic redemption. The Gush Emunim (Block of the Faithful) movement emerged from within the younger generation of the National Religious Party. The purpose of this new movement was to launch an aggressive settlement drive in the West Bank (Lustick 1988). Though its justification for the continued occupation of the West Bank was religious and messianic, Gush Emunim took great pride in presenting itself, in the words of one of its leaders, Rabbi Moshe Levinger, as "the direct and legitimate offspring of the pioneers of Zionism" (*Yediot Aharonot,* June 18, 1976). As a settlement movement, Gush Emunim was supported by nonreligious groups and individuals as well, precisely because it successfully claimed the mantle of the virtuous republican community that works selflessly for the common good (Shafir 1984). The movement also received considerable financial, military, and political support from the state. Thus, 51 percent of the settlers are currently employed by state agencies, including (Jewish) local governments in the West Bank, compared to 33 percent of the population in Israel proper (*Haaretz* weekly magazine, December 15, 1995).

The assassination of Prime Minister Yitzhak Rabin on November 4, 1995, has demonstrated that the peace process does not go unopposed by powerful forces in society. While most of the opposition to the peace process is general and diffuse, and seems to resign itself to each stage in the process as a fait accompli, its hard core, comprised mostly of settlers and their religious Zionist backers, would go to almost any length to stop and even reverse the process. Their vehement opposition stems from a mixture of ideological and instrumental concerns, but significantly also from their fear of losing their elevated status as a virtuous republican citizen community, true heirs to the legacy of the Labor Zionist pioneers. In this hard core are rabbis who issued religious injunctions against relinquishing Israeli control over any part of the Land of Israel and who have called on religious soldiers to refuse orders to evacuate settlements (which the government has not decided to do yet) and military bases. It is from these circles that the application of the religious categories of *rodef* (persecutor) and *mosser* (collaborator), punishable by death, to the Rabin government and to the prime minister personally emerged and his assassin came.

## CONCLUSION

At the heart of our analysis is the claim that as a democratic frontier society, the Israeli polity has operated under two partially contradictory imperatives: the exclusionary imperative of settlement and nation-building, and the universalist imperative of democratic state-building. As a result, a fragmented, hierarchical citizenship structure was constructed through which the various ethnic and religious groups within Israel and the occupied territories were differentially incorporated in the society. Under this citizenship the tension between exclusion and universalism was sustained, so long as the mobilizational capacity of the state was high and resistance on the part of the lowest-placed group — noncitizen Palestinians — was low.

In recent years both of these conditions have been changing. The mobilizational capacity of the state has been weakening as a result of liberalizing pressures in the economy, and noncitizen Palestinians have launched a national uprising in the occupied territories. Attacked from both the top and the bottom, the entire edifice of Israeli citizenship has begun to unravel, making room for liberal reforms in all spheres of social life. It is this unraveling that led the Rabin-Peres government to reassess and drastically moderate its opposition to Palestinian nationalism.

The decline of republican citizenship and the colonial practices that correspond to it opened the way for the rise of the liberal and the eth-nonationalist citizenship discourses that appear now not as subsidiary or subordinate to republican citizenship but as comprehensive alternatives in their own right. It is on the struggle between the proponents of liberal and *völkisch* citizenship that the future of the peace process depends. Israel's considerable dependence on foreign aid, its myriad economic and cultural ties with Western countries and institutions, and the growth of the socioeconomic sectors within Israel whose continued expansion depend on the flourishing of civil society and liberal citizenship seem to justify a cautious optimism that the supporters of the peace process, and the moderation on which its is based, will prevail.

## BIBLIOGRAPHY

Benvenisti, Eyal. 1990. *Legal Dualism: The Absorption of the Occupied Territories into Israel.* West Bank Data Project. Boulder, Colo.: Westview.

Bernstein, Deborah, and Shlomo Swirski. 1982. "The Rapid Economic Development of Israel and the Emergence of the Ethnic Division of Labour." *British Journal of Sociology* 33, no. 1.

Kimmerling, Baruch. 1985. "Between the Primordial and the Civil Definitions of the Collective Identity: Eretz Israel or the State of Israel?" In *Comparative Social Dynamics,* ed. Erik Cohen et al. Boulder, Colo.: Westview.

Kraus, Vered, and R. W. Hodge. 1990. *Promises in the Promised Land.* New York: Greenwood.

Kretzmer, David. 1990. *The Legal Status of the Arabs in Israel.* Boulder, Colo.: Westview.

Lamar, Howard, and Leonard Thompson. 1981. *The Frontier in History: North America and Southern Africa Compared.* New Haven, Conn.: Yale University Press.

Lustick, Ian S. 1988. *For the Land and the Lord: Jewish Fundamentalism in Israel.* New York: Council on Foreign Relations.

Peled, Yoav. 1992. "Ethnic Democracy and the Legal Construction of Citizenship: Arab Citizens of the Jewish State." *American Political Science Review* 86, no. 2 (June):432–43.

Razin, Assaf, and Efraim Sadka. 1993. *The Economy of Modern Israel: Malaise and Promise.* Chicago: University of Chicago Press.

Semyonov, Moshe, and Noah Lewin-Epstein. 1987. *Hewers of Wood and Drawers of Water: Noncitizen Arabs in the Israeli Labor Market.* Ithaca, N.Y.: Cornell University School of Industrial and Labor Relations.

Shafir, Gershon. 1984. "Changing Nationalism and Israel's 'Open Frontier' on the West Bank." *Theory and Society* 13, no. 6 (Nov.): 803–27.

———. 1996. *Land, Labor and the Origins of the Israeli-Palestinian Conflict, 1882–1914.* Rev. ed. Berkeley: University of California Press.

Shalev, Michael. 1992. *Labour and the Political Economy in Israel.* Oxford: Oxford University Press.

———. 1993. "The Death of the 'Bureaucratic' Labor Market? Structural Change in the Israeli Political Economy." Unpublished paper, Department of Sociology, The Hebrew University, Jerusalem.

Shapiro, Yonathan. 1976. *The Formative Years of the Israeli Labour Party: The Organization of Power, 1919–1930.* London: Sage.

Smooha, Sammy. 1978. *Israel: Pluralism and Conflict.* Berkeley: University of California Press.

Zucker, Norman L. 1983. *The Coming Crisis in Israel: Private Faith and Public Policy.* Cambridge, Mass.: MIT Press.

# 13

## Polity and Group Difference:
## A Critique of the Ideal of Universal Citizenship

IRIS MARION YOUNG

An ideal of universal citizenship has driven the emancipatory momentum of modern political life. Ever since the bourgeoisie challenged aristocratic privileges by claiming equal political rights for citizens as such, women, workers, Jews, blacks, and others have pressed for inclusion in that citizenship status. Modern political theory asserted the equal moral worth of all persons, and social movements of the oppressed took this seriously as implying the inclusion of all persons in full citizenship status under the equal protection of the law.

Citizenship for everyone, and everyone the same qua citizen. Modern political thought generally assumed that the universality of citizenship in the sense of citizenship for all implies a universality of citizenship in the sense that citizenship status transcends particularity and difference. Whatever the social or group differences among citizens, whatever their inequalities of wealth, status, and power in the everyday activities of civil society, citizenship gives everyone the same status as peers in the political public. With equality conceived as sameness, the ideal of universal citizenship carries at least two meanings in addition to the extension of citizenship to everyone: (a) [generality:] universality defined as general in opposition to particular; what citizens have in common as opposed to how they differ, and (b) [equal treatment:] universality in the sense of laws and rules that say the same for all and apply to all in the same way; laws and rules that are blind to individual and group differences.

During this angry, sometimes bloody, political struggle in the nineteenth and twentieth centuries, many among the excluded and disadvantaged thought that winning full citizenship status, that is, equal political and civil rights, would lead to their freedom and equality. Now, in the late twentieth century, however, when citizenship rights have been formally extended to all groups in liberal capitalist societies, some groups still find themselves treated as second-class citizens. Social movements of oppressed and excluded groups have recently asked why extension of equal citizenship rights has not led to social justice and equality. Part of the answer is straightforwardly Marxist: those social activities that most determine the status of individuals and groups are anarchic and oligarchic; economic life is not sufficiently under the control of citizens to affect the unequal status and treatment of groups. I think this is an important and correct diagnosis of why equal citizenship has not eliminated oppression, but in this essay I reflect on another reason more intrinsic to the meaning of politics and citizenship as expressed in much modern thought.

The assumed link between citizenship for everyone, on the one hand, and the two other senses of citizenship — having a common life with and being treated in the same way as the other citizens — on the other, is itself a problem. Contemporary social movements of the oppressed have weakened the link. They assert a positivity and pride in group specificity against ideals of assimilation. They have also questioned whether justice always means that law and policy should enforce equal treatment for all groups. Embryonic in these challenges lies a concept of *differentiated* citizenship as the best way to realize the inclusion and participation of everyone in full citizenship.

In this essay I argue that far from implying one another, the universality of citizenship, in the sense of the inclusion and participation of everyone, stands in tension with the other two meanings of universality embedded in modern political ideas: universality as generality, and universality as equal treatment. First, the ideal that the activities of citizenship express or create a general will that transcends the particular differences of group affiliation, situation, and interest has in practice excluded groups judged not capable of adopting that general point of view; the idea of citizenship as expressing a general will has tended to enforce a homogeneity of citizens. To the degree that contemporary proponents of revitalized citizenship retain that idea of a general will and common life, they implicitly support the same exclusions and homogeneity. Thus I argue that the inclusion and participation of everyone in public discussion and decision making requires mechanisms for group representation. Second, where differences in capacities, culture, values, and behavioral styles exist among groups, but some of these groups are privileged, strict adherence to a principle of equal treatment tends to perpetuate oppression or disadvantage. The inclusion and participation of everyone in social and political institutions therefore sometimes requires the articulation of special rights that attend to group differences in order to undermine oppression and disadvantage.

## CITIZENSHIP AS GENERALITY

Many contemporary political theorists regard capitalist welfare society as depoliticized. Its interest group pluralism privatizes policy making, consigning it to backroom deals and autonomous regulatory agencies and groups. Interest group pluralism fragments both policy and the interests of the individual, making it difficult to assess issues in relation to one another and set priorities. The fragmented and privatized nature of the political process, moreover, facilitates the dominance of the more powerful interests.[1]

In response to this privatization of the political process, many writers call for a renewed public life and a renewed commitment to the virtues of citizenship. Democracy requires that citizens of welfare corporate society awake from their privatized consumerist slumbers, challenge the experts who claim the sole right to rule, and collectively take control of their lives and institutions through processes of active discussion that aim at reaching collective decisions.[2] In participatory democratic institutions citizens develop and exercise capacities of reasoning, discussion, and socializing that otherwise lie dormant, and they move out of their private existence to address others and face them with respect and concern for justice. Many who invoke the virtues of citizenship in opposition to the privatization of politics in welfare capitalist society assume as models for contemporary public life the civic humanism of thinkers such as Machiavelli or, more often, Rousseau.[3]

With these social critics I agree that interest group pluralism, because it is privatized and fragmented, facilitates the domination of corporate, military, and other powerful interests. With them I think democratic processes require the institutionalization of genuinely public discussion. There are serious problems, however, with uncritically assuming as a model the ideals of the civic public that come to us from the tradition of modern political thought.[4] The ideal of the public realm of citizenship as expressing a general will, a point of view and interest that citizens have in common that transcends their differences, has operated in fact as a demand for homogeneity among citizens. The exclusion of groups defined as different was explicitly acknowledged before this century. In our time, the excluding consequences of the universalist ideal of a public that embodies a common will are more subtle, but they still obtain.

The tradition of civic republicanism stands in critical tension with the individualist contract theory of Hobbes or Locke. Where liberal individualism regards the state as a necessary instrument to mediate conflict and regulate action so that individuals can have the freedom to pursue their private ends, the republican tradition locates freedom and autonomy in the actual public activities of citizenship. By participating in public discussion and collective decision making, citizens transcend their particular self-interested lives and the pursuit of private interests to adopt a general point of view from which they agree on the common good. Citizenship is an expression of the universality of human life; it is a realm of rationality and freedom as opposed to the heteronomous realm of particular need, interest, and desire.

Nothing in this understanding of citizenship as universal as opposed to particular, common as opposed to differentiated, implies extending full citizenship status to all groups. Indeed, at least some modern republicans thought just the contrary. While they extolled the virtues of citizenship as expressing the universality of humanity, they consciously excluded some people from citizenship on the grounds that they could not adopt the general point of view, or that their inclusion would disperse and divide the public. The ideal of a common good, a general will, a shared public life leads to pressures for a homogeneous citizenry.

Feminists in particular have analyzed how the discourse that links the civic public with fraternity is not merely metaphorical. Founded by men, the modern state and its public realm of citizenship paraded as universal values and norms that were derived from specifically masculine experience: militarist norms of honor and homoerotic camaraderie; respectful competition and bargaining among independent agents; discourse framed in unemotional tones of dispassionate reason.

Several commentators have argued that in extolling the virtues of citizenship as participation in a universal public realm, modern men expressed a flight from sexual difference, from having to recognize another kind of existence that they could not entirely understand, and from the embodiment, dependency on nature, and morality that women represent.[5] Thus the opposition between the universality of the public realm of citizenship and the particularity of private interest became conflated with oppositions between reason and passion, masculine and feminine.

The bourgeois world instituted a moral division of labor between reason and sentiment, identifying masculinity with reason and femininity with sentiment, desire, and the needs of the body. Extolling a public realm of manly virtue and citizenship as independence, generality, and dispassionate reason entailed creating the private sphere of the family as the place to which emotion, sentiment, and bodily needs must be confined.[6] The generality of the public thus depends on excluding women, who are responsible for tending to that private realm, and who lack the dispassionate rationality and independence required of good citizens.

In his social scheme, for example, Rousseau excluded women from the public realm of citizenship because they are the caretakers of affectivity, desire, and the body. If we allowed appeals to desires and bodily needs to move public debates, we would undermine public deliberation by fragmenting its unity. Even within the domestic realm, moreover, women must be dominated. Their dangerous, heterogeneous sexuality must be kept chaste and confined to marriage. Enforcing chastity on women will keep each family a separated unity, preventing the chaos and blood mingling that would be produced by illegitimate children. Chaste, enclosed women in turn oversee men's desire by tempering its potentially disruptive impulses through moral education. Men's desire for women itself threatens to shatter and disperse the universal, rational realm of the public, as well as to disrupt the neat distinction between the public and private. As guardians of the private realm of need, desire, and affectivity, women must ensure that men's impulses do not subvert the universality of reason. The moral neatness of the female-tended hearth, moreover, will temper the possessively individualistic impulses of the particularistic realm of business and commerce, since competition, like sexuality, constantly threatens to explode the unity of the polity.[7]

It is important to recall that universality of citizenship conceived as generality operated to exclude not only women, but other groups as well. European and American republicans found little contradiction in promoting a universality of citizenship that excluded some groups, because the idea that citizenship is the same for all translated in practice to the requirement that all citizens be the same. The white male bourgeoisie conceived republican virtue as rational, restrained, and chaste, not yielding to passion or desire for luxury, and thus able to rise above desire and need to a concern for the common good. This implied excluding poor people and wage workers from citizenship on the grounds that they were too motivated by need to adopt a general perspective. The designers of the American Constitution were no more egalitarian than their European brethren in this respect; they specifically intended to restrict the access of the laboring class to the public, because they feared disruption of commitment to the general interests.

These early American republicans were also quite explicit about the need for the homogeneity of citizens, fearing that group differences would tend to undermine commitment to the general interest. This meant that the presence of blacks and Indians, and later Mexicans and Chinese, in the territories of the republic posed a threat that only assimilation, extermination, or dehumanization could thwart. Various combinations of these three were used, of course, but recognition of these groups as peers in the public was never an option. Even such republican fathers as Jefferson identified the red and black people in their territories with wild nature and passion, just as they feared that women outside the domestic realm were wanton and avaricious. They defined moral, civilized republican life in opposition to this backward-looking, uncultivated desire that they identified with women and nonwhites.[8] A similar logic of exclusion operated in Europe, where Jews were particular targets.[9]

These republican exclusions were not accidental, nor were they inconsistent with the ideal of universal citizenship as understood by these theorists. They were a direct consequence of a dichotomy between public and private that defined the public as a realm of generality in which all particularities are left behind, and defined the private as the particular, the realm of affectivity, affiliation, need, and the body. As long as that dichotomy is in place, the inclusion of the formerly excluded — women, workers, Jews, blacks, Asians, Indians, Mexicans — in the definition of citizenship imposes a homogeneity that suppresses group differences in the public and in practice forces the formerly excluded groups to be measured according to norms derived from and defined by privileged groups.

Contemporary critics of interest group liberalism who call for a renewed public life certainly do not intend to exclude any adult persons or groups from citizenship. They are democrats, convinced that only the inclusion and participation of all citizens in political life will make for wise and fair decisions and a polity that enhances rather than inhibits the capacities of its citizens and their relations with one another. The emphasis by such participatory democrats on generality and commonness, however, still threatens to suppress differences among citizens.

I shall focus on the text of Benjamin Barber, who, in his book *Strong Democracy,* produces a compelling and concrete vision of participatory democratic processes. Barber recognizes the need to safeguard a democratic public from intended or inadvertent group exclusions, though he offers no proposals for safeguarding the inclusion and participation of everyone. He also argues fiercely against contemporary political theorists who construct a model of political discourse purified of affective dimensions. Thus Barber does not fear the disruption of the generality and rationality of the public by desire and the body in the way that nineteenth-century republican theorists did. He retains, however, a conception of the civic public as defined by generality, as opposed to group affinity and particular need and interest. He makes a clear distinction between the public realm of citizenship and civic activity on the one hand, and a private realm of particular identities, roles, affiliations, and interests on the other. Citizenship by no means exhausts people's social identities, but it takes moral priority over all social activities in a strong democracy. The pursuit of particular interests, the pressing of the claims of particular groups, all must take place within a framework of community and common vision established by the public realm. Thus Barber's vision of participatory democracy continues to rely on an opposition between the public sphere of a general interest and a private sphere of particular interest and affiliation.[10]

While recognizing the need for majority rule procedures and means of safeguarding minority rights, Barber asserts that "the strong democrat regrets every division and regards the existence of majorities as a sign that mutualism has failed" (207). A community of citizens, he says, "owes the character of its existence to what its constituent members have in common" (232), and this entails transcending the order of individual needs and wants to recognize that "we are a moral body whose existence depends on the common ordering of individual needs and wants into a single vision of the future in which all can share" (224). This common vision is not imposed on individuals from above, however, but is forged by them in talking and working together. Barber's models of such common projects, however, reveal his latent biases: "Like players on a team or soldiers at war, those who practice a common politics may come to feel ties that they never felt before they commenced their common activity. This sort of bonding, which emphasizes common procedures, common work, and a shared sense of what a community needs to succeed, rather than monolithic purposes and ends, serves strong democracy most successfully" (244).

The attempt to realize an ideal of universal citizenship that finds the public embodying generality as opposed to particularity, commonness versus difference, will tend to exclude or to put at a disadvantage some groups, even when they have formally equal citizenship status. The idea of the public as universal and the concomitant identification of particularity with privacy makes homogeneity a requirement of public participation. In exercising their citizenship, all citizens should assume the same impartial, general point of view transcending all particular interests, perspectives, and experiences.

But such an impartial general perspective is a myth.[11] People necessarily and properly consider public issues in terms influenced by their situated experience and perception of social relations. Different social groups have different needs, cultures, histories, experiences, and perceptions of social relations, which influence their interpretation of the meaning and consequences of policy proposals and influence the form of their political reasoning. These differences in political interpretation are not merely or even primarily a result of differing or conflicting interests, for groups have differing interpretations even when they seek to promote justice and not merely their own self-regarding ends. In a society where some groups are privileged while others are oppressed, insisting that as citizens persons should leave behind their particular affiliations and experiences to adopt a general point of view serves only to reinforce that privilege; for the perspectives and interests of the privileged will tend to dominate this unified public, marginalizing or silencing those of other groups.

Barber asserts that responsible citizenship requires transcending particular affiliations, commitments, and needs, because a public cannot function if its members are concerned only with their private interests. Here he makes an important confusion between plurality and privatization. The interest group pluralism that he and others criticize indeed institutionalizes and encourages an egoistic, self-regarding view of the political process, one that sees parties entering the political competition for scarce goods and privileges only in order to maximize their own gain, and therefore they need not listen to or respond to the claims of others who have their own point of view. The processes and often the outcomes of interest group bargaining, moreover, take place largely in private; they are neither revealed nor discussed in a forum that genuinely involves all those potentially affected by decisions.

Privacy in this sense of private bargaining for the sake of private gain is quite different from plurality, in the sense of the differing group experiences, affiliations, and commitments that operate in any large society. It is possible for persons to maintain their group identity and to be influenced by their perceptions of social events derived from their group-specific experience, and at the same time to be public-spirited, in the sense of being open to listening to the claims of others and not being concerned for their own gain alone. It is possible and necessary for people to maintain a critical distance from their own immediate desires and gut reactions in order to discuss public proposals. Doing so, however, cannot require that citizens abandon their particular affiliations, experiences, and social locations. As I will discuss in the next section, having the voices of particular group perspectives other than one's own explicitly represented in public discussion best fosters the maintenance of such critical distance without the pretense of impartiality.

A repoliticization of public life should not require the creation of a unified public realm in which citizens leave behind their particular group affiliations, histories, and needs to discuss a general interest or common good. Such a desire for unity suppresses but does not eliminate differences and tends to exclude some perspectives from the public.[12] Instead of a universal citizenship in the sense of this generality, we need a group-differentiated citizenship and a heterogeneous public. In a heterogeneous public, differences are publicly recognized and acknowledged as irreducible, by which I mean that persons from one perspective or history can never completely understand and adopt the point of view of those with other group-based perspectives and histories. Yet commitment to the need and desire to decide together the society's policies fosters communication across those differences.

## DIFFERENTIATED CITIZENSHIP AS
## GROUP REPRESENTATION

In her study of the functioning of a New England town meeting government, Jane Mansbridge discusses how women, blacks, working-class people, and poor people tend to participate less and have their interests represented less than whites, middle-class professionals, and men. Even though all citizens have the right to participate in the decision-making process, the experience and perspectives of some groups tend to be silenced for many reasons. White middle-class men assume authority more than others, and they are more practiced at speaking persuasively; mothers and old people often find it more difficult than others to get to meetings.[13] Amy Gutmann also discusses how participatory democratic structures tend to silence disadvantaged groups. She offers the example of community control of schools, where increased democracy led to increased segregation in many cities because the more privileged and articulate whites were able to promote their perceived interests against blacks' just demand for equal treatment in an integrated system.[14] Such cases indicate that when participatory democratic structures define citizenship in universalistic and unified terms, they tend to reproduce existing group oppression.

Gutmann argues that such oppressive consequences of democratization imply that social and economic equality must be achieved before political equality can be instituted. I cannot quarrel with the value of social and economic equality, but I think its achievement depends on increasing political equality as much as the achievement of political equality depends on increasing social and economic equality. If we are not to be forced to trace a utopian circle, we need to solve now the "paradox of democracy" by which social power makes some citizens more equal than others, and equality of citizenship makes some people more powerful citizens. That solution lies at least in part in providing institutionalized means for the explicit recognition and representation of oppressed groups. Before discussing principles and practices involved in such a solution, however, it is necessary to say something about what a group is and when a group is oppressed.

The concept of a social group has become politically important because recent emancipatory and leftist social movements have mobilized around group identity rather than exclusively class or economic interests. In many cases such mobilization has consisted in embracing and positively defining a despised or devalued ethnic or racial identity. In the women's movement, gay rights movement, or elders' movements, differential social status based on age, sexuality, physical capacity, or the division of labor has been taken up as a positive group identity for political mobilization.

I shall not attempt to define a social group here, but I shall point to several marks that distinguish a social group from other collectivities of people. A social group involves first of all an affinity with other persons by which they identify with one another, and by which other people identify them. A person's particular sense of history, understanding of social relations and personal possibilities, her or his mode of reasoning, values, and expressive styles are constituted at least partly by her or his group identity. Many group definitions come from the outside, from other groups that label and stereotype certain people. In such circumstances the despised group members often find their affinity in their oppression. The concept of social group must be distinguished from two concepts with which it might be confused: aggregate and association.

An aggregate is any classification of persons according to some attribute. Persons can be aggregated according to any number of attributes, all of them equally arbitrary — eye color, the make of car we drive, the street we live on. At times the groups that have emotional and social salience in our society are interpreted as aggregates, as arbitrary classifications of persons according to attributes of skin color, genitals, or years lived. A social group, however, is not defined primarily by a set of shared attributes, but by the sense of identity that people have. What defines black Americans as a social group is not primarily their skin color; this is exemplified by the

fact that some persons whose skin color is fairly light, for example, identify as black. Though sometimes objective attributes are a necessary condition for classifying oneself or others as a member of a certain social group,
it is the identification of certain persons with a social status, a common
history that social status produces, and a self-identification that defines the
group as a group.

Political and social theorists tend more often to elide social groups
with associations rather than with aggregates. By an association I mean a
collectivity of persons who come together voluntarily — such as a club, corporation, political party, church, college, union, lobbying organization, or
interest group. An individualist contract model of society applies to associations but not to groups. Individuals constitute associations; they come together as already formed persons and set them up, establishing rules, positions, and offices.

Since one joins an association, even if membership in it fundamentally affects one's life, one does not take that association membership to define one's very identity in the way that, for example, being Navajo might.
Group affinity, on the other hand, has the character of what Heidegger calls
"thrownness": one finds oneself as a member of a group, whose existence
and relations one experiences as always already having been. For a person's
identity is defined in relation to how others identify him or her, and others
do so in terms of groups that always already have specific attributes, stereotypes, and norms associated with them, in reference to which a person's
identity will be formed. From the thrownness of group affinity it does not
follow that one cannot leave groups and enter new ones. Many women become lesbian after identifying as heterosexual, and anyone who lives long
enough becomes old. These cases illustrate thrownness precisely in that
such changes in group affinity are experienced as a transformation in one's
identity.

A social group should not be understood as an essence or nature
with a specific set of common attributes. Instead, group identity should be
understood in relational terms. Social processes generate groups by creating relational differentiations, situations of clustering and affective bonding in which people feel affinity for other people. Sometimes groups define
themselves by despising or excluding others whom they define as other, and
whom they dominate and oppress. Although social processes of affinity and
separation define groups, they do not give groups a substantive identity.
There is no common nature that members of a group have.

As products of social relations, groups are fluid; they come into being and may fade away. Homosexual practices have existed in many soci-

eties and historical periods, for example, but gay male group identification exists only in the West in the twentieth century. Group identity may become salient only under specific circumstances, in interaction with other groups. Most people in modern societies have multiple group identifications, moreover, and therefore groups themselves are not discrete unities. Every group has group differences cutting across it.

I think that group differentiation is an inevitable and desirable process in modern societies. We need not settle that question, however. I merely assume that ours is now a group-differentiated society, and that it will continue to be so for some time to come. Our political problem is that some of our groups are privileged and others are oppressed.

But what is oppression? In another place I give a fuller account of the concept of oppression.[15] Briefly, a group is oppressed when one or more of the following conditions occurs to all or a large portion of its members: (1) the benefits of their work or energy go to others without those others reciprocally benefiting them (exploitation); (2) they are excluded from participation in major social activities, which in our society means primarily a workplace (marginalization); (3) they live and work under the authority of others, and have little work autonomy and authority over others themselves (powerlessness); (4) as a group they are stereotyped at the same time that their experience and situation is invisible in the society in general, and they have little opportunity and little audience for the expression of their experience and perspective on social events (cultural imperialism); (5) group members suffer random violence and harassment motivated by group hatred or fear. In the United States today at least the following groups are oppressed in one or more of these ways: women, blacks, Native Americans, Chicanos, Puerto Ricans and other Spanish-speaking Americans, Asian Americans, gay men, lesbians, working-class people, poor people, old people, and mentally and physically disabled people.

Perhaps in some utopian future there will be a society without group oppression and disadvantage. We cannot develop political principles by starting with the assumption of a completely just society, however, but must begin from within the general historical and social conditions in which we exist. This means that we must develop participatory democratic theory not on the assumption of an undifferentiated humanity, but rather on the assumption that there are group differences and that some groups are actually or potentially oppressed or disadvantaged.

I assert, then, the following principle: a democratic public, however that is constituted, should provide mechanisms for the effective representation and recognition of the distinct voices and perspectives of those of its constituent groups that are oppressed or disadvantaged within it. Such group representation implies institutional mechanisms and public resources supporting three activities: (1) self-organization of group members so that they gain a sense of collective empowerment and a reflective understanding of their collective experience and interests in the context of the society; (2) voicing a group's analysis of how social policy proposals affect them, and generating policy proposals themselves, in institutionalized contexts where decision makers are obliged to show that they have taken these perspectives into consideration; (3) having veto power regarding specific policies that affect a group directly, for example, reproductive rights for women or use of reservation lands for Native Americans.

The principles call for specific representation only for oppressed or disadvantaged groups, because privileged groups already are represented. Thus the principles would not apply in a society entirely without oppression. I do not regard the principles as merely provisional, or instrumental, however, because I believe that group difference in modern complex societies is both inevitable and desirable, and that wherever there is group difference, disadvantage or oppression always looms as a possibility. Thus a society should always be committed to representation for oppressed or disadvantaged groups and ready to implement such representation when it appears. These considerations are rather academic in our own context, however, since we live in a society with deep group oppressions, the complete elimination of which is only a remote possibility.

Social and economic privilege means, among other things, that the groups that have it behave as though they have a right to speak and be heard, that others treat them as though they have that right, and that they have the material, personal, and organizational resources that enable them to speak and be heard in public. The privileged are usually not inclined to protect and further the interests of the oppressed partly because their social position prevents them from understanding those interests, and partly because to some degree their privilege depends on the continued oppression of others. So a major reason for explicit representation of oppressed groups in discussion and decision making is to undermine oppression. Such group representation also exposes in public the specificity of the assumptions and experience of the privileged. For unless they are confronted with different perspectives on social relations and events, different values and language, most people tend to assert their own perspective as universal.

Theorists and politicians extol the virtues of citizenship because through public participation persons are called on to transcend merely self-centered motivation and acknowledge their dependence on and responsibility to others. The responsible citizen is concerned not merely with interests but with justice, with acknowledging that each other person's interest and point of view is as good as his or her own, and that the needs and interests of everyone must be voiced and be heard by the others, who must acknowledge, respect, and address those needs and interests. The problem of universality has occurred when this responsibility has been interpreted as transcendence into a general perspective.

I have argued that defining citizenship as generality avoids and obscures this requirement that all experiences, needs, and perspectives on social events have a voice and are respected. A general perspective that all persons can adopt and from which all experiences and perspectives can be understood and taken into account does not exist. The existence of social groups implies different, though not necessarily exclusive, histories, experiences, and perspectives on social life that people have, and it implies that they do not entirely understand the experience of other groups. No one can claim to speak in the general interest, because no one of the groups can speak for another, and certainly no one can speak for them all. Thus the only way to have all group experience and social perspectives voiced, heard, and taken account of is to have them specifically represented in the public.

Group representation is the best means to promote just outcomes to democratic decision-making processes. The argument for this claim relies on Habermas's conception of communicative ethics. In the absence of a philosopher king who reads transcendent normative verities, the only ground for a claim that a policy or decision is just is that it has been arrived at by a public that has truly promoted free expression of all needs and points of view. In his formulation of a communicative ethic, Habermas retains inappropriately an appeal to a universal or impartial point of view from which claims in a public should be addressed. A communicative ethic that does not merely articulate a hypothetical public that would justify decisions, but proposes actual conditions tending to promote just outcomes of decision-making processes, should promote conditions for the expression of the concrete needs of all individuals in their particularity.[16] The concreteness of individual lives, their needs and interests, and their perception of the needs and interests of others, I have argued, are structured partly through group-based experience and identity. Thus full and free expression of concrete needs and interests under social circumstances where some groups are silenced or marginalized requires that they have a specific voice in deliberation and decision making.

The introduction of such differentiation and particularity into democratic procedures does not encourage the expression of narrow self-interest; indeed, group representation is the best antidote to self-deceiving self-interest masked as an impartial or general interest. In a democratically structured public where social inequality is mitigated through group representation, individuals or groups cannot simply assert that they want something; they must say that justice requires or allows that they have it. Group representation provides the opportunity for some to express their needs or interests who would not likely be heard without that representation. At the same time, the test of whether a claim on the public is just, or a mere expression of self-interest, is best made when persons making it must confront the opinion of others who have explicitly different, though not necessarily conflicting, experiences, priorities, and needs. As a person of social privilege, I am not likely to go outside of myself and have a regard for social justice unless I am forced to listen to the voice of those my privilege tends to silence.

Group representation best institutionalizes fairness under circumstances of social oppression and domination. But group representation also maximizes knowledge expressed in discussion, and thus promotes practical wisdom. Group differences involve not only different needs, interests, and goals, but probably more importantly, different social locations and experiences from which social facts and policies are understood. Members of different social groups are likely to know different things about the structure of social relations and the potential and actual effects of social policies. Because of their history, their group-specific values or modes of expression, their relationship to other groups, the kind of work they do, and so on, different groups have different ways of understanding the meaning of social events, which can contribute to the others' understanding if they are expressed and heard.

Emancipatory social movements in recent years have developed some political practices committed to the idea of a heterogeneous public, and they have at least partly or temporarily instituted such publics. Some political organizations, unions, and feminist groups have formal caucuses for groups (such as blacks, Latinos, women, gay men and lesbians, and disabled or old people) whose perspectives might be silenced without them. Frequently these organizations have procedures for caucus voice in organization discussion and caucus representation in decision making, and some organizations also require representation of members of specific groups in leadership bodies. Under the influence of these social movements asserting group difference, during some years even the Democratic Party, at both national and state levels, has instituted delegate rules that include provisions for group representation.

Though its realization is far from assured, the ideal of a "rainbow coalition" expresses such a heterogeneous public with forms of group representation. The traditional form of coalition corresponds to the idea of a unified public that transcends particular differences of experience and concern. In traditional coalitions, diverse groups work together for ends that they agree interest or affect them all in a similar way, and they generally agree that the differences of perspective, interests, or opinion among them will not surface in the public statements and actions of the coalition. In a rainbow coalition, by contrast, each of the constituent groups affirms the presence of the others and affirms the specificity of its experience and perspective on social issues.[17] In the rainbow public, blacks do not simply tolerate the participation of gays, labor activists do not grudgingly work alongside peace movement veterans, and none of them paternalistically allow feminist participation. Ideally, a rainbow coalition affirms the presence and supports the claims of each of the oppressed groups or political movements constituting it, and it arrives at a political program not by voicing some "principles of unity" that hide differences but rather by allowing each constituency to analyze economic and social issues from the perspective of its experience. This implies that each group maintains autonomy in relating to its constituency, and that decision-making bodies and procedures provide for group representation.

To the degree that there are heterogeneous publics operating according to the principles of group representation in contemporary politics, they exist only in organizations and movements resisting the majority politics. Nevertheless, in principle participatory democracy entails commitment to institutions of a heterogeneous public in all spheres of democratic decision making. Until and unless group oppression and disadvantages are eliminated, political publics, including democratized workplaces and government decision-making bodies, should include the specific representation of those oppressed groups, through which those groups express their specific understanding of the issues before the public and register a group-based vote. Such structures of group representation should not replace structures of regional or party representation but should exist alongside them.

Implementing principles of group representation in national politics in the United States, or in restructured democratic publics within particular institutions such as factories, offices, universities, churches, and social service agencies, would require creative thinking and flexibility. There are no models to follow. European models of consociational democratic institutions, for example, cannot be taken outside of the contexts in which they have evolved, and even within them they do not operate in a very democratic fashion. Reports of experiments with publicly institutionalized self-organization among women, indigenous peoples, workers, peasants, and students in contemporary Nicaragua offer an example closer to the conception I am advocating.[18]

The principle of group representation calls for such structures of representation for oppressed or disadvantaged groups. But what groups deserve representation? Clear candidates for group representation in policy making in the United States are women, blacks, Native Americans, old people, poor people, disabled people, gay men and lesbians, Spanish-speaking Americans, young people, and nonprofessional workers. But it may not be necessary to ensure specific representation of all these groups in all public contexts and in all policy discussions. Representation should be designated whenever the group's history and social situation provide a particular perspective on the issues, when the interests of its members are specifically affected, and when its perceptions and interests are not likely to receive expression without that representation.

An origin problem that no philosophical argument can solve emerges in proposing a principle such as this. To implement this principle a public must be constituted to decide which groups deserve specific representation in decision-making procedures. What are the principles guiding the composition of such a "constitutional convention"? Who should decide what groups should receive representation, and by what procedures should this decision take place? No program or set of principles can found a politics, because politics is always a process in which we are already engaged. Principles can be appealed to in the course of political discussion; they can be accepted by a public as guiding their action. I propose a principle of group representation as a part of such potential discussion, but it cannot replace that discussion or determine its outcome.

What should be the mechanisms of group representation? Earlier I stated that the self-organization of the group is one of the aspects of a principle of group representation. Members of the group must meet together in democratic forums to discuss issues and formulate group positions and proposals. This principle of group representation should be understood as part of a larger program for democratized decision-making processes. Public life and decision-making processes should be transformed so that all citizens have significantly greater opportunities for participation in discussion and decision making. All citizens should have access to neighborhood or district assemblies where they participate in discussion and decision making. In such a more participatory democratic scheme, members of oppressed groups would also have group assemblies, which would delegate group representatives.

One might well ask how the idea of a heterogeneous public that encourages self-organization of groups and structures of group representation in decision making is different from the interest group pluralism criticism I endorsed earlier in this essay. First, in the heterogeneous public not any collectivity of persons that chooses to form an association counts as a candidate for group representation. Only those groups that describe the major identities and major status relationships constituting the society or particular institution, and that are oppressed or disadvantaged, deserve specific representation in a heterogeneous public. In the structures of interest group pluralism, Friends of the Whales, the National Association for the Advancement of Colored People, the National Rifle Association, and the National Freeze Campaign all have the same status, and each influences decision making to the degree that its resources and ingenuity can win out in the competition for policy makers' ears. While democratic politics must maximize freedom of the expression of opinion and interest, that is a different issue from ensuring that the perspective of all groups has a voice.

Second, in the heterogeneous public the groups represented are not defined by some particular interest or goal, or some particular political position. Social groups are comprehensive identities and ways of life. Because of their experiences their members may have some common interests that they seek to press in the public. Their social location, however, tends to give them distinctive understandings of all aspects of the society and unique perspectives on social issues. For example, many Native Americans argue that their traditional religion and relation to land gives them a unique and important understanding of environmental problems.

Finally, interest group pluralism operates precisely to forestall the emergence of public discussion and decision making. Each interest group promotes only its specific interest as thoroughly and forcefully as it can, and it need not consider the other interests competing in the political marketplace except strategically, as potential allies or adversaries in the pursuit of its own. The rules of interest group pluralism do not require justifying one's interest as right or as compatible with social justice. A heterogeneous public, however, is a public, where participants discuss together the issues before them and are supposed to come to a decision that they determine is best or most just.

## UNIVERSAL RIGHTS AND SPECIAL RIGHTS

A second aspect of the universality of citizenship is today in tension with the goal of full inclusion and participation of all groups in political and social institutions: universality in the formulation of law and policies. Modern and contemporary liberalism hold as basic the principle that the rules and policies of the state, and in contemporary liberalism also the rules of private institutions, ought to be blind to race, gender, and other group differences. The public realm of the state and law properly should express its rules in general terms that abstract from the particularities of individual and group histories, needs, and situations to recognize all persons equally and treat all citizens in the same way.

As long as political ideology and practice persisted in defining some groups as unworthy of equal citizenship status because of supposedly natural differences from white male citizens, it was important for emancipatory movements to insist that all people are the same in respect of their moral worth and deserve equal citizenship. In this context, demands for equal rights that are blind to group differences were the only sensible way to combat exclusion and degradation.

Today, however, the social consensus is that all persons are of equal moral worth and deserve equal citizenship. With the near achievement of equal rights for all groups, with the important exception of gay men and lesbians, group inequalities nevertheless remain. Under these circumstances, many feminists, black liberation activists, and others struggling for the full inclusion and participation of all groups in this society's institutions and positions of power, reward, and satisfaction, argue that rights and rules that are universally formulated and thus blind to differences of race, culture, gender, age, or disability perpetuate rather than undermine oppression.

Contemporary social movements seeking full inclusion and participation of oppressed and disadvantaged groups now find themselves faced with a dilemma of difference.[19] On the one hand, they must continue to deny that there are any essential differences between men and women, whites and blacks, able-bodied and disabled people that justify denying women, blacks, or disabled people the opportunity to do anything that others are free to do or to be included in any institution or position. On the other hand, they have found it necessary to affirm that there are often group-based differences between men and women, whites and blacks, able-bodied and disabled people that make application of a strict principle of equal treatment, especially in competition for positions, unfair because these differences put those groups at a disadvantage. For example, white middle-class men as a group are socialized into the behavioral styles of a particular kind of articulateness, coolness, and competent authoritativeness that are most rewarded in professional and managerial life. To the degree that there are group differences that disadvantage, fairness seems to call for acknowledging rather than being blind to them.

Though in many respects the law is now blind to group differences, the society is not, and some groups continue to be marked as deviant and as the other. In everyday interactions, images, and decision making, assumptions continue to be made about women, blacks, Latinos, gay men, lesbians, old people, and other marked groups that continue to justify exclusions, avoidances, paternalism, and authoritarian treatment. Continued racist, sexist, homophobic, ageist, and ableist behaviors and institutions create particular circumstances for these groups, usually disadvantaging them in their opportunity to develop their capacities and giving them particular experiences and knowledge. Finally, in part because they have been segregated and excluded from one another, and in part because they have particular histories and traditions, there are cultural differences among social groups — differences in language, style of living, body comportment and gesture, values, and perspectives on society.

Acknowledging group difference in capacities, needs, culture, and cognitive styles poses a problem for those seeking to eliminate oppression only if difference is understood as deviance or deficiency. Such understanding presumes that some capacities, needs, cultures, or cognitive styles are normal. I suggested earlier that their privilege allows dominant groups to assert their experience of and perspective on social events as impartial and objective. In a similar fashion, their privilege allows some groups to project their group-based capacities, values, and cognitive and behavioral styles as the norm to which all persons should be expected to conform. Feminists in particular have argued that most contemporary workplaces, especially the most desirable, presume a life rhythm and behavioral style typical of men, and that women are expected to accommodate to the workplace expectations that assume those norms.

Where group differences in capacities, values, and behavioral or cognitive styles exist, equal treatment in the allocation of reward according to rules of merit composition will reinforce and perpetuate disadvantage. Equal treatment requires everyone to be measured according to the same norms, but in fact there are no "neutral" norms of behavior and performance. Where some groups are privileged and others oppressed, the formulation of law, policy, and the rules of private institutions tend to be biased in favor of the privileged groups, because their particular experience implicitly sets the norm. Thus, where there are group differences in capacities, socialization, values, and cognitive and cultural styles, only attending to such differences can enable the inclusion and participation of all groups in political and economic institutions. This implies that instead of always formulating rights and rules in universal terms that are blind to difference, some groups sometimes deserve special rights.[20] In what follows, I shall review several contexts of contemporary policy debate where I argue such special rights for oppressed or disadvantaged groups are appropriate.

The issue of a right to pregnancy and maternity leave, and the right to special treatment for nursing mothers, is highly controversial among feminists today. I do not intend here to wind through the intricacies of what has become a conceptually challenging and interesting debate in legal theory. As Linda Krieger argues, the issue of rights for pregnant and birthing mothers in relation to the workplace has created a paradigm crisis for our understanding of sexual equality, because the application of a principle of equal treatment on this issue has yielded results whose effects on women are at best ambiguous and at worst detrimental.[21]

In my view, an equal treatment approach on this issue is inadequate because it either implies that women do not receive any right to leave and job security when they are having babies, or it assimilates such guarantees under a supposedly gender-neutral category of "disability." Such assimilation is unacceptable because pregnancy and childbirth are normal conditions of normal women, they themselves count as socially necessary work, and they have unique and variable characteristics and needs.[22] Assimilating pregnancy into disability gives a negative meaning to these processes as "unhealthy." It suggests, moreover, that the primary or only reason that a woman has a right to leave and job security is that she is physically unable to work at her job, or that doing so would be more difficult than when she is not pregnant and recovering from childbirth. While these are important reasons, depending on the individual woman, another reason is that she ought to have the time to establish breast-feeding and develop a relationship and routine with her child, if she chooses.

The pregnancy leave debate has been heated and extensive because both feminists and nonfeminists tend to think of biological sex difference as the most fundamental and irradicable difference. When difference slides into deviance, stigma, and disadvantage, this impression can engender the fear that sexual equality is not attainable. I think it is important to emphasize that reproduction is by no means the only context in which issues of same versus different treatment arise. It is not even the only context where it arises for issues involving bodily difference. The last twenty years have seen significant success in winning special rights for persons with physical and mental disabilities. Here is a clear case where promoting equality in participation and inclusion requires attending to the particular needs of different groups.

Another bodily difference that has not been as widely discussed in law and policy literature, but should be, is age. With increasing numbers of old people who are willing and able to work now marginalized in our society, the issue of mandatory retirement has been increasingly discussed. This discussion has been muted because serious consideration of working rights for all people able and willing to work implies major restructuring of the allocation of labor in an economy with already socially volatile levels of unemployment. Forcing people out of their workplaces solely on account of their age is arbitrary and unjust. Yet I think it is also unjust to require old people to work on the same terms as younger people. Old people should have different working rights. When they reach a certain age they should be allowed to retire and receive income benefits. If they wish to continue working, they should be allowed more flexible and part-time schedules than most workers currently have.

Each of these cases of special rights in the workplace — pregnancy and birthing, physical disability, and being old — has its own purposes and structures. They all challenge, however, the same paradigm of the "normal, healthy" worker and the "typical work situation." In each case the circumstance that calls for different treatment should be understood as lodged not in the differently treated workers per se, but in their interaction with the structure and norms of the workplace. Even in cases such as these, that is, difference does not have its source in natural, unalterable biological attributes, but in the relationship of bodies to conventional rules and practices. In each case the political claim for special rights emerges not from a need to compensate for an inferiority, as some would interpret it, but from a positive assertion of specificity in different forms of life.[23]

Issues of difference arise for law and policy not only regarding bodily being, but just as importantly for cultural integrity and invisibility. By culture I mean group-specific phenomena of behavior, temperament, or meaning. Cultural differences include phenomena of language, speaking style or dialect, body comportment, gesture, social practices, values, group-specific socialization, and so on. To the degree that groups are culturally different, however, equal treatment in many issues of social policy is unjust because it denies these cultural differences or makes them a liability. There are a vast number of issues where fairness involves attention to cultural differences and their effects, but I shall briefly discuss three: affirmative action, comparable worth, and bilingual, bicultural education and service.

Whether they involve quotas or not, affirmative action programs violate a principle of equal treatment because they are race- or gender-conscious in setting criteria for school admissions, jobs, or promotions. These policies are usually defended in one of two ways. Giving preference to race or gender is understood either as just compensation for groups that have suffered discrimination in the past, or as compensation for the present disadvantage these groups suffer because of that history of discrimination and exclusion.[24] I do not wish to quarrel with either of these justifications for the differential treatment based on race or gender implied by affirmative action policies. I want to suggest that in addition we can understand affirmative action policies as compensating for the cultural biases of standards and evaluators used by the schools or employers. These standards and evaluators reflect at least to some degree the specific life and cultural experience of dominant groups — whites, Anglos, men. In a group-differentiated society, moreover, the development of truly neutral standards and evaluations is difficult or impossible, because female, black, or Latino cultural experience and the dominant cultures are in many respects not reducible to a common measure. Thus affirmative action policies compensate for the dominance of one set of cultural attributes. Such an interpretation of affirmative action locates the "problem" that affirmative action solves partly in the understandable biases of evaluators and their standards, rather than only in specific differences of the disadvantaged group.

Although they are not a matter of different treatment as such, comparable worth policies similarly claim to challenge cultural biases in traditional evaluation in the worth of female-dominated occupations, and in doing so require attending to differences. Schemes of equal pay for work of comparable worth require that predominantly male and predominantly female jobs have similar usage structures if they involve similar degrees of skill, difficulty, stress, and so on. The problem in implementing these policies, of course, lies in designing methods of comparing the jobs, which often are very different. Most schemes of comparison choose to minimize sex differences by using supposedly gender-neutral criteria, such as educational attainment, speed of work, whether it involves manipulation of symbols, decision making, and so on. Some writers have suggested, however, that standard classifications of job traits may be systematically biased to keep specific kinds of tasks involved in many female-dominated occupations hidden.[25] Many female-dominated occupations involve gender-specific kinds of labor — such as nurturing, smoothing over social relations, or the exhibition of sexuality — which most task observation ignores.[26] A fair assessment of the skills and complexity of many female-dominated jobs may therefore involve paying explicit attention to gender differences in kinds of jobs rather than applying gender-blind categories of comparison.

Finally, linguistic and cultural minorities ought to have the right to maintain their language and culture and at the same time be entitled to all the benefits of citizenship, as well as valuable education and career opportunities. This right implies a positive obligation on the part of governments and other public bodies to print documents and to provide services in the native language of recognized linguistic minorities, and to provide bilingual instruction in schools. Cultural assimilation should not be a condition of full social participation, because it requires a person to transform his or her sense of identity, and when it is realized on a group level it means altering or annihilating the group's identity. This principle does not apply to any persons who do not identify with majority language or culture within a society, but only to sizeable linguistic or cultural minorities living in distinct though not necessarily segregated communities. In the United States, then, special rights for cultural minorities applies at least to Spanish-speaking Americans and Native Americans.

The universalist finds a contradiction in asserting both that formerly segregated groups have a right to inclusion and that these groups have a right to different treatment. There is no contradiction here, however, if attending to difference is necessary in order to make participation and inclusion possible. Groups with different circumstances or forms of life should be able to participate together in public institutions without shedding their distinct identities or suffering disadvantage because of them. The goal is not to give special compensation to the deviant until they achieve normality, but rather to denormalize the way institutions formulate their rules by revealing the plural circumstances and needs that exist, or ought to exist, within them.

Many opponents of oppression and privilege are wary of claims for special rights because they fear a restoration of special classifications that can justify exclusion and stigmatization of the specially marked groups. Such fear has been particularly pronounced among feminists who oppose affirming sexual and gender difference in law and policy. It would be foolish for me to deny that this fear has some significant basis.

Such fear is founded, however, on accession to traditional identification of group difference with deviance, stigma, and inequality. Contemporary movements of oppressed groups, however, assert a positive meaning to group difference, by which a group claims its identity as a group and rejects the stereotypes and labeling by which others mark it as inferior or inhuman. These social movements engage the meaning of difference itself as a terrain of political struggle, rather than leave difference to be used to jus-tify exclusion and subordination. Supporting policies and rules that attend to group difference in order to undermine oppression and disadvantage is, in my opinion, a part of that struggle.

Fear of claims to special rights points to a connection of the prin-ciple of group representation with the principle of attending to difference in policy. The primary means of defense from the use of special rights to oppress or exclude groups is the self-organization and representation of those groups. If oppressed and disadvantaged groups are able to discuss among themselves what procedures and policies they judge will best further their social and political equality, and have access to mechanisms to make their judgments known to the larger public, then policies that attend to differ-ence are less likely to be used against them than for them. If they have the institutionalized right to veto policy proposals that directly affect them, and them primarily, moreover, such danger is further reduced.

In this essay I have distinguished three meanings of universality that have usually been collapsed in discussions of the universality of citi-zenship and the public realm. Modern politics properly promotes the uni-versality of citizenship in the sense of the inclusion and participation of everyone in public life and democratic processes. The realization of gen-uinely universal citizenship in this sense today is impeded rather than fur-thered by the commonly held conviction that when they exercise their citi-zenship, persons should adopt a universal point of view and leave behind the perceptions they derive from their particular experience and social po-sition. The full inclusion and participation of all in law and public life is also sometimes impeded by formulating laws and rules in universal terms that apply to all citizens in the same way.

In response to these arguments, some people have suggested to me that such challenges to the ideal of universal citizenship threaten to leave no basis for rational normative appeals. Normative reason, it is suggested, entails universality in a Kantian sense: when a person claims that some-thing is good or right he or she is claiming that everyone in principle could consistently make that claim, and that everyone should accept it. This refers to a fourth meaning of universality, more epistemological than political. There may indeed be grounds for questioning a Kantian-based theory of the universality of normative reason, but this is a different issue from the substantive political issues I have addressed here, and the arguments in this essay neither imply nor exclude such a possibility. In any case, I do not be-lieve that challenging the ideal of a unified public or the claim that rules should always be formally universal subverts the possibility of making rational normative claims.

## NOTES

1. Theodore Lowi's classic analysis of the privatized operations of interest group liberalism remains descriptive of American politics; see *The End of Liberalism* (New York: Norton, 1969). For more recent analyses, see Jürgen Habermas, *Legitimation Crisis* (Boston: Beacon, 1973); Claus Offe, *Contradictions of the Welfare State* (Cambridge, Mass.: MIT Press, 1984); John Keane, *Public Life in Late Capitalism* (Cambridge, Mass.: MIT Press, 1984); Benjamin Barber, *Strong Democracy* (Berkeley: University of California Press, 1984).

2. For an outstanding recent account of the virtues of and conditions for such democracy, see Philip Green, *Retrieving Democracy* (Totowa, N.J.: Rowman & Allanheld, 1985).

3. Barber and Keane both appeal to Rousseau's understanding of civic activity as a model for contemporary participatory democracy, as does Carole Pateman in her classic work, *Participation and Democratic Theory* (Cambridge: Cambridge University Press, 1970). (Pateman's position has, of course, changed.) See also James Miller, *Rousseau: Dreamer of Democracy* (New Haven, Conn.: Yale University Press, 1984).

4. Many who extol the virtues of the civic public, of course, appeal also to a model of the ancient *polis*. For a recent example, see Murray Bookchin, *The Rise of Urbanization and the Decline of Citizenship* (San Francisco: Sierra Club Books, 1987). In this essay, however, I choose to restrict my claims to modern political thought. The idea of the ancient Greek *polis* often functions in both modern and contemporary discussion as a myth of lost origins, the paradise from which we have fallen and to which we desire to return; in this way, appeals to the ancient Greek *polis* are often contained within appeals to modern ideas of civic humanism.

5. Hannah Pitkin performs a most detailed and sophisticated analysis of the virtues of the civic public as a flight from sexual difference through a reading of the texts of Machiavelli; see *Fortune Is a Woman* (Berkeley: University of California Press, 1984). Carole Pateman's recent writing also focuses on such analysis; see, for example, Carole Pateman, *The Social Contract* (Stanford, Calif.: Stanford University Press, 1988). See also Nancy Hartsock, *Money, Sex and Power* (New York: Longman, 1983), chapters 7 and 8.

6. See Susan Okin, "Women and the Making of the Sentimental Family," *Philosophy and Public Affairs* 11 (1982):65–88; see also Linda Nicholson, *Gender and History: The Limits of Social Theory in the Age of the Family* (New York: Columbia University Press, 1986).

7. For analyses of Rousseau's treatment of women, see Susan Okin, *Women in Western Political Thought* (Princeton, N.J.: Princeton University Press, 1978); Lynda Lange, "Rousseau: Women and the General Will," in *The Sexism of Social and Political Theory,* ed. Lorenne M. G. Clark and Lynda Lange (Toronto:

University of Toronto Press, 1979); Jean Bethke Elshtain, *Public Man, Private Woman* (Princeton, N.J.: Princeton University Press, 1981), chapter 4. Mary Dietz develops an astute critique of Elshtain's "maternalist" perspective on political theory; in so doing, however, she also seems to appeal to a universalist ideal of the civic public in which women will transcend their particular concerns and become general; see "Citizenship with a Feminist Face: The Problem with Maternal Thinking," *Political Theory* 13 (1985):19–37. On Rousseau on women, see also Joel Schwartz, *The Sexual Politics of Jean-Jacques Rousseau* (Chicago: University of Chicago Press, 1984).

     8. See Ronald Takaki, *Iron Cages: Race and Culture in 19th Century America* (New York: Knopf, 1979). Don Herzog discusses the exclusionary prejudices of some other early American republicans; see "Some Questions for Republicans," *Political Theory* 14 (1986):473–93.

     9. George Mosse, *Nationalism and Sexuality* (New York: Fertig, 1985).

     10. Barber, *Strong Democracy,* chapters 8 and 9. Page references in parentheses in the text refer to this book.

     11. I have developed this account more thoroughly in my paper "Impartiality and the Civic Public: Some Implications of Feminist Critiques of Moral and Political Theory," in *Feminism as Critique,* ed. S. Benhabib and D. Cornell (Oxford: Polity Press, 1987), pp. 56–76.

     12. On feminism and participatory democracy, see Pateman, *Social Contract.*

     13. Jane Mansbridge, *Beyond Adversarial Democracy* (New York: Basic Books, 1980).

     14. Amy Gutmann, *Liberal Equality* (Cambridge: Cambridge University Press, 1980), pp. 191–202.

     15. See Iris Marion Young, "Five Faces of Oppression," *Philosophical Forum* 19 (1988):270–90.

     16. Jürgen Habermas, *Reason and the Rationalization of Society* (Boston: Beacon, 1983), part 3. For criticism of Habermas as retaining too universalist a conception of communicative action, see Seyla Benhabib, *Critique, Norm and Utopia* (New York: Columbia University Press, 1986), and Young, "Impartiality and the Civic Public."

     17. The Mel King for mayor campaign organization [in Boston in 1983] exhibited the promise of such group representation in practice, which was only partially and haltingly realized; see the special double issue of *Radical American* 17, no. 6, and 18, no. 1 (1984). Sheila Collins discusses how the idea of a rainbow coalition challenges traditional American political assumptions of a "melting pot," and she shows how lack of coordination between the national-level rainbow departments and the grassroots campaign committees prevented Jesse Jackson's 1984 campaign from realizing the promise of group representation; see *The Rainbow Challenge: The Jackson Campaign and the Future of U.S. Politics* (New York: Monthly Review Press, 1986).

18. See Gary Ruchwarger, *People in Power: Forging a Grassroots Democracy in Nicaragua* (Hadley, Mass.: Bergin & Garvey, 1985).

19. Martha Minow, "Learning to Live with the Dilemma of Difference: Bilingual and Special Education," *Law and Contemporary Problems*, no. 48 (1985):157–211.

20. I use the term "special rights" in much the same way that Elizabeth Wolgast uses it in *Equality and the Rights of Women* (Ithaca, N.Y.: Cornell University Press, 1980). Like Wolgast, I wish to distinguish a class of rights that all persons should have, general rights, and a class of rights that categories of persons should have by virtue of particular circumstances. That is, the distinction should refer only to different levels of generality, where "special" means only "specific." Unfortunately, "special rights" tends to carry a connotation of *exceptional*, that is, specially marked and deviating from the norm. As I assert later in this essay, however, the goal is not to compensate for deficiencies in order to help people be "normal," but to denormalize, so that in certain contexts and at certain levels of abstraction, everyone has "special" rights.

21. Linda J. Krieger, "Through a Glass Darkly: Paradigms of Equality and the Search for a Women's Jurisprudence," *Hypatia: A Journal of Feminist Philosophy* 2 (1987):45–62.

22. See Ann Scales, "Towards a Feminist Jurisprudence," *Indiana Law Journal* 56 (1980):375–444. Christine Littleton provides a very good analysis of the feminist debate about equal versus different treatment regarding pregnancy and childbirth, among other legal issues for women, in "Reconstructing Sexual Equality," *California Law Review* 25 (1987):1279–337. Littleton suggests, as I have stated, that only the dominant male conception of work keeps pregnancy and birthing from being conceived of as work.

23. Littleton suggests that difference should be understood not as a characteristic of particular sorts of people, but of the interaction of particular sorts of people with specific institutional structures. Minow expresses a similar point by saying that difference should be understood as a function of the relationship among groups, rather than located in attributes of a particular group.

24. For one among many discussions of such "backward looking" and "forward looking" arguments, see Bernard Boxill, *Blacks and Social Justice* (Totowa, N.J.: Rowman & Allanheld, 1984), chapter 7.

25. See R. W. Beatty and J. R. Beatty, "Some Problems with Contemporary Job Evaluation Systems," and Ronnie Steinberg, "A Want of Harmony: Perspectives on Wage Discrimination and Comparable Worth," both in *Comparable Worth and Wage Discrimination: Technical Possibilities and Political Realities*, ed. Helen Remick (Philadelphia: Temple University Press, 1981), and D. J. Treiman and H. I. Hartmann, eds., *Women, Work and Wages* (Washington, D.C.: National Academy Press, 1981), p. 81.

26. David Alexander, "Gendered Job Traits and Women's Occupations," Ph.D. dissertation, University of Massachusetts, Department of Economics, 1987.

# 14

## *The Civil Society Argument*

### MICHAEL WALZER

### I

My aim here is to defend a complex, imprecise, and, at crucial points, uncertain account of society and politics. I have no hope of theoretical simplicity, not at this historical moment when so many stable oppositions of political
and intellectual life have collapsed; but I also have no desire for simplicity,
since a world that theory could fully grasp and neatly explain would not, I suspect, be a pleasant place. In the nature of things, then, my argument will not
be elegant, and though I believe that arguments should march, the sentences
following one another like soldiers on parade, the route of my march today
will be twisting and roundabout. I shall begin with the idea of civil society, recently revived by Central and East European intellectuals, and go on to discuss the state, the economy, and the nation, and then civil society and the
state again. These are the crucial social formations that we inhabit, but we do
not at this moment live comfortably in any of them. Nor is it possible to imagine, in accordance with one or another of the great simplifying theories, a way
to choose among them—as if we were destined to find, one day, the best
social formation. I mean to argue against choosing, but I shall also claim
that it is from within civil society that this argument is best understood.

The words *civil society* name the space of uncoerced human association and also the set of relational networks—formed for the sake of fam-

ily, faith, interest, and ideology — that fill this space. Central and East European dissidence flourished within a highly restricted version of civil society, and the first task of the new democracies created by the dissidents, so we are told, is to rebuild the networks: unions, churches, political parties and movements, cooperatives, neighborhoods, schools of thought, societies for promoting or preventing this and that. In the West, by contrast, we have lived in civil society for many years without knowing it. Or, better, since the Scottish Enlightenment, or since Hegel, the words have been known to the knowers of such things, but they have rarely served to focus anyone else's attention. Now writers in Hungary, Czechoslovakia, and Poland invite us to think about how this social formation is secured and invigorated.

We have reasons of our own for accepting the invitation. Increasingly, associational life in the "advanced" capitalist and social democratic countries seems at risk. Publicists and preachers warn us of a steady attenuation of everyday cooperation and civic friendship. And this time it is possible that they are not, as they usually are, foolishly alarmist. Our cities really are noisier and nastier than they once were. Familial solidarity, mutual assistance, political like-mindedness — all these are less certain and less substantial than they once were. Other people, strangers on the street, seem less trustworthy than they once did. The Hobbesian account of society is more persuasive than it once was.

Perhaps this worrisome picture follows — in part, no more, but what else can a political theorist say? — from the fact that we have not thought enough about solidarity and trust or planned for their future. We have been thinking too much about social formations different from, in competition with, civil society. And so we have neglected the networks through which civility is produced and reproduced. Imagine that the following questions were posed, one or two centuries ago, to political theorists and moral philosophers: What is the preferred setting, the most supportive environment, for the good life? What sorts of institutions should we work for? Nineteenth-and twentieth-century social thought provides four different, by now familiar, answers to these questions. Think of them as four rival ideologies, each with its own claim to completeness and correctness. Each of them is importantly wrong. Each of them neglects the necessary pluralism of any civil society. Each of them is predicated on an assumption I mean to attack: that such questions must receive a singular answer.

## II

I shall begin, since this is for me the best-known ground, with two leftist answers. The first of the two holds that the preferred setting for the good life is the political community, the democratic state, within which we can be citizens: freely engaged, fully committed, decision-making members. And a citizen, on this view, is much the best thing to be. To live well is to be politically active, working with our fellow citizens, collectively determining our common destiny — not for the sake of this or that determination but for the work itself, in which our highest capacities as rational and moral agents find expression. We know ourselves best as persons who propose, debate, and decide.

This argument goes back to the Greeks, but we are most likely to recognize its neoclassical versions. It is Rousseau's argument, or the standard leftist interpretation of Rousseau's argument. His understanding of citizenship as moral agency is one of the key sources of democratic idealism. We can see it at work in liberals like John Stuart Mill, in whose writings it produced an unexpected defense of syndicalism (what is today called "workers' control") and, more generally, of social democracy. It appeared among nineteenth- and twentieth-century democratic radicals, often with a hard populist edge. It played a part in the reiterated demand for social inclusion by women, workers, blacks, and new immigrants, all of whom based their claims on their capacity as agents. And this same neoclassical idea of citizenship resurfaced in the 1960s in New Left theories of participation, where it was, however, like many latter-day revivals, highly theoretical and without local resonance.

Today, perhaps in response to the political disasters of the late 1960s, "communitarians" in the United States struggle to give Rousseauian idealism a historical reference, looking back to the early American republic and calling for a renewal of civic virtue. They prescribe citizenship as an antidote to the fragmentation of contemporary society — for these theorists, like Rousseau, are disinclined to value the fragments. In their hands, republicanism is still a simplifying creed. If politics is our highest calling, then we are called away from every other activity (or, every other activity is redefined in political terms); our energies are directed towards policy formation and decision making in the democratic state.

I don't doubt that the active and engaged citizen is an attractive figure — even if some of the activists that we actually meet carrying placards and shouting slogans aren't all that attractive. The most penetrating criticism of this first answer to the question about the good life is not that the life isn't good but that it isn't the "real life" of very many people in the modern world. This is so in two senses. First, though the power of the democratic state has grown enormously, partly (and rightly) in response to the demands of engaged citizens, it cannot be said that the state is fully in the hands of its citizens. And the larger it gets, the more it takes over those smaller associations still subject to hands-on control. The rule of the *demos* is in significant ways illusory; the participation of ordinary men and women in the activities of the state (unless they are state employees) is largely vicarious; even party militants are more likely to argue and complain than actually to decide.

Second, despite the single-mindedness of republican ideology, politics rarely engages the full attention of the citizens who are supposed to be its chief protagonists. They have too many other things to worry about. Above all, they have to earn a living. They are more deeply engaged in the economy than in the political community. Republican theorists (like Hannah Arendt) recognize this engagement only as a threat to civic virtue. Economic activity belongs to the realm of necessity, they argue; politics to the realm of freedom. Ideally, citizens should not have to work; they should be served by machines, if not by slaves, so that they can flock to the assemblies and argue with their fellows about affairs of state. In practice, however, work, though it begins in necessity, takes on value of its own — expressed in commitment to a career, pride in a job well done, a sense of camaraderie in the workplace. All of these are competitive with the values of citizenship.

### III

The second leftist position on the preferred setting for the good life involves a turning away from republican politics and a focus instead on economic activity. We can think of this as the socialist answer to the questions I began with; it can be found in Marx and also, though the arguments are somewhat different, among the utopians he hoped to supersede. For Marx, the preferred setting is the cooperative economy, where we can all be producers — artists (Marx was a romantic), inventors, and craftsmen. (Assembly-line workers don't quite seem to fit.) This again is much the best thing to be. The picture Marx paints is of creative men and women making useful and beautiful objects, not for the sake of this or that object but for the sake of creativity itself, the highest expression of our "species-being" as *homo faber,* man-the-maker.

The state, in this view, ought to be managed in such a way as to set productivity free. It doesn't matter who the managers are so long as they are committed to this goal and rational in its pursuit. Their work is technically important but not substantively interesting. Once productivity is free, politics simply ceases to engage anyone's attention. Before that time, in the Marxist here and now, political conflict is taken to be the superstructural enactment of economic conflict, and democracy is valued mainly because it enables socialist movements and parties to organize for victory. The value is instrumental and historically specific. A democratic state is the preferred setting not for the good life but for the class struggle; the purpose of the struggle is to win, and victory brings an end to democratic instrumentality. There is no intrinsic value in democracy, no reason to think that politics has, for creatures like us, a permanent attractiveness. When we are all engaged in productive activity, social division and the conflicts it engenders will disappear, and the state, in the once-famous phrase, will wither away.

In fact, if this vision were ever realized, it is politics that would wither away. Some kind of administrative agency would still be necessary for economic coordination, and it is only a Marxist conceit to refuse to call this agency a state. "Society regulates the general production," Marx wrote in *The German Ideology,* "and thus makes it possible for me to do one thing today and another tomorrow... just as I have a mind." Since this regulation is nonpolitical, the individual producer is freed from the burdens of citizenship. He attends instead to the things he makes and to the cooperative relationships he establishes. Exactly how he can work with other people and still do whatever he pleases is unclear to me and probably to most other readers of Marx. The texts suggest an extraordinary faith in the virtuosity of the regulators. No one, I think, quite shares this faith today, but something like it helps to explain the tendency of some leftists to see even the liberal and democratic state as an obstacle that has to be, in the worst of recent jargons, "smashed."

The seriousness of Marxist antipolitics is nicely illustrated by Marx's own dislike of syndicalism. What the syndicalists proposed was a neat amalgam of the first and second answers to the question about the good life: for them, the preferred setting was the worker-controlled factory, where men and women were simultaneously citizens and producers, making decisions and making things. Marx seems to have regarded the combination as impossible; factories could not be both democratic and productive. This is the point of Engels's little essay on authority, which I take to express Marx's view also. More generally, self-government on the job called into question the legitimacy of "social regulation" or state planning, which alone, Marx thought, could enable individual workers to devote themselves, without distraction, to their work.

But this vision of the cooperative economy is set against an unbelievable background — a nonpolitical state, regulation without conflict, "the administration of things." In every actual experience of socialist politics, the state has moved rapidly into the foreground, and most socialists, in the West at least, have been driven to make their own amalgam of the first and second answers. They call themselves *democratic* socialists, focusing on the state as well as (in fact, much more than) on the economy and doubling the preferred settings for the good life. Since I believe that two are better than one, I take this to be progress. But before I try to suggest what further progress might look like, I need to describe two more ideological answers to the question about the good life, one of them capitalist, the other nationalist. For there is no reason to think that only leftists love singularity.

## IV

The third answer holds that the preferred setting for the good life is the marketplace, where individual men and women, consumers rather than producers, choose among a maximum number of options. The autonomous individual confronting his, and now her, possibilities—this is much the best thing to be. To live well is not to make political decisions or beautiful objects; it is to make personal choices. Not any particular choices, for no choice is substantively the best: it is the activity of choosing that makes for autonomy. And the market within which choices are made, like the socialist economy, largely dispenses with politics; it requires at most a minimal state—not "social regulation," only the police.

Production, too, is free even if it isn't, as in the Marxist vision, freely creative. More important than the producers, however, are the entrepreneurs, heroes of autonomy, consumers of opportunity, who compete to supply whatever all the other consumers want or might be persuaded to want. Entrepreneurial activity tracks consumer preference. Though not without its own excitements, it is mostly instrumental: the aim of all entrepreneurs (and all producers) is to increase their market power, maximize their options. Competing with one another, they maximize everyone else's options too, filling the marketplace with desirable objects. The market is preferred (over the political community and the cooperative economy) because of its fullness. Freedom, in the capitalist view, is a function of plenitude. We can only choose when we have many choices.

It is also true, unhappily, that we can only make effective (rather than merely speculative or wistful) choices when we have resources to dispose of. But people come to the marketplace with radically unequal resources—some with virtually nothing at all. Not everyone can compete successfully in commodity production, and therefore not everyone has access to commodities. Autonomy turns out to be a high-risk value, which many men and women can only realize with help from their friends. The market, however, is not a good setting for mutual assistance, for I cannot help someone else without reducing (for the short term, at least) my own options. And I have no reason, as an autonomous individual, to accept any reductions of any sort for someone else's sake. My argument here is not that autonomy collapses into egotism, only that autonomy in the marketplace provides no support for social solidarity. Despite the successes of capitalist production, the good life of consumer choice is not universally available. Large numbers of people drop out of the market economy or live precariously on its margins.

Partly for this reason, capitalism, like socialism, is highly dependent on state action—not only to prevent theft and enforce contracts but also to regulate the economy and guarantee the minimal welfare of its participants. But these participants, insofar as they are market activists, are not active in the state: capitalism in its ideal form, like socialism again, does not make for citizenship. Or, its protagonists conceive of citizenship in economic terms, so that citizens are transformed into autonomous consumers, looking for the party or program that most persuasively promises to strengthen their market position. They need the state, but have no moral relation to it, and they control its officials only as consumers control the producers of commodities, by buying or not buying what they make.

Since the market has no political boundaries, capitalist entrepreneurs also evade official control. They need the state but have no loyalty to it; the profit motive brings them into conflict with democratic regulation. So arms merchants sell the latest military technology to foreign powers and manufacturers move their factories overseas to escape safety codes or minimum wage laws. Multinational corporations stand outside (and to some extent against) every political community. They are known only by their brand names, which, unlike family names and country names, evoke preferences but not affections or solidarities.

## V

The fourth answer to the question about the good life can be read as a response to market amorality and disloyalty, though it has, historically, other sources as well. According to the fourth answer, the preferred setting is the nation, within which we are loyal members, bound to one another by ties of blood and history. And a member, secure in his membership, literally part of an organic whole—this is much the best thing to be. To live well is to participate with other men and women in remembering, cultivating, and passing on a national heritage. This is so, on the nationalist view, without reference to the specific content of the heritage, so long as it is one's own, a matter of birth, not choice. Every nationalist will, of course, find value in his own heritage, but the highest value is not in the finding but in the willing: the firm identification of the individual with a people and a history.

Nationalism has often been a leftist ideology, historically linked to democracy and even to socialism. But it is most characteristically an ideology of the right, for its understanding of membership is ascriptive; it requires no political choices and no activity beyond ritual affirmation. When nations find themselves ruled by foreigners, however, ritual affirmation is not enough. Then nationalism requires a more heroic loyalty: self-sacrifice in the struggle for national liberation. The capacity of the nation to elicit such sacrifices from its members is proof of the importance of this fourth answer. Individual members seek the good life by seeking autonomy not for themselves but for their people. Ideally this attitude ought to survive the liberation struggle and provide a foundation for social solidarity and mutual assistance. Perhaps, to some extent, it does: certainly the welfare state has had its greatest successes in ethnically homogeneous countries. It is also true, however, that once liberation has been secured, nationalist men and women are commonly content with a vicarious rather than a practical participation in the community. There is nothing wrong with vicarious participation, on the nationalist view, since the good life is more a matter of identity than activity — faith, not works, so to speak, though both of these are understood in secular terms.

In the modern world, nations commonly seek statehood, for their autonomy will always be at risk if they lack sovereign power. But they don't seek states of any particular kind. No more do they seek economic arrangements of any particular kind. Unlike religious believers who are their close kin and (often) bitter rivals, nationalists are not bound by a body of authoritative law or a set of sacred texts. Beyond liberation, they have no program, only a vague commitment to continue a history, to sustain a "way of life." Their own lives, I suppose, are emotionally intense, but in relation to society and economy this is a dangerously free-floating intensity. In time of trouble, it can readily be turned against other nations, particularly against the internal others: minorities, aliens, strangers. Democratic citizenship, worker solidarity, free enterprise, and consumer autonomy — all these are less exclusive than nationalism but not always resistant to its power. The ease with which citizens, workers, and consumers become fervent nationalists is a sign of the inadequacy of the first three answers to the question about the good life. The nature of nationalist fervor signals the inadequacy of the fourth.

## VI

All these answers are wrong-headed because of their singularity. They miss the complexity of human society, the inevitable conflicts of commitment and loyalty. Hence I am uneasy with the idea that there might be a fifth and finally correct answer to the question about the good life. Still, there is a fifth answer, the newest one (it draws upon less central themes of nineteenth- and twentieth-century social thought), which holds that the good life can only be lived in civil society, the realm of fragmentation and struggle but also of concrete and authentic solidarities, where we fulfill E. M. Forster's injunction "only connect," and become sociable or communal men and women. And this is, of course, much the best thing to be. The picture here is of people freely associating and communicating with one another, forming and reforming groups of all sorts, not for the sake of any particular formation—family, tribe, nation, religion, commune, brotherhood or sisterhood, interest group or ideological movement—but for the sake of sociability itself. For we are by nature social, before we are political or economic, beings.

I would rather say that the civil society argument is a corrective to the four ideological accounts of the good life—part denial, part incorporation—rather than a fifth to stand alongside them. It challenges their singularity, but it has no singularity of its own. The phrase "social being" describes men and women who are citizens, producers, consumers, members of the nation, and much else besides—and none of these by nature or because it is the best thing to be. The associational life of civil society is the actual ground where all versions of the good are worked out and tested . . . and proven to be partial, incomplete, ultimately unsatisfying. It cannot be the case that living on this ground is good in itself; there isn't any other place to live. What is true is that the quality of our political and economic activity and of our national culture is intimately connected to the strength and vitality of our associations.

Ideally, civil society is a *setting of settings:* all are included, none is preferred. The argument is a liberal version of the four answers, accepting them all, insisting that each leave room for the others, therefore not finally accepting any of them. Liberalism appears here as an anti-ideology, and this is an attractive position in the contemporary world. I shall stress this attractiveness as I try to explain how civil society might actually incorporate and deny the four answers. Later on, however, I shall have to argue that this position too, so genial and benign, has its problems.

Let's begin with the political community and the cooperative economy, taken together. These two leftist versions of the good life systematically undervalued all associations except the *demos* and the working class. Their protagonists could imagine conflicts between political communities and between classes, but not within either; they aimed at the abolition or transcendence of particularism and all its divisions. Theorists of civil society, by contrast, have a more realistic view of communities and economies. They are more accommodating to conflict — that is, to political opposition and economic competition. Associational freedom serves for them to legitimate a set of market relations, though not necessarily the capitalist set. The market, when it is entangled in the network of associations, when the forms of ownership are pluralized, is without doubt the economic formation most consistent with the civil society argument. This same argument also serves to legitimate a kind of state, liberal and pluralist more than republican (not so radically dependent upon the virtue of its citizens). Indeed, a state of this sort, as we will see, is necessary if associations are to flourish.

Once incorporated into civil society, neither citizenship nor production can ever again be all-absorbing. They will have their votaries, but these people will not be models for the rest of us — or they will be partial models only, for some people at some time of their lives, not for other people, not at other times. This pluralist perspective follows in part, perhaps, from the lost romance of work, from our experience with the new productive technologies and the growth of the service economy. Service is more easily reconciled with a vision of man as a social animal than with *homo faber*. What can a hospital attendant or a schoolteacher or a marriage counselor or a social worker or a television repairman or a government official be said to *make*? The contemporary economy does not offer many people a chance for creativity in the Marxist sense. Nor does Marx (or any socialist thinker of the central tradition) have much to say about those men and women whose economic activity consists entirely of helping other people. The helpmate, like the housewife, was never assimilated to the class of workers.

In similar fashion, politics in the contemporary democratic state does not offer many people a chance for Rousseauian self-determination. Citizenship, taken by itself, is today mostly a passive role: citizens are spectators who vote. Between elections, they are served, well or badly, by the civil service. They are not at all like those heroes of republican mythology, the citizens of ancient Athens meeting in assembly and (foolishly, as it turned out) deciding to invade Sicily. But in the associational networks of civil society, in unions, parties, movements, interest groups, and so on, these same people make many smaller decisions and shape to some degree the more distant determinations of state and economy. And in a more densely organized, more egalitarian civil society, they might do both these things to greater effect.

These socially engaged men and women — part-time union officers, movement activists, party regulars, consumer advocates, welfare volunteers, church members, family heads — stand outside the republic of citizens as it is commonly conceived. They are only intermittently virtuous; they are too caught up in particularity. They look, most of them, for many partial fulfillments, no longer for one clinching fulfillment. On the ground of actuality (unless the state usurps the ground), citizenship shades off into a great diversity of (sometimes divisive) decision-making roles; and, similarly, production shades off into a multitude of (sometimes competitive) socially useful activities. It is, then, a mistake to set politics and work in opposition to one another. There is no ideal fulfillment and no essential human capacity. We require many settings so that we can live different kinds of good lives.

All this is not to say, however, that we need to accept the capitalist version of competition and division. Theorists who regard the market as the preferred setting for the good life aim to make it the actual setting for as many aspects of life as possible. Their single-mindedness takes the form of market imperialism; confronting the democratic state, they are advocates of privatization and laissez-faire. Their ideal is a society in which all goods and services are provided by entrepreneurs to consumers. That some entrepreneurs would fail and many consumers find themselves helpless in the marketplace — this is the price of individual autonomy. It is, obviously, a price we already pay: in all capitalist societies, the market makes for inequality. The more successful its imperialism, the greater the inequality. But were the market to be set firmly within civil society, politically constrained, open to communal as well as private initiatives, limits might be fixed on its unequal outcomes. The exact nature of the limits would depend on the strength and density of the associational networks (including, now, the political community).

The problem with inequality is not merely that some individuals are more capable, others less capable, of making their consumer preferences effective. It's not that some individuals live in fancier apartments than others, or drive better-made cars, or take vacations in more exotic places. These are conceivably the just rewards of market success. The problem is that inequality commonly translates into domination and radical deprivation. But the verb *translates* here describes a socially mediated process, which is fostered or inhibited by the structure of its mediations. Dominated and deprived individuals are likely to be disorganized as well as impoverished, whereas poor people with strong families, churches, unions, political parties, and ethnic alliances are not likely to be dominated or deprived for long. Nor need these people stand alone even in the marketplace. The capitalist answer assumes that the good life of entrepreneurial initiative and consumer choice is a life led most importantly by individuals. But civil society en-compasses or can encompass a variety of market agents: family businesses, publicly owned or municipal companies, worker communes, consumer co-operatives, nonprofit organizations of many different sorts. All these func-tion in the market though they have their origins outside. And just as the experience of democracy is expanded and enhanced by groups that are in but not of the state, so consumer choice is expanded and enhanced by groups that are in but not of the market.

It is only necessary to add that among the groups in but not of the state are market organizations, and among the groups in but not of the market are state organizations. All social forms are relativized by the civil society ar-gument—and on the actual ground too. This also means that all social forms are contestable; moreover, contests can't be won by invoking one or another account of the preferred setting—as if it were enough to say that market organizations, insofar as they are efficient, do not have to be democratic or that state firms, insofar as they are democratically controlled, do not have to operate within the constraints of the market. The exact character of our associational life is something that has to be argued about, and it is in the course of these arguments that we also decide about the forms of democ-racy, the nature of work, the extent and effects of market inequalities, and much else.

The quality of nationalism is also determined within civil society, where national groups coexist and overlap with families and religious com-munities (two social formations largely neglected in modernist answers to the question about the good life) and where nationalism is expressed in schools and movements, organizations for mutual aid, cultural and histori-cal societies. It is because groups like these are entangled with other groups, similar in kind but different in aim, that civil society holds out the hope of a domesticated nationalism. In states dominated by a single nation, the mul-tiplicity of the groups pluralizes nationalist politics and culture; in states with more than one nation, the density of the networks prevents radical polarization.

Civil society as we know it has its origin in the struggle for reli-gious freedom. Though often violent, the struggle held open the possibility of peace. "The establishment of this one thing," John Locke wrote about toleration, "would take away all ground of complaints and tumults upon account of conscience." One can easily imagine groundless complaints and tumults, but Locke believed (and he was largely right) that tolerance would dull the edge of religious conflict. People would be less ready to take risks once the stakes were lowered. Civil society simply is that place where the stakes are lower, where, in principle, at least, coercion is used only to keep the peace and all associations are equal under the law. In the market, this formal equality often has no substance, but in the world of faith and identity, it is real enough. Though nations do not compete for members in the same way as religions (sometimes) do, the argument for granting them the associational freedom of civil society is similar. When they are free to celebrate their histories, remember their dead, and shape (in part) the education of their children, they are more likely to be harmless than when they are unfree. Locke may have put the claim too strongly when he wrote that "there is only one thing which gathers people into seditious commotions, and that is oppression," but he was close enough to the truth to warrant the experiment of radical tolerance.

But if oppression is the cause of seditious commotion, what is the cause of oppression? I don't doubt that there is a materialist story to tell here, but I want to stress the central role played by ideological single-mindedness: the intolerant universalism of (most) religions, the exclusivity of (most) nations. The actual experience of civil society, when it can be had, seems to work against these two. Indeed, it works so well, some observers think, that neither religious faith nor national identity is likely to survive for long in the network of free associations. But we really don't know to what extent faith and identity depend upon coercion or whether they can reproduce themselves under conditions of freedom. I suspect that they both respond to such deep human needs that they will outlast their current organizational forms. It seems, in any case, worthwhile to wait and see.

# VII

But there is no escape from power and coercion, no possibility of choosing, like the old anarchists, civil society alone. A few years ago, in a book called *Anti-Politics,* the Hungarian dissident George Konrad described a way of living alongside the totalitarian state but, so to speak, with one's back turned towards it. He urged his fellow dissidents to reject the very idea of seizing or sharing power and to devote their energies to religious, cultural, economic, and professional associations. Civil society appears in his book as an alternative to the state, which he assumes to be unchangeable and irredeemably hostile. His argument seemed right to me when I first read his book. Looking back, after the collapse of the communist regimes in Hungary and elsewhere, it is easy to see how much it was a product of its time — and how short that time was! No state can survive for long if it is wholly alienated from civil society. It cannot outlast its own coercive machinery; it is lost, literally, without its firepower. The production and reproduction of loyalty, civility, political competence, and trust in authority are never the work of the state alone, and the effort to go it alone—one meaning of totalitarianism—is doomed to failure. . . .

This is, indeed, the experience of the dissidents; the state could not destroy their unions, churches, free universities, illegal markets, samizdat publications. Nonetheless, I want to warn against the antipolitical tendencies that commonly accompany the celebration of civil society. The network of associations incorporates, but it cannot dispense with, the agencies of state power; neither can socialist cooperation or capitalist competition dispense with the state. That's why so many dissidents are ministers now. It is indeed true that the new social movements in the East and the West—concerned with ecology, feminism, the rights of immigrants and national minorities, workplace and product safety, and so on—do not aim, as the democratic and labor movements once aimed, at taking power. This represents an important change, in sensibility as much as in ideology, reflecting a new valuation of parts over wholes and a new willingness to settle for something less than total victory. But there can be no victory at all that does not involve some control over, or use of, the state apparatus. The collapse of totalitarianism is empowering for the members of civil society precisely because it renders the state accessible.

Here is the paradox of the civil society argument. Citizenship is one of many roles that members play, but the state itself is unlike all the other associations. It both frames civil society and occupies space within it. It fixes the boundary conditions and the basic rules of all associational activity (including political activity). It compels association members to think about a common good, beyond their own conceptions of the good life. Even the failed totalitarianism of, say, the Polish communist state had this much impact upon the Solidarity union: it determined that Solidarity was a Polish union, focused on economic arrangements and labor policy within the borders of Poland. A democratic state, which is continuous with the other associations, has at the same time a greater say about their quality and vitality. It serves, or it doesn't serve, the needs of the associational networks as these are worked out by men and women who are simultaneously members and citizens. I will give only a few obvious examples, drawn from American experience.

Families with working parents need state help in the form of publicly funded day care and effective public schools. National minorities need help in organizing and sustaining their own educational programs. Worker-owned companies and consumer cooperatives need state loans or loan guarantees; so (even more often) do capitalist entrepreneurs and firms. Philanthropy and mutual aid, churches and private universities, depend upon tax exemptions. Labor unions need legal recognition and guarantees against "unfair labor practices." Professional associations need state support for their licensing procedures. And across the entire range of association, individual men and women need to be protected against the power of officials, employers, experts, party bosses, factory supervisers, directors, priests, parents, patrons; and small and weak groups need to be protected against large and powerful ones. For civil society, left to itself, generates radically unequal power relationships, which only state power can challenge.

Civil society also challenges state power, most importantly when associations have resources or supporters abroad: world religions, pan-national movements, the new environmental groups, multinational corporations. We are likely to feel differently about these challenges, especially after we recognize the real but relative importance of the state. Multinational corporations, for example, need to be constrained, much like states with imperial ambitions; and the best constraint probably lies in collective security, that is, in alliances with other states that give economic regulation some international effect. The same mechanism may turn out to be useful to the new environmental groups. In the first case, the state pressures the corporation; in the second it responds to environmentalist pressure. The two cases suggest, again, that civil society requires political agency. And the state is an indispensable agent — even if the associational networks also, always, resist the organizing impulses of state bureaucrats.

Only a democratic state can create a democratic civil society; only a democratic civil society can sustain a democratic state. The civility that makes democratic politics possible can only be learned in the associational networks; the roughly equal and widely dispersed capabilities that sustain the networks have to be fostered by the democratic state. Confronted with an overbearing state, citizens, who are also members, will struggle to make room for autonomous associations and market relationships (and also for local governments and decentralized bureaucracies). But the state can never be what it appears to be in liberal theory, a mere framework for civil society. It is also the instrument of the struggle, used to give a particular shape to the common life. Hence citizenship has a certain practical preeminence among all our actual and possible memberships. That's not to say that we must be citizens all the time, finding in politics, as Rousseau urged, the greater part of our happiness. Most of us will be happier elsewhere, involved only sometimes in affairs of state. But we must have a state open to our sometime involvement.

Nor need we be involved all the time in our associations. A democratic civil society is one controlled by its members, not through a single process of self-determination but through a large number of different and uncoordinated processes. These need not all be democratic, for we are likely to be members of many associations, and we will want some of them to be managed in our interests, but also in our absence. Civil society is sufficiently democratic when in some, at least, of its parts we are able to recognize ourselves as authoritative and responsible participants. States are tested by their capacity to sustain this kind of participation — which is very different from the heroic intensity of Rousseauian citizenship. And civil society is tested by its capacity to produce citizens whose interests, at least sometimes, reach further than themselves and their comrades, who look after the political community that fosters and protects the associational networks.

## VIII

I mean to defend a perspective that might be called, awkwardly, "critical associationalism." I want to join, but I am somewhat uneasy with, the civil society argument. It cannot be said that nothing is lost when we give up the single-mindedness of democratic citizenship or socialist cooperation or individual autonomy or national identity. There was a kind of heroism in those projects — a concentration of energy, a clear sense of direction, an unblinking recognition of friends and enemies. To make one of them one's own was a serious commitment. The defense of civil society does not quite seem comparable. Associational engagement is conceivably as important a project as any of the others, but its greatest virtue lies in its inclusiveness, and inclusiveness does not make for heroism. "Join the associations of your choice" is not a slogan to rally political militants, and yet that is what civil society requires: men and women actively engaged — in state, economy, and nation, and also in churches, neighborhoods, and families, and in many other settings too. To reach this goal is not as easy as it sounds; many people, perhaps most people, live very loosely within the networks, and a growing number of people seem to be radically disengaged — passive clients of the state, market dropouts, resentful and posturing nationalists. And the civil society project doesn't confront an energizing hostility, as all the others do; its protagonists are more likely to meet sullen indifference, fear, despair, apathy, and withdrawal.

In Central and Eastern Europe, civil society is still a battle cry, for it requires a dismantling of the totalitarian state and it brings with it the exhilarating experience of associational independence. Among ourselves what is required is nothing so grand; nor does it lend itself to a singular description (but this is what lies ahead in the East too). The civil society project can only be described in terms of all the other projects, against their singularity. Hence my account here, which suggests the need (1) to decentralize the state, so that there are more opportunities for citizens to take responsibility for (some of) its activities; (2) to socialize the economy, so that there is a greater diversity of market agents, communal as well as private; and (3) to pluralize and domesticate nationalism, on the religious model, so that there are different ways to realize and sustain historical identities.

None of this can be accomplished without using political power to redistribute resources and to underwrite and subsidize the most desirable associational activities. But political power alone cannot accomplish any of it. The kinds of "action" discussed by theorists of the state need to be supplemented (not, however, replaced) by something radically different: more like union organizing than political mobilization, more like teaching in a school than arguing in the assembly, more like volunteering in a hospital than joining a political party, more like working in an ethnic alliance or a feminist support group than canvassing in an election, more like shaping a co-op budget than deciding on national fiscal policy. But can any of these local and small-scale activities ever carry with them the honor of citizenship? Sometimes, certainly, they are narrowly conceived, partial and particularist; they need political correction. The greater problem, however, is that they seem so ordinary. Living in civil society, one might think, is like speaking in prose.

But just as speaking in prose implies an understanding of syntax, so these forms of action (when they are pluralized) imply an understanding of civility. And that is not an understanding about which we can be entirely confident these days. There is something to be said for the neoconservative argument that in the modern world we need to recapture the density of associational life and relearn the activities and understandings that go with it. And if this is the case, then a more strenuous argument is called for from the left: we have to reconstruct that same density under new conditions of freedom and equality. It would appear to be an elementary requirement of social democracy that there exist a *society* of lively, engaged, and effective men and women — where the honor of "action" belongs to the many and not to the few.

Against a background of growing disorganization — violence, homelessness, divorce, abandonment, alienation, and addiction — a society of this sort looks more like a necessary achievement than a comfortable reality. In truth, however, it was never a comfortable reality, except for the few. Most men and women have been trapped in one or another subordinate relationship, where the "civility" they learned was deferential rather than independent and active. That is why democratic citizenship, socialist production, free enterprise, and nationalism were all of them liberating projects. But none of them has yet produced a general, coherent, or sustainable liberation. And their more single-minded adherents, who have exaggerated the effectiveness of the state or the market or the nation and neglected the networks, have probably contributed to the disorder of contemporary life. The projects have to be relativized and brought together, and the place to do that is in civil society, the setting of settings, where each can find the partial fulfillment that is all it deserves.

Civil society itself is sustained by groups much smaller than the *demos* or the working class or the mass of consumers or the nation. All these are necessarily pluralized as they are incorporated. They become part of the world of family, friends, comrades, and colleagues, where people are connected to one another and made responsible for one another. Connected and responsible: without that, "free and equal" is less attractive than we once thought it would be. I have no magic formula for making connections or strengthening the sense of responsibility. These are not aims that can be underwritten with historical guarantees or achieved through a single unified struggle. Civil society is a project of projects; it requires many organizing strategies and new forms of state action. It requires a new sensitivity for what is local, specific, contingent—and, above all, a new recognition (to paraphrase a famous sentence) that the good life is in the details.

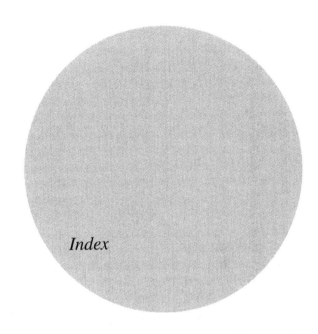

# Index

GERSHON SHAFIR is a professor in the department of sociology at the University of California, San Diego. He is the author of *Land, Labor, and the Origins of the Israeli-Palestinian Conflict* and *Nationalists and Immigrants: Ethnic Conflict and Accommodation in Catalonia, the Basque Country, Latvia, and Estonia.*